PARTY POLITICS IN CANADA

SECOND EDITION
edited by

HUGH G. THORBURN

Department of Political Studies
Queen's University, Kingston, Ontario

P
PRENTICE-HALL ✦ OF CANADA LTD.
Scarborough h *Ontario*

Preface to the First Edition

*

While there is no book currently in print devoted to Canadian political parties, there are many articles, dissertations, monographs, and biographies which contain excellent material relating to the subject. This little book presents a selection of these, or excerpts from them, arranged to present a balanced picture of the background, organization, and policy of the four parties presently dominating the national stage. Since it is too soon for definitive studies to be done on the New Democratic party, I have decided to rely on two excellent articles on the C.C.F. rather than attempt to cover the newer movement, whose position and role are not yet firmly established. The Social Credit party in Quebec is also too young to have been carefully analysed, so no article devoted to it is included.

For practical reasons, the book has been held to two hundred pages; hence much material has had to be left out. For the reader who wishes to pursue a subject beyond these essays, suggested readings for each section are listed at the end of the book.

I wish to thank the authors and publishers who have generously granted me permission to reproduce their material. Knowing readers will discern gaps, which I regret. In some cases space was limited and difficult decisions had to be made not to include some pieces in order to include others. In still other cases permission to reprint could not be secured. I am grateful for the helpful advice and suggestions of my colleagues and friends; Professors F. W. Gibson and N. M. Ward, Senator C. G. Power, and my wife were especially helpful.

The work of others gives this book its strength. Its faults are mine.

H.G.T.

Preface to the Second Edition

*

This second edition is an enlarged and updated presentation. In the four years since *Party Politics in Canada* first appeared valuable additions to the literature on parties in Canada, and changes in the party system itself have been made. I have tried to make this edition express these changes as completely as space permits. The two articles by Professors Meisel and Horowitz are analyses which give insight to the political structure of Canada. The report of the Committee on Election Expenses presents the most valuable analysis of party finance yet undertaken in Canada. Professor Black casts new light on the internal strains between the federal and provincial levels of the Progressive Conservative Party. The essay by Messrs. Baker and Price was especially written for this edition to present an up-to-date picture of the New Democratic Party. Professor Robin casts new light on the politics of British Columbia. Quebec politics have grown so complex that available space could not hope to cover them; I decided to let Professor Guindon explain the social bases of change and to let the reader look elsewhere for the details. Professor Porter's comments on party leadership and responsiveness to interests are extremely revealing interpretations of the rationale of Canadian politics. I am deeply indebted to these authors and their publishers, whose co-operation has made this new edition possible. The publisher is cited at the bottom of the first page of each essay.

Canada has experienced two federal elections since the first edition of this book appeared; they are reported in the statistical appendix. The bibliography has been enlarged to bring it up-to-date.

H.G.T.

Contents

PARTY
POLITICS
IN CANADA

Historical Background

*

The growth of national parties in Canada is interpreted in different ways in the following essays. Mr. Hougham looks at the local and regional interests that came together to form the Liberal and Conservative parties and analyses the programmes they developed to unite the new country behind them. Mr. Reid, on the other hand, finds that national parties were slow to develop, for parochialism persisted and members of parliament tended to trade their support of the government for local patronage. Mr. Hougham focuses his attention on the activities, hopes, and ideas of the men at the centre of political life; Mr. Reid is concerned with the political conditions in the country at large during the years of slow party growth before the turn of the century.

1

The Background and Development of National Parties

GEORGE M. HOUGHAM

*

The story of national politics in Canada begins with the establishment of a federal union by act of the British Parliament in 1867. The passage of the British North America Act produced a new and larger arena for party manoeuvre and created new and more complex problems for political manipulation and solution.

*   *   *   *   *

John A. Macdonald['s] . . . ministry . . . was based on an earlier coalition of which Macdonald had been one of the leaders; it was committed to support of the Confederation settlement and to the fulfillment of the purposes which Confederation was designed to serve. In its constituent elements and its programme, moreover, it was to provide a prototype for the successful organization of a major party in Canada.

The Conservative party and ministry of 1867 derived from an alliance between the supporters of John A. Macdonald and Georges Etienne Cartier in 1854, one of the bewildering series of coalitions that had characterized government under the Act of Union. At its inception, the coalition contained four important elements—two from Lower Canada and two from Upper Canada. The Montreal commercial and industrial interests, with able spokesmen in Alexander Galt and the Montreal *Gazette*, were the economically important element from Lower Canada. The politically important element was the French Canadian majority. Although at cross-purposes during the fight for responsible government, the French Canadian voting bloc and the business community of Montreal now joined forces in a union made possible by the political astuteness of the Catholic Church. In those days of ultramontanism, the French Canadian "habitants" were accustomed to conform to the wishes, if not the dictates, of the ecclesiastical hierarchy. When the Church decided that its interests would be more adequately protected in alliance with, rather than in opposition to, the Conservative business community, most of the

*Based on *Minor Parties in Canadian National Politics, 1867-1940*, Ph.D. Dissertation, University of Pennsylvania, 1954.

"habitants" could be relied upon to act accordingly. Georges E. Cartier, a French Canadian faithful son of the Church and an outstanding corporation counsel, was the natural spokesman of this Lower Canada Conservatism.

The larger of the two elements from Upper Canada included anti-American United Empire Loyalists and anti-Catholic Orangemen who were followers of the Tory "Family Compact" leaders during the fight for responsible government; . . . the second was composed of the moderate Reformers who earlier had followed the leadership of Robert Baldwin. The introduction of a series of reforms . . . had fulfilled the objectives of these moderate Reformers. . . . The two groups had no real difficulty in joining forces. And, as in Lower Canada, they represented the more settled and conservative sections of the rural community and the urban interests of trade and commerce. By 1867 John A. Macdonald had become their acknowledged spokesman.

The Conservative victory of 1867 was to a considerable degree manufactured from these four elements. In the Dominion House of Commons, Ontario and Quebec possessed approximately 75 per cent of the seats. The four elements in the Macdonald-Cartier alliance carried a solid majority of these seats for the Conservative party. Central Canada alone gave the government the hard core of a parliamentary majority. New Brunswick, by electing a majority of pro-Confederation candidates, did nothing to disturb the balance. Thus, under the circumstances, the election of eighteen Nova Scotian members (out of a total of nineteen) on an anti-Union platform was unfortunate, but not disastrous. . . . Once it became obvious that the union was destined to endure, the Nova Scotian members could be, and were, absorbed into the fabric of national party politics.

An enumeration of the diverse interests represented in the Conservative party coalition reads like a recipe for friction and discord rather than for co-operation and constructive achievement. In fact, the combination of interests—Protestant and Catholic, English and French, urban and rural—was, and has remained, the standard formula for the construction of a national party in Canada. The Conservative party was simply the first to discover and apply the formula, to develop the technique and possess the leadership necessary for its successful application. The technique was theoretically simple but practically complex: the development and pursuit of some unifying programme; the conciliation (if not the satisfaction) of opposing interests and attitudes; and, in an emergency, a not-too-high standard of political ethics—a readiness "to buy love and purchase peace."[1] The leadership was epitomized in the career and character of John A. Macdonald.

The unifying programme was all ready to hand, in the objectives of Confederation. In order to provide an adequate channel of trade and communication between central Canada and the Maritimes,

---

[1] Quoted in D. G. Creighton, *Dominion of the North* (Boston: Houghton Mifflin Co., 1944), p. 327.

completion of the old Intercolonial Railway project was an immediate necessity and a recognized obligation. To set a northern limit to American expansion, to provide an artery for Canadian expansion to the west, and to create a link between the Dominion and the colony of British Columbia, construction of an all-Canadian railway from central Canada to the Pacific was accepted as an equally important, if less pressing, responsibility. Establishment of a protective tariff was, likewise, almost inevitable in order to counteract the geographically derived tendency toward north-south trade and communication, to provide a protected market for domestic industry, and to guarantee an adequate financial return on the proposed transportation projects.

The Conservative administration began to implement this programme almost immediately. In 1869 the Dominion government acquired the tremendous territorial holdings of the Hudson's Bay Company in the Northwest. Two years later the colony of British Columbia became a province in the expanding federal union. Committed to the construction of a railway to the new province within ten years, the Dominion granted a charter to the Canadian Pacific Railway Company in 1872. The Intercolonial Railway, begun in the pre-Confederation period, was continued under national auspices in 1867 and completed in 1876. The national tariff, the famous National Policy of 1878, completed the process. The term "National Policy" could, with justice, be applied to all aspects of the programme. It was a policy uniting business and government in the pursuit of material and national advantage. . . . In its nationalistic appeal, it might override, where it did not eliminate, local interests and sectional jealousies.

Given the divisive elements in the Canadian community and the formidable topography of the Canadian countryside, success in the prosecution of the National Policy demanded political leadership of a high order. In the leadership provided by John A. Macdonald, the Conservative party and the nation were fortunate. By his contemporaries, Macdonald was likely to be either praised as a national statesman or damned as a rank political opportunist—there was an element of validity in both attitudes. . . . Through his personal magnetism, through his ability as a conciliator of individual and group antagonisms, and through his readiness to utilize the power and patronage of the national government when necessary, Macdonald preserved a semblance of unity among the disparate elements of his party. The Conservative party reaped the benefits in an almost unbroken tenure of power while the National Policy was implemented. In the process the original coalition of 1854 was transformed into an efficient and powerful national party.

The Liberal party was unable to match the impressive performance of the Conservatives. When the Macdonald-Cartier coalition of 1854 embraced elements from all points of the political compass, it left only two significant political groups in the colony of Canada. These provided the nucleus of the Liberal opposition to Macdonald Conservatism. The Clear Grits of western Ontario were the numerically important element. With an able spokesman in George Brown, editor of the Toronto *Globe*, they were the spiritual heirs of the radicalism that had sought expression in the revolt of 1837. Grittism, in fact, reflected the democratic biases of the agrarian frontier: a deep and abiding suspicion of the commercial and transportation monopoly of Montreal; and a belief in egalitarianism and rugged individualism, in free trade and free land, in representation by population, and in strict supervision of, if not a limitation on, government support to business enterprise. The Clear Grits were almost exclusively Protestant, and their latent anti-Catholicism found expression and stimulation in the writings of George Brown.

The French Canadian element in the Liberal coalition was the Parti Rouge. Although the Parti Rouge shared the Clear Grits' bias toward democracy and against big business, it did not, unfortunately, share the latter group's religious beliefs and prejudices. The French Canadian membership of the Parti Rouge combined allegiance to Roman Catholicism with a tendency toward anticlericalism. This ambivalence was a dual source of weakness in the Liberal cause. On the one hand, it precluded anything more substantial than an uneasy alliance between the Parti Rouge and the Clear Grits. On the other, by ensuring the hostility of the politically powerful Catholic Church it blocked the recruitment of a significant number of French Canadian supporters.

The coming of Confederation increased the size of the Liberal coalition, but it did nothing to facilitate the transformation of the coalition into an effective national political party. The numerical strength of the Liberal opposition in the new Parliament was augmented by the addition of Maritime opponents of Confederation and of the Conservative party. The unity of the party neverthless remained in doubt. The parliamentary opposition might distrust and criticize the grandiose nation-building programme of the Conservatives—might, indeed, doubt the wisdom of the federal union itself. Was it, however, united behind an acceptable and a workable alternative?

Just six years after Confederation, the Liberals were provided with an opportunity to essay an answer to this question. The opportunity arose out of the famous "Pacific Scandal." During the spring and summer of 1873, it became increasingly evident that the Conservative party had won the general election the previous year with the help of a substantial campaign contribution from the financiers of the Canadian Pacific Railway. Threatened with defeat in the House of Commons as a result of the scandal, the Conservative administration resigned in the fall of 1873. Suddenly and unexpectedly the Liberal party found itself in possession of national office.

The achievements of the Liberal administration during the ensuing five years showed that the Liberal party had a number of worthwhile reforms to offer, but almost no positive programme. The government passed badly needed legislation that required the secret ballot and simultaneous voting in federal elections. It established a federal judicial system and an independent audit of government accounts. Groundwork was laid for a territorial government in the area newly acquired from the Hudson's Bay Company. A system that permitted local option on the contentious issue of prohibition was instituted. In the field where the Conservatives had been most successful, however, the Liberals largely failed. Instead of adopting a fiscal policy to promote Canadian business and win its electoral support, the Liberal administration attempted to negotiate a reciprocity treaty with the United States. Failing to take aggressive action toward the completion of the Canadian Pacific Railway, the administration leaned toward a policy of public ownership of the railway. The consequent delay in construction helped to promote a seccessionist movement in British Columbia. Whereas the Conservatives had consciously utilized the patronage and power of office to construct a national party, the Liberal leadership resolutely refused to use the perquisites of office to build a party organization.[2]

During their term of office, the Liberals . . . also disclosed their lack of dynamic leadership. In contrast to the easygoing tolerance and imaginative direction of John A. Macdonald, they offered the puritanical and common-sense approach of Alexander Mackenzie.

*   *   *   *   *

In programme and leadership the Liberal party of the 1870's failed to meet the demands of the times. The onslaught of depression, coincident with the party's accession to power in 1873, only sealed the Liberals' doom. The Liberal antidote to depression was reform and retrenchment; the Conservative prescription was a national tariff, the coping stone of the National Policy edifice. In 1878 the Canadian voters chose the more speculative, but more potent, Conservative remedy.

If conservatism is associated with preservation of the *status quo* and resistance to change, then the Conservative party's reliance on protection, public works, and private enterprise reflected a more liberal philosophy than that of the doctrinaire, free-trade Liberals. The Conservative programme, moreover, was better calculated to command popular support. Through a series of general elections spanning eighteen years, the Conservative party reaped the electoral benefit of its National Policy. Lacking such a vote-catching national programme, the Liberal party became more and more the instrument of a "provincial rights" opposition to Tory nation-building and centralization. The Liberals discovered that in a federal system there might be countervailing advantages for a major party which failed to produce an immediate key to national office. Relegated to the opposition at the national level, the Liberal party maintained itself by steadily increasing its influence and power in the provinces.[3]

*   *   *   *   *

In politics, as in other fields of human endeavour, the appearance of things may be deceiving. Blessed with strong leadership and a positive programme, and nourished by the fruits of national power, the Conservatives established an apparently invincible national party in the three decades following Confederation. During the same period, nevertheless, the groundwork was laid for their defeat in 1896. Concurrently, the Liberal party recovered from its 1878 defeat and, in spite of the barrier to a united effort provided by a "provincial rights" orientation, gradually transformed itself into an efficient national organization. By the time the Conservative party was finally defeated, the Liberal party had found effective leadership and evolved an acceptable national programme.

The National Policy of the Conservative party was expected to produce an integrated national economy.[4] Designed primarily to command the support of, and to produce benefits for, the commercial and industrial centre of Canada, it was expected to produce sufficient incidental benefits in the other regions of the Dominion to make possible the maintenance of economic and political equilibrium. Transportation development would make feasible large-scale immigration and the settlement of the Canadian West. The western farmer would produce grain for export to foreign markets and would use the proceeds to purchase the industrial products of eastern Canada. The shipment of grain in one direction and of manufactured goods in the other would make the railway venture profitable. And the protective tariff would stimulate the growth of native industry, encourage east-west trade, and prevent the economic returns of the whole process from filtering out of the country. Because this grand design ultimately depended upon the export of staples, its success was contingent on world prosperity. Unfortunately, world prosperity was the one factor that was unaffected by, and never occurred during, the Conservative tenure of office. Consequently, the Tory National Policy was never completely successful.

The inauguration of the Liberal administration in 1873 had coincided with the onslaught of a world-wide depression [which] . . . continued unabated until almost the end of the nineteenth century. Originally designed primarily for revenue purposes, the Canadian tariff was revised upwards by the Tories in 1879 in an attempt to counteract economic stagnation and to complete the design of the National Policy. The tariff did stimulate industrialization in central Canada but simply provided a focus of economic discontent for the farmers of Ontario, Manitoba, and the other regions. After the 1878 election, the Conservative administration again sponsored legislation designed to promote the rapid completion of the Canadian Pacific Railway. The railway was completed in 1885, but the national government's railway policy produced friction and discord in both Manitoba and British Columbia.

* * * * *

---

[2]F. H. Underhill, "The Development of National Political Parties in Canada," *Canadian Historical Review*, XVI (1935), 383-84.

[3]By 1886 four provincial administrations were Liberal, by 1891 six were Liberal, and when the Liberal party was re-elected to national office in 1896, only the province of Quebec had a Conservative administration.

[4]For greater detail concerning the following, see the *Report of the Royal Commission on Dominion-Provincial Relations* (Ottawa: 1940), Book I, pp. 47-55.

At first, the policies developed by the Conservative administration reflected and reinforced a burgeoning national spirit in the Dominion. When, however, the policies failed to produce all of their anticipated benefits, incipient nationalism, was submerged in a recrudescence of local interests and loyalties. The success of the Liberal party in the provinces during the 1880's and 1890's was a reflection of this trend. A growing "provincial rights" movement encouraged and justified opposition by the provincial governments to the centralization trend inherent in the constitutional structure of Confederation and in the policies of the federal government.

The failure of the Conservative party to evolve an economic policy that would keep the diverse interests of the Canadian economy in dynamic equilibrium was paralleled by a failure to produce compromise policies to keep the divergent interests of race and religion in balance. In normal times, John A. Macdonald maintained harmony among his ill-assorted followers by means of a judicious mixture of personal magnetism and patronage. In a crisis, he was wont to rely on procrastination or compromise. . . .

Confederation was no sooner achieved than the Conservative party was confronted with an issue that involved both race and religion. The first problem originated in the Canadian Northwest. A large element in the population of the future province of Manitoba consisted of the Métis "nation," a people of mixed (Indian and French) blood, whose religion was Roman Catholic. When the national government, in the inauguration of its policies for the development of the West, appeared to ignore their interests, the Métis became aroused. And when verbal protests had no effect . . . the agitation quickly flared into open revolt. Despite the leadership of their brilliant but unstable Louis Riel, the half-breeds were no match for the federal authorities. The revolt collapsed as rapidly as it had begun.

. . . During the relatively short period of lawlessness in the Northwest, a "provisional government" established by the rebels had ordered the execution of a Protestant Orangeman from Ontario who had been acting on behalf of the Dominion government. The resultant outburst of racial and religious feeling in central Canada completely overshadowed the original dispute. French-Catholic Quebec was inclined to champion the Metis cause; a large body of opinion in Ontario demanded the execution of Louis Riel and the punishment of his followers; and the national Conservative party was threatened with a deep schism between its French and English elements. . . . Riel escaped to the United States, and the schism did not materialize.

The escape of Louis Riel only postponed settlement of the basic issue. Discontent continued in the Canadian Northwest . . . and in 1885 reached a new climax with the second Northwest Rebellion. Again, the rebel leader was Louis Riel, and again the rebels—half-breeds and Indians—were defeated by the more powerful forces of the national government. Louis Riel was captured. This time, yielding to pressure from

Protestant Ontario, the national government sanctioned his execution. Riel . . . had by then become an accepted champion of . . . Canada's racial and religious minority. When the government . . . allowed the execution to take place, many adherents of the Conservative party in French Canada were outraged. . . . The biracial fabric of the Conservative party and of Canadian unity had been seriously weakened.

Although the Macdonald administration managed to survive the execution of Louis Riel, the Conservative administration in the province of Quebec was less fortunate. . . . Honoré Mercier, leader of the Nationalist movement . . . became Premier of Quebec and embarked upon a policy destined to subject the bicultural framework of the Conservative party to new strains. A bill to compensate the Jesuit order for estates confiscated by the British government years before was passed by the Quebec legislature in 1888. Although the measure was supported by both races in the province, the more militant Protestants in Ontario saw in it evidence of papal machinations and a negation of the principle of separation of church and state. They demanded that the national government. . . disallow the provincial legislation.

John A. Macdonald and the Conservative government . . . refused to interfere with the provincial act. The decision helped to counteract the adverse reaction in Quebec to Riel's execution, but it eventually weakened the Conservative party in Ontario. . . . Thus was laid the groundwork for the Equal Rights Association and for its successor, the Protestant Protective Association. When the Conservative party was defeated in 1896, this anti-Catholic bloc broke completely with the conservatives and supported the Liberals.

* * * * *

The Manitoba school question arose in 1890 with an act of the Manitoba provincial legislature designed to establish a single, nonsectarian, public school system in the province. The act evoked an immediate protest from the Roman Catholic minority. . . . Although the minority claimed that the legislation infringed its constitutional rights, the national government at first decided against intervention. When, subsequently, the administration reversed itself and passed an order-in-council directing the Manitoba government to restore the rights of the Catholic minority, the provincial government refused to obey. Finally, the national government decided to pass remedial legislation, but the decision came too late. A well-organized filibuster prevented the passage of the remedial bill before the expiration of the parliamentary term, and the Manitoba school question was carried over into the 1896 election campaign. The Conservative party, once more confronted with an issue involving both race and religion, had again failed to develop a satisfactory compromise.

The defeat of the Conservative party in 1896 was not unexpected. The National Policy had not produced all the benefits expected of it. The racial and religious conflicts of the previous twenty-five years had steadily undermined the party's bicultural strength. And the party's shortcomings in both spheres had led to a reaction against centralization of power and a resurgence of provincial and regional particularism. Deterioration in the national leadership and disclosures of administrative corruption sealed the Conservative's doom.

*   *   *   *   *

The transformation of the Liberal party began as early as the 1870's. Its weak element at that time was the Parti Rouge bloc in the province of Quebec. The only Liberal group in Quebec, the Rouges were more of a liability than an asset to the national party. Their reputation for anti-clericalism, superficially confirmed by their alliance with the Clear Grits from the province of Ontario, made widespread popular support in the province of Quebec impossible. The Rouge leaders, moreover, were frequently at odds with the Liberal party's national leadership. . .

Before the Liberal party could make significant inroads into Tory strength in Quebec, the Rouges had to become identified with a programme acceptable to both the Catholic Church and the average, conservative French Canadian. Speaking at Quebec city, June 26, 1877, Wilfrid Laurier, one of the younger leaders of the Parti Rouge, attempted to produce such a new orientation. On behalf of French Canadian Liberalism, Laurier vigorously rejected the political and religious radicalism that, associated with nineteenth-century European liberalism, was anathema to the Church in Quebec. . . . Laurier simultaneously rejected the ultramontane pretensions of a large segment of the French Canadian hierarchy. Denying the claims of the clergy to a special and controlling voice in politics, he denounced the current identification of religious orthodoxy with political Conservatism and demanded the separation of religion and politics. Canadian political liberalism was associated by Laurier with moderate reformist liberalism in the British tradition, and the radical and anticlerical bias of the old Rouge party was disowned.

Laurier's eloquent statement . . . was not long in producing dividends. The hostility of the Church toward the Liberal party . . . gradually declined as the old Rouge leaders were retired. By identifying itself with French Canadian nationalism (stimulated by rising dissatisfaction with the handling of racial and religious issues by the national government), the Liberal party was able to enhance its reputation for respectability without surrendering its reform programme. Through the 1880's and 1890's, it became an increasingly acceptable vehicle for protest against the policies of the Conservative party and the Dominion government.

If the first major step in the resurgence of the Liberal party was Wilfrid Laurier's address on "Political Liberalism," the second was the selection of the same Wilfrid Laurier as the party's national leader. After the 1878 election, the party leadership passed from Alexander Mackenzie to another Ontarian, the brilliant but unpredictable Edward Blake. . . . When the party was defeated once more in 1887, he resigned . . . . The party caucus decided to pass over the two leading contenders and to offer the position to Edward Blake's own nominee, Wilfrid Laurier.

The choice was . . . a happy one. As he had demonstrated in his 1877 speech, Wilfrid Laurier was a man of courage and conviction. He also possessed rhetorical ability, the flexibility and facility in compromise of the politician, and the "sunny ways" of the popular leader—qualities which had been conspicuously lacking in Mackenzie and Blake. Indeed, Wilfrid Laurier had a capacity for leadership more like that of John A. Macdonald than that of his two Liberal predecessors. . . . By 1896 the party had evolved an appealing and acceptable national platform. Reflecting the motivating forces in Canadian politics, that platform contained two important planks—one, racial and religious; the other, economic.

*   *   *   *   *

In the spring of 1896 the Conservatives introduced their remedial bill on the Manitoba school question. Laurier Liberals denounced the measure as an attempt to coerce the Manitoba provincial government and succeeded in filibustering it to death. In the ensuing election campaign, this strategy paid handsome dividends. Since the Roman Catholic Church favoured the remedial bill, the Liberal party's opposition in English Canada catered to anti-Catholic sentiment. In Quebec, on the other hand, Liberal opposition to the Church-supported remedial bill was more than offset by the ability of Laurier himself to appeal to the racial pride of the French Canadian voter. To elect one of their number to the highest office in the land, the French Canadians were ready to vote against the dictates of their own Church and the apparent interests of their co-religionists in the western province. In both communities, morevover, Liberal opposition to a policy of federal coercion appealed to the rising spirit of provincialism and regionalism. Whereas the Conservatives had attempted to settle the issue by coercion, the Liberals . . . promised to seek an acceptable solution by compromise. Thus they had established, at last, a strong position on the contentious issue of race and religion.

The Liberal party achieved a satisfactory economic policy in 1893. In the National Policy of a protective tariff, the Conservatives discovered . . . a fiscal formula commanding popular support. During the intervening years, the Liberals experimented with a number of competing programmes—free trade, reciprocity with the United States, and even the Conservatives' protective tariff. None proved able to command the whole-hearted support of Canadian Liberals; none proved able to command a majority in a general election. At the Liberal convention in 1893, the party finally united behind a compromise policy—a revenue tariff.

. . . To the agrarian, low-tariff enthusiasts, a revenue tariff seemed to promise a reduction in the existing import duties, the maximum of free trade consistent with fiscal need. To the business community, on the other hand, it seemed to promise that a Liberal government would make no radical change in the tariff structure to which business and industry had become accustomed. And, to the Liberal party itself, it offered a tariff plank that could be distinguished from that of the Conservatives but that did not embrace any radical proposal. The Liberal party now had what it heretofore lacked—a moderate economic programme.

With its victory in 1896 the Liberal party not only attained national power for the first time in almost a generation but also, like the Conservative party in 1878, embarked upon a long tenure of national office. What were the ingredients in the success of the Liberal party? Both in the achievement of victory and in its consolidation the Liberal party paid tribute to its Conservative opponent. In both instances, the success of the party reflected that subtlest form of flattery—imitation! By imitating the leadership and programme of the Conservative party during its era of strength, the Liberals defeated a faltering Conservative administration in 1896. By similarly imitating Conservative policy, the Liberals proceeded to consolidate their newly won position.

Settlement of the Manitoba school question came first. As the Liberal party had promised during the election campaign, a compromise, unacceptable only to the extremists, was worked out almost immediately with the government of Manitoba. The tariff plank in the Liberal platform came next. In 1897-98, the commitment to a revenue tariff was fulfilled by a moderate reduction in import duties. Finally, the whole performance was climaxed by "the most brilliant political coup in Canadian history"[5]—the introduction of preferential duties on British imports. In "British preference" the Liberal party had devised a fiscal formula comparable to the Conservative National Policy. It not only enabled the party to offer a concession to its low-tariff, agrarian wing without unduly exciting the suspicions of the business community, but also laid to rest the spectre of disloyalty within the Liberal party and appealed to the widespread pro-British sentiment in the Dominion. Canadian Liberalism had become thoroughly respectable.

The return of world prosperity and rapid increases in the populations of western Europe and the United States now created for the Liberal party an economic milieu that the Conservatives had lacked. Under Liberal auspices the Dominion of Canada began to fulfil both the expectations of the architects of Confederation and the expectations of the draftsmen of Conservative policies during the latter half of the nineteenth century. While world prosperity, population increase, and urbanization were creating a tremendous demand for foodstuffs, the Laurier administration instituted a vigorous programme of immigration and settlement designed to populate western Canada. The resulting Canadian wheat boom produced a buoyant national economy and created many opportunities for the investment of foreign capital in Canada. The government responded with policies directed toward the encouragement of new transportation development and of business expansion. The Provincialism of the 1880's and 1890's was forgotten in the new, expansive atmosphere, and the Liberal party reaped the benefits of a fresh outburst of Canadian nationalism. By adopting the Conservative party's formula for success and adapting it to new conditions, the Liberal party had, in fact, come of age.

*   *   *   *   *

The two-party system which emerged in Canada at the beginning of the twentieth century was the natural product of a British and French inheritance operating in a North American environment. As these influences have continued to operate impartially on both parties, so also the formula for the successful organization and operation of a national party in the Dominion, developed by the Macdonald Conservatives and the Laurier Liberals, has remained substantially the same through the years. What are the main ingredients in that formula?

Sectional diversity precluded the establishment of a unitary state in 1867. Sectional diversity has, likewise, precluded the establishment of unitary party organizations. Both party organizations and government have been . . . federal in form. In the early years, indeed, both the Liberal and Conservative parties were nothing more than loose alliances of sectional groups. And although national organizations were gradually superimposed upon sectional factions, even today the national organizations tend to become quiescent, if they do not disppear altogether, in the intervals between elections. The continuing and effective units in the political party are, consequently, the provincial organizations. Even in federal elections, the party will rely heavily on its provincial organizations to conduct the campaign and to get out the vote.

Sectional diversity has been equally influential in other ways. In the competition for national power, the major parties inevitably seek programmes which can override sectional interests and jealousies. At a particular point of time, the greater success of one party in this respect leaves the other free to act as a vehicle of (if not deliberately to incite) sectional discontent. Provincial victory offers compensation for national defeat. Provincial patronage nourishes the party that is in opposition at the national level, while the loss of provincial power tends to weaken the provincial organizations of the party currently holding national office. Finally, the opposition party at Ottawa develops a new synthesis of sectional attitudes, a new national programme—the federal government is defeated, and the process begins all over again. A continuous, long-run tendency toward dominion-provincial political equilibrium is the result.

The attributes necessary for party leadership and the attitude of the party toward its leader reflect in like manner the influence of sectional diversity. To be successful, the party leader must possess a marked ability to compromise differences, to reconcile conflicting interests, and to make of himself the indispensable, unifying symbol of the party's national pretensions. Despite differences in personality and temperament, John A. Macdonald, Wilfrid Laurier, and Mackenzie King were alike in this respect. And the party reciprocates by giving such men its continuing support. The position of the leader who exhibits facility in achieving party unity and winning national power is remarkably secure. Conversely, the tenure of the leader who fails to "deliver the goods" is

---

[5]Underhill, *op cit.*, 385.

likely to be of short duration. While Macdonald was Prime Minister, the Liberal opposition experimented with three different leaders; while King was Prime Minister, the Conservative opposition tried no less than seven.

Canada's major parties must, of necessity, encompass a wide variety of interests: economic, racial, religious, and social. As a result, both parties are "great, nation-wide, easygoing, omnibus vehicles whose occupants often have difficulty in recognizing their fellow passengers or in understanding why the driver of the vehicle let them in."[6]

Neither party can afford to espouse rigid doctrines for long, when divergence of opinion may be as great within one major party as between the two. On a specific issue, therefore, the difference between the major parties is likely to turn more on emphasis than on a basic difference in outlook. The Liberal party, it is true, has been more prone to emphasize Canadian autonomy and free trade, has appeared more sensitive to the interests of French Canada and the farmer. And the Conservative party has been more prone to emphasize the British connection and protection, has appeared more sensitive to the interests of English Canada and the business man. At various times, nevertheless, both parties have espoused public ownership and social security, have defended provincial rights and private enterprise.

Faced with the task of attracting a wide variety of followers and of encompassing a wide variety of attitudes and convictions, the major party must constantly seek a policy that promises to induce political equilibrium and some semblance of national unity. In the past, the search has always led in the same direction. The heavy concentration of industry and population in Ontario and Quebec means that a major party must obtain financial and voting support in at least one of these provinces. The successful party articulates its policies in terms of the interests of Canada's industrial heart. The compliance, if not the support, of other regions may then be purchased more or less openly by a process of political and economic bargaining.

In past periods of economic expansion, the high cost of national unity has been charged against Canada's tremendous natural wealth. In periods of economic stagnation or contraction, the price has not always been paid. National policies have then been accompanied by the rumblings of regional discontent, sometimes successfully channelled through the major party in opposition at the moment, sometimes finding overt expression only through a minor party movement. Canada, a country whose wide diversity and bicultural heritage has made it extremely susceptible to sectionalism and sectarian passions, a country whose economy has been extremely sensitive to world economic fluctuations, is, indeed, a formidable challenge to any national political party.

---

[6]G. V. Ferguson, "Parties of Protest," *Annals of the American Academy of Political and Social Science*, CCLIII (1947), 32.

2

The Rise of National Parties
in Canada

ESCOTT M. REID

*

To understand Canadian politics during the first quarter century or so of the Dominion's history one must constantly bear in mind certain differences between the conduct of general elections then and now. The two most important points of difference are that in the first three general elections, those of 1867, 1872, and 1874, voting was open throughout all the provinces and the polling in the various constituencies did not take place at the same time. A Toronto constituency might elect its member one day and the neighbouring York constituency six weeks later. The grosser abuses of the system of non-simultaneous elections were remedied in 1874 but not till 1878 was the ballot used and simultaneous voting established in all but a few of the constituencies of the five eastern provinces. In 1882 Manitoba voted simultaneously with the east and by 1908 deferred elections had been discontinued in the great majority of the remaining western constituencies. It is also worth noting that open voting was resurrected for use in the first two federal general elections held in the North-West Territories, those of 1887 and 1891.

Deferred elections and open voting are important in a study of the rise of national political parties in that they make it possible for government to exercise a great measure of control over the results of elections—and the greater this control of government over elections, the weaker the political parties. Under the old system of open voting, civil servants, contractors, anyone who wanted to obtain favours from the government could not vote against the candidates it supported without losing their jobs or their expectations of favours should the government be returned to power. On the other hand if they voted for the government and the opposition were successful their fate would be equally unhappy. As a natural consequence they disliked partisan electoral contests. This dislike was shared by many of their neighbours who, though they did not expect to be the direct recipients of government favours, had the interests of the whole constituency at heart and did not want its chances of obtaining a new post office, wharf or railway spoilt by its unintentional support

*Reprinted from *Papers and Proceedings of the Canadian Political Science Association*, IV, 1932.

of the weaker party at an election. Even after vote by ballot was adopted these people continued to disapprove of partisan electoral contests which committed the constituency to the support of one side or another before they knew which side would constitute the government. The ideal election of these political realists was an uncontested one in which the member was not definitely committed to any party and could therefore make good terms for his constituency in return for giving his support to the strongest party in the House.[1] Such members constituted an important fraction of all the early parliaments; Macdonald called them "loose fish," George Brown, "the shaky fellows" and Cartwright, "waiters on Providence." These appellations are hardly dispassionate enough for us so we shall call them for want of a better term, "ministerialists," because their politics were not to support a party but a ministry and any ministry would do. These ministerialists were inverted Irishmen. They were always "agin" the opposition. Their counterpart in ecclesiastical politics was the Vicar of Bray.

It was because of the strength of this political realism that non-simultaneous elections threw such power into the hands of the ministry. The government could bring on the elections first in those constituencies in which they were safe, and having carried them, tackle those where they had some chance against the opposition, and leave the dangerous seats till the last. At the close of the election of 1872, *The* Toronto *Globe* wrote that: "The sole object of this nefarious trickery was to enable the Ministerialists to raise a grand howl over their pretended success and cheat the people into the belief that the Opposition were bring awfully beaten."[2]

The Globe knew that if the people believed the opposition were being awfully beaten many of them would rally to the government camp and the opposition would be badly beaten. The illusion of victory would create victory. For if the voting in a ministerially minded constituency, in our sense of the word, were deferred until it seemed pretty clear which party would form the government, that constituency need no longer return an avowed "loose fish"; it could return a proper party candidate. Nevertheless that would not mean that it cared at all for parties—that parties had any real existence in that constituency.

*   *   *   *   *

National political parties certainly did not exist under the Macdonald government from 1867 to 1873. Confederation saw group government established at Ottawa. The dominant groups or parties in the coalition government were the several branches of Ontario Conservatism under Galt, Macdonald and others, and the French Conservative groups under Cartier. This dual alliance was supported by the Ontario Liberals under McDougall, Howland and Blair, the English minority in Quebec under Galt, and a large group of ministerialists mostly from Eastern Ontario, Quebec and New Brunswick. The Ontario coalition Liberals and the Cartier followers were not members of a coalition party because they owed their allegiance entirely to their own sectional leaders. They appear to have been willing to support an alternative administration which would have excluded Macdonald and his supporters, and Macdonald in 1871 had to use all his cunning to prevent a successful alliance arising out of the "coquetting," as he called it, which was going on between his French followers and the two wings of Ontario Liberalism.[3] By 1872 the coalition Liberals had returned to the Reform party or had been swallowed up by one of the Conservative groups, and consequently the government followers in Ontario were slightly more homogeneous, though the number of parties which made up Ontario Conservatism was still great if we can judge from the events of 1873. Certainly in that year it appeared as if the Conservative sectional leaders in Ontario could transfer their personal following to the support of another administration at their own mere pleasure. If Galt, for example, had entered Mackenzie's cabinet, as at one time seemed likely, he would have brought over the Conservative members from the Cobourg district and this, according to his adviser (the Conservative editor in Cobourg) would have given him "the strongest personal following of any member of the Cabinet."[4]

The members from New Brunswick in the first two parliaments were either ministerialists or independents. The election of 1867 in that province was fought not between an anti-government party and a pro-government party but between so-called anti-unionists under Smith and Anglin and so-called unionists under Mitchell and Tilley. These terms apparently meant nothing and when the respective groups got to Ottawa the former did not consistently vote with the opposition nor the latter with the government. As a group they gave a "fair trial to the administration" (that over-worked phrase of early dominion politics) but occasionally they would show their complete independence as, for example, when they voted unanimously in favour of an amendment to the first dominion tariff debated in parliament.[5] In the election of 1872 only one successful can-

---

[1]An example of such an election was that in the constituency of Cornwall (eastern Ontario) in 1872. Candidates of both parties were nominated but the Conservative who was a son of John Sandfield withdrew and allowed the nominal Liberal, Bergin, to be elected by acclamation. In withdrawing Macdonald said that "he believed that when Dr. Bergin got into Parliament he would throw over all ties and follow the crowd if the Government had a majority in the House. He thought that he would show good judgment in doing so, because he would get more favours by going with the majority than he could from the minority." *The* Toronto *Globe*, August 24, 1872.

[2]Ibid., August 8, 1872.

[3]Sir John Macdonald to Hon. Alex. Morris, April 21, 1871, in Sir Joseph Pope, *Correspondence of Sir John Macdonald* (Toronto: Doubleday & Co., Inc., 1921), p. 145.

[4]H. J. Ruttan to Sir Alex. Galt, November 17, 1873, in O. D. Skelton, *Life and Times of Sir A. T. Galt* (Toronto: Oxford University Press, 1920), pp. 465-466.

[5]Amendment of McDonald (Lunenburg) of December 14, 1867 "for the purpose of placing wheat and rye flour, cornmeal and corn in the free list," *Journals of the House of Commons* (Canada), 1867-68, p. 92.

didate appears to have committed himself to the support of the government or opposition. The others professed varying degrees of independence of party ties.

The Nova Scotians in 1867 constituted a separate political party and its very *raison d'etre,* opposition to confederation, signified that it owed no loyalty to any party or leader outside Nova Scotia. According to Howe even the beaten Tupper party had not taken sides in the party politics of Ontario. "No man in this county," said Howe in the first session of parliament, "went to the hustings pledged to any side of any question in the politics of Canada."[6] When Howe entered the cabinet his followers became still another group within the coalition for they continued to owe their allegiance to their sectional leader not to Macdonald. In 1872 in Nova Scotia as in New Brunswick the issues were mainly personal and the candidates were unpledged to any party. Their general attitude was that they had no affection for the government but that the Reformers were even less likeable for they were a selfish Ontario party.[7]

It follows from this analysis of the government supporters in the first two parliaments that there was then no national Liberal party. The Brownite Liberals of Ontario possessed the unity of adversity—all who were not truly loyal had deserted to join the winning side—but they, like the conservatives, did not even extend over the whole province for Ontario east of Kingston was a hotbed of ministerialism. Members from that district might call themselves Liberal or Conservative but they almost unanimously supported the government. There was also a Liberal or Rouge party in Quebec but the Ontario and Quebec Liberal parties were not united. There was between them little more than an entente cordiale, at most a dual alliance. Not until 1872 were they able to draw close enough together to choose a common leader in parliament. This dual alliance of Ontario and Quebec Liberals did not even have an entente with the New Brunswick independents or the Nova Scotian party. The leaders of the Liberals, Mackenzie and Dorion, tried to co-operate with the maritimers but they could carry only about half their supporters with them on a division.[8] The Liberals did not even possess enough cohesion to pursue a tactically sound policy.

The election of 1872 increased the number of votes the Liberal alliance could muster on a division but it did this rather by increasing the number of groups and perplexed ministerialists who attached themselves to its standard than by adding to the strength of the real party. The reason for ministerialists supporting an opposition party was that as the returns came in during the long six weeks of polling they were so close that both parties claimed the victory and the ministerialists were not certain on which side of the fence to jump. The wiser of them concluded that even if Macdonald had won his was but a temporary triumph and his tenure of office would be brief. Consequently it was good policy to support the opposition so that they would be remembered when the opposition came into its own. In Quebec there were interesting developments which showed how thin was the veneer of party unity which had covered the fissures between the various groups under Cartier, now weakened by the intrigues of church politics, by the Riel rising and the New Brunswick school law. He lost support on the right to the Ultramontanes or Programmists, and on the left to the Parti National, and both dissident groups attached themselves to the Rouges. Thus the Quebec oppositionists constituted no longer a fairly united party but a heterogeneous collection of groups. The parallel with 1896 is interesting.

After the downfall of Macdonald over the Pacific scandal one coalition government succeeded another. The dominant groups in the new coalition were the Ontario Liberals and the Quebec Rouges. They were supported by a few Ontario Conservatives who had left their party because of the scandal, by the Parti National and the Programmists, and by the usual assortment of ministerialists from eastern Ontario and Quebec and by almost unanimous ministerial groups from the maritimes and the west. The personnel of the cabinet gives convincing evidence of the coalition's heterogeneity. The Ontario members were Mackenzie, Blake, Cartwright, D. A. Macdonald, Scott, and Christie. Of these Cartwright and Scott had been avowed Conservatives as late as two years before and D. A. Macdonald was an eastern Ontario "wobbler." The original Quebec representation of three were all Rouges but not one of the five maritime members could have been called a Mackenzie supporter in the previous election. A. J. Smith of New Brunswick had declared at his nomination meeting that he had said to Sir John Macdonald and Sir George Cartier that even if he had the power he would not turn them out for the sake of office, for he thought no other could do any better than they.[9] Burpee, the other cabinet minister from that province, had denounced the Liberal opposition because they were engrossed by the sectional interests of Ontario.[10] Ross of Nova Scotia had not even supported the remonstrance to the Governor-General on August 12th, 1873, when a dozen of the usual government supporters had bolted, and though Coffin of Nova Scotia had joined in the remonstrance he had previously supported Macdonald in the two party divisions on the charges of corruption. Laird of Prince Edward Island had not taken part in the campaign of 1872 since the Island was

[6]*House of Commons Debates* (Canada), November 8, 1867.

[7]For example Killam, the member for Yarmouth from 1867 to 1882, said in his campaign according to an editorial in the *St. John Daily Telegraph*, August 17, 1872: "I have not had much confidence in the Government in many respects; but am sorry to say that I have no confidence in the Opposition. They . . . have attempted to treat the interests of these Maritime Provinces as mere make-weights in the scale, to further the selfish aims of great parties in Ontario."

[8]Examples of such divisions are those on the amendment of McDonald (Lunenburg) of December 14, 1867, mentioned above, and on the Holton amendment of April 29, 1868, moving the House into Committee of the Whole "to consider the alleged grievances of [Nova Scotia]." *Journals of the House of Commons* (Canada), 1867-68, pp. 92, 249.

[9]*St. John Daily Telegraph*, August 6, 1872.

[10]*Ibid.*, August 5, 1872.

not then a member of Confederation. Thus even counting D. A. Macdonald as a Liberal, the Liberals constituted only half the Mackenzie
cabinet.

It was only by 1878 that the Ontario-Quebec parties had
conquered most of eastern Canada. That was the election, it will be remembered, in which the ballot was introduced and elections were held
simultaneously in all but four of the eastern constituencies. Of the 141
eastern members of parliament who sought re-election all but one did so as
supporters of that leader whom they had supported in the first session of
the parliament of 1874, and the great majority of the other candidates
committed themselves in their election speeches to following one of the
two party leaders. The result was that the Toronto *Globe* and the Montreal
Gazette disputed over the party affiliations of only five members-elect
instead of the thirty-five of 1872, and it was thus possible to discover the
approximate strength of the parties in the House as soon as the ballots
were counted, whereas previously that knowledge could only be gained
after the first party division had taken place. There flowed from this the
establishment of a constitutional precedent, for Mackenzie resigned before
meeting the new parliament. This break with tradition did not go uncon-
demned. The *Dominion Annual Register* for that year summed up the
criticism which was directed against his action: "To count up the results
of an election according to the success of certain candidates who were
represented to hold certain views on public affairs and to accept that
result as the will of the people constitutionally expressed was . . . a dangerous approach to the plebiscite."[11]

The critics were right. General elections were becoming
dangerously like plebiscites but the reason was not Mackenzie's break
with constitutional precedent but the establishment of the two-party system in eastern Canada. Every advance towards national political parties
was to mean a further step towards making general elections plebiscites.

We must not think of the two parties as being as firmly
established in eastern Canada in 1878 as they were by 1896. The Conservative party in Quebec in 1878 was still made up of a union of groups
and it is possible that the only loyalty which a member of one of these
groups owed was to his own sectional leader. Certainly in 1887 the
ultramontane members did not seem to experience any violent conflict of
loyalties when they broke with Macdonald and sought to destroy him in
revenge for the murdered Riel, and were so nearly successful that Macdonald was only saved by the extra seats his gerrymander had given him
in Ontario. It would appear, however, that from 1891 on the federal
Conservative party did possess a measure of sovereignty in Quebec, for
Chapleau was not certain enough of the loyalty of his followers to risk an
open break with Macdonald. Instead he kept one foot in each camp.

In the seventies partisanship had been making no progress
in the western provinces. The politics of Manitoba and British Columbia
in the three general elections of that decade can be explained as the result
of two forces: their desire for the Pacific Railway, and the holding of

their elections some weeks after the results in the east had been declared. Until the railway was completed the west could not afford the luxury of party politics. It had to be ministerialist. And as it always knew which party had been sustained by the east, it could be ministerialist without difficulty. All parliamentary candidates in the west in the seventies were unanimous in their opposition to the opposition. Opposition candidates did not appear in Manitoba until 1882 nor in British Columbia until 1891. Western ministerialism was, however, of a different nature from the *politique de pourboire* of the eastern ministerialists. The westerners did not sell their support in return for the petty favours of the patronage machine and the pork barrel but only in return for the railway, the whole railway, and nothing but the railway. This attitude of political realism, dictated by the economic needs of the frontier, did not triumph in Manitoba without a struggle against the partisan political attitudes of the Ontario settlers. The struggle was short and not severe. The economic necessities of the present triumphed over the political institutions of the past.[12] The British Columbians had no such struggle, for few of them had any interest in the party politics of the east until the completion of the railway in 1885 brought eastern immigrants and with them eastern political ideas. This difference in the composition of the population of the two provinces meant that Manitoba declared its allegiance to the eastern parties as soon as it was safe for it to do so, that is in 1882 or 1887, while British Columbia delayed till 1891 or 1896. The North-West Territories did not swear loyalty to the parties till 1896 in spite of a false appearance of partisanship in 1887—the result of perplexed ministerialism. The *Globe* told them that the Liberals had won and the *Gazette* that the Conservatives had again triumphed.

With the conquest of the west completed in 1896 the Conservative and the Liberal parties had at last become national and thus a national two-party system was established in Canada for the first time. In becoming national the two parties did not lose all their old characteristics. 1878 and 1896 do not mark breaks in the evolution of political parties in Canada, for the development of such extra-legal political institutions is a gradual process. Consequently it is not surprising to find today sectionalism in parties, heterogeneity in cabinets, and ministerialism in constituencies—veiled and modified as they are by the party system. Bargaining between sectional groups still takes place but nowadays more often in caucus and cabinet than on the floor of the House of Commons. In caucus the party is sectional. In public it is homogeneous. In reality it is federal.

What is the force which has made out of the loose coalitions of Macdonald and Mackenzie the federated unions of sectional groups which have constituted the national parties from 1896 to the

---

[11]H. J. Morgan, *Dominion Annual Register 1878* (Montreal: Dawson Brothers, 1879), p. 211.

[12]This struggle is reflected in the editorials of *The Manitoba Free Press*, January 10, 17, and February 7, 1874.

present day? The loose coalitions had as their core dual alliances of Quebec and Ontario groups. Whichever of these alliances proved to be the more powerful ruled with the assistance of the maritime and western groups which remained neutral until the struggle in the central provinces had been resolved and then made as good terms as possible with the victors. There came a time when the neutral groups had to choose before the struggle of the rival dual alliances which one they would support. As some chose one and some another the dual alliances would have become quintuple had not other forces been working to make them two federations of five or more groups. For when allied and associated powers are fighting a war for supreme power—and political combinations are always fighting a war for supreme power—the alliance tends to become itself the direct object of the devotion and loyalty of the citizens of the separate powers or, in other words, there is a tendency for the alliance to acquire sovereignty and so become a super or federal state. The other force making for closer union is the result of the actions of the leaders of the groups who find from bitter experience that an alliance is most effective in attack or defence when it is united under a supreme command. These two forces meet, the force of individual devotion pushing up from the bottom and the force of political strategy pushing down from above, and what was once a loose dual alliance is compressed into a federal union. The cement which made this union durable is furnished from non political sources. Better means of communication bind the sections together; inter-migration breaks down sectional differences; new territories are settled as a common enterprise; a national feeling struggles into existence. Out of the alliances of sectional parties are created the federations of sectional groups—the national Conservative and the national Liberal parties.

The Canadian Party System

*

Thibaudet remarked: "La politique, ce sont des idées." This certainly does not apply to Canadian politics. Some observers have seen our politics as a struggle of the "Ins" versus the "Outs," with no difference between the parties. Mr. Mallory, however, does distinguish between them. One party succeeds because, through its leader, it creates a mood which is in tune with that of the country at the time.

Professor Meisel looks at how changes in social organization and in the governmental process have altered the Canadian party structure in the direction of a multiple party system. Each party is assessed on a schema, and individually analysed.

Professor Horowitz shows how Canada has both a Lockean Liberal tradition and a Tory organic one. It is the latter which makes Canada more accepting of socialist ideas than the U.S.A.

3

The Structure of Canadian Politics

J. R. MALLORY

*

. . . Parliament—the agency which makes and controls government—performs its essential functions because political parties translate it from a chaotic mob to an organized and disciplined body. . . . Political parties are the operating units in a game played under definite rules, and played for a definite object. The object is power—but not absolute power. It is power conditionally held and exercised subject to law and subject to the freedom of others playing within the rules to gain it. Consequently political parties whose objects are revolutionary and whose operations are clandestine are playing the game without regard for the rules, and with the object of getting power and retaining it by changing the rules to suit themselves. Thus a communist or a fascist party is not a party in the same sense as is the Conservative Party or the Co-operative Commonwealth Federation.

Our party system operates also on another important assumption: that there is a certain optimum number of parties. . . . "The party system, and particulary the party system under cabinet government, will find the best conditions for its operation where there are only two parties, or, at least, two parties sufficiently large to provide as a rule a clear majority in the legislature."[1]. . . .

One of the things that a party system is supposed to do is to offer to the elector a reasonably clear cut choice. One of the conventional ways in which political choice is expressed in the modern world is between left and right, or between conservative and liberal. This is not a very definite distinction but I think most people konw what it means. Conservatives are expected to be more satisfied with the status quo than liberals: they are contented, somnolent, skeptical of the need for change. Liberals are inclined to favour change because to them there is nothing particularly sacred about the past. To a liberal, rights acquired by prescription are no better than any other kind of rights, and reform is always justified if it will enlarge the area of liberty. This is the classic distinction

*Reprinted from *Canadian Politics*, Mount Allison University Publications No. 4, Sackville, N.B., 1959.

between conservative and liberal. It corresponds to a division both by temperament and interest which exists in most countries. It is a ready explanation of nineteenth century English politics.

How far is it true of politics in Canada? . . . A reader of party platforms and of leaders' speeches will find that there is a remarkable similarity in what the parties profess to want. They claim to seek the same objectives, the very wording of some of their declared aims is almost identical. Each is in favour of everything which will attract votes: each, at least in public, is against sin. But where does the difference lie?

Part of the explanation is well-known, and I will not spend time over it. In Canada and in the United States, political parties are engaged in a struggle for power in vast sprawling countries which occupy half a continent and people of diverse origins. Among such groups no sharp division on readily intelligible principles is easy. The task of building a successful political party is essentially that of building an uneasy coalition of sectional interests whose common body of doctrine is bound to be slight. For example, forty years ago the Liberal Party, as we have recently been reminded by reading a life of Mackenzie King, included not only a radical agrarian group which wished to get rid of the tariff and to extend the degree of democracy everywhere, but also a very right-wing, big-business dominated, high tariff group in Quebec. The task of reconciliation between these two and the many other divergent interests in the party was the principal task of a party leader.

. . . .It has been argued that there is only one North American tradition—the radical one—and that a genuine conservative politics is alien to North American political conditions.[2] What I mean is best summed up in an observation of Gunnar Myrdal's that "America . . . is . . . conservative . . . But the principles conserved are liberal, and some, indeed, are radical."[3]

This notion that newness is all, that there is no good thing but a new good thing, that tradition and prescription are not essential values: this is appropriate to the United States whose very foundations are based on a violent revolutionary overthrow of the past, advocated by the most respected names in American history. We up here are Americans too in that we live in a new country where to be new and radical is, in a certain sense, to be respectable. I draw your attention to the name of the Progressive Conservative Party. And yet there are parts of Canada to which this generalization does not apply. There can be no doubt that, in Quebec and the Maritime Provinces, there remains a conservative outlook on life as characterized by an attachment to the values of the past and a scorn for the material and the temporary. In Canada there are at least

---

[1]R. M. Dawson, *The Government of Canada* (Toronto: University of Toronto Press, 1954) p. 492.

[2]See, for example, Bernard Crick, "The Strange Quest for an American Conservatism," *Review of Politics*, XVII, No. 3, July, 1955, 359-376.

[3]Gunnar Myrdal, *An American Dilemma* (New York: Harper & Row, Publishers, 1944), p. 7.

conservative *regions*, though it is clear that this is only of accidental benefit to a political party which calls itself conservative.

There are two possible theories of the party system in Canada which I have so far mentioned. There is first the "literary" theory of a two-party system of liberals and conservatives more or less evenly balanced, alternating in and out of power in part as the mood of the country shifts from optimism to pessimism. Over a century of careful search has led most observers to abandon the view that our main parties differ in any sure and consistent way by the litmus test of political doctrine. They both stand for a congeries of objectives, without any real regard to whether these objectives are consistent with the underlying theory of liberalism and conservatism. It is only fair to say that I think this was less true before 1900 than it has been since. The issues that divided Macdonald and his party from the Grit and reform elements in the Liberal party were such questions as the tariff, the franchise, and the imperial connection. On these the parties divided in a way which was consistent with the notions of liberal and conservative.

Secondly we can look at our political parties as mere collections of interest groups, held together by a more or less cynical bargain of political bosses. Indeed, if we look at Canadian parties at any particular time, it is easy to find evidence to support this view. They are great national coalitions with their leaders meeting at the summit.[4] I think it probable that this view of the nature of political parties, which shows a healthy lack of respect for the propaganda of party leaders, is neverthless too materialistic. It is not true, most of the time, that the voters will vote for the party that promises the biggest benefits. Public works do not necessarily win elections, though no responsible political leader is advised to neglect them. Voters do not like to think of themselves as calculating hedonists, any more than the buyers of soap will buy the cheapest good soap.

*   *   *   *   *

I am here concerned only with the political consequences of a constant regimen of necessary compromise. From time to time, when political or economic conditions are particularly unsatisfactory, a very large number of people become disillusioned with the whole political system. They lose faith not only in the leaders and the existing parties, but in the system in which they operate. Thus the various successive protest parties in the West were in revolt not only against the old parties but against the rules of the game. They wished to impose "constituency autonomy" on the parliamentary representative so that he became a mere delegate of his constituents—a measure which would have made the operation of disciplined parties in the legislature impossible and would have destroyed cabinet government. The Social Crediters went further, and sought to place the main areas of government policy in the hands of "technicians" who were free from the usual constitutional and political controls. It was, if you will, political fundamentalism. But in the early days of Social Credit, as with the Progressive party and the C.C.F., the dominant motive was to clean out the political temple, and to bring about good government by good men, uncorrupted by the vested interests of wealth and special privilege.

Such parties, of course, soon learn from the responsibilities of power that the new Jerusalem is not easy to attain, and that they themselves must adopt the organization and methods of their opponents or give up the struggle. But nevertheless it should be recognized that these periodic eruptions of new parties on the fringes of our political system are a healthy thing.

Political parties operate in an unstable market, a sort of monopolistic competition which is subject to the same objections as monopolistic competition in the production of soap or motor cars. The competing parties are desperately afraid of making mistakes and as a consequence they resort to the principle of minimum differentiation of the product. They cling hopefully to the same ideas and policies which have stood them in good stead in the past. A political party which prematurely adopts an unpalatable policy may suffer frightful damage, just as Chrysler Motors did when it introduced a streamlined car twenty years too soon. The result is that old parties become poor in ideas, and desperately afraid of new ones. New parties, with nothing to lose and everything to gain, can afford to advocate new ideas. In the process they may gain supporters, and at the same time the public receives a gradual awareness of some new policy. Then, when the time is ripe, the old parties calmly adopt the more durable reforms of the third parties and carry them into law. This has been true of almost every significant reform of the last thirty years. It has been advocated by the Progressives and the C.C.F., and then turned into law by Liberal, or sometimes, Conservative governments.

There is a second way in which third parties are a healthy influence. They are movements of protest from the grass roots which get their initial momentum from the anxious and urgent participation of many humble people in political affairs. Most of the time in Canada there is a tendency for people to leave politics to the "professionals" so that the average voter in Canada is becoming increasingly passive and has little or no direct participation in the internal affairs of his own political party. As the country gets bigger and more urban the divorce of the average voter from any meaningful participation in politics is increasing. A new party which stirs up popular interest has the effect of countering this trend and bringing actual democracy closer to more of the people.

The accepted American theory about third parties assigns them a necessary but unrewarding role in the party system. No American

---

'Thus Mr. Bruce Hutchison describes the last Mackenzie King administration as "a congeries of separate groups in coalition. Men like Gardiner as the spokesman of agriculture, Howe as the representative of industry, Mitchell as the delegate of labour, St. Laurent as the leader of Quebec, possessed almost autonomous and sovereign power within the party and could apply, when necessary, a veto on government policy by Calhoun's ancient Law of Concurrent Majority." *The Incredible Canadian* (Toronto: Longmans, Green & Co., Inc., 1952), 414.

third party since the Republican Party has succeeded in becoming firmly established in the national system in the last century. All the rest—the Greenbacks, the Progressives, the Prohibitionists, and the Socialists, have withered on the vine. It has been their destiny to play a role similar to that of the male bee—they have fertilized another party with their ideas and then passed into oblivion. The reason that American third parties are confined to the role of creative innovators is the nature of the American system of government, which has built-in obstacles against third parties which tend to keep them off the ballot. The major obstacle of all is that supreme power comes to a party only with the capture of the presidency —and the president is a single man who can hardly take the form of a coalition. American third parties are denied by the nature of the American electoral system the possibility of reaching the critical size—which is big enough to stay alive.

It is easy to argue that this theory is equally applicable to Canadian politics, but I think we should accept it with caution. There are several characteristics of our system which give a third party rather more of a fighting chance to survive. One of these is that there are only ten provinces, so that a party which captures one or more of them has a better organizational base from which to continue to fight elections than a comparable party in the United States. In the second place, a third party in Canada is probably more necessary, in the sense that there are deep political cleavages within our national life which justify a regional party for a considerable time as a necessary safety-valve for pent-up local feeling which would be inadequately expressed were there only two national parties. Finally, the nature of cabinet government gives a third party more leverage than does the presidential system. For a third party which holds the balance of power in the legislature is not excluded necessarily from a share of power. Coalitions are possible, and the rules of legislative procedure are adapted to make it easy for third parties to make their position clear. Since our federal system makes it possible for a third party to gain experience of power, and thus demonstrate its capacity to govern, a Canadian third party has at least a fighting chance of forcing its way into the party system.

*   *   *   *   *

It may be that to the skeptical eye there is no real difference between Conservative and Liberal, and therefore the conclusion should follow that it really does not matter who wins an election. But the party contest in Canada is not just a sham battle between Tweedledum and Tweedledee. There is a difference between parties. This difference is not one of programme, though there may be minor differences in emphasis. For example, the Conservatives and Liberals may in practice be a little different in the attitude toward protective tariff measures. But these differences are not great.

What I think is important is that at any given time only one party is in tune with a national mood—and that party is likely to stay in power until the mood changes and leaves it politically high and dry. Macdonald was in his way the perfect expression of the national spirit in the nineteenth century—raffish, careless, tough and pliable. Laurier expressed the character of the new Liberal Party which he was able to create out of what had been merely a series of doctrinaire and local provincial parties. Laurier combined an elegant and eloquent idealism with the embodiment of a spirit of compromise—of healing the scars of conflicts of race, religion and region which had grown up since the seventies. The time came when much of the glamour of the Liberal position wore off, when compromise appeared merely the inaction of old, tired men in office. The earnest, precise Borden represented the reaction in a time of deep national trial. Again Mackenzie King, with his earnest preaching about the virtue of conciliation, represented the tortured doubts of an age of national frustration, when constitutional difficulties, the baffling new problems of an industrial age and a shattered world, combined to create an atmosphere of cautious despair. With Louis St. Laurent a new look came to the Liberal party: toughminded, bland, sophisticated, and confident in managing a growing society bursting at the seams with growth. But mere prosperity and competent government is not enough. There is plenty of evidence that the pace of modern living produces a host of frustrations and a mixture of guilt and insecurity. Into this atmosphere was skilfully projected the personality of John Diefenbaker, solemnly intoning evangelical phrases about a national vision and a national dedication. It does not matter whether these "thoughts" have much meaning —they did catch a mood—and it is a mood which is still upon us.

I do not mean to say that political success is just a matter of the "right" personality—of the leader who uniquely symbolizes his age. Elections are won by party workers with money to spend. But mere money and organization are not enough unless a party can project an image of itself which gets a strong response from the voters. The invention of television has undoubtedly brought much closer together the visible personality of the Prime Minister or party leader and the image which the party wishes to project of itself to the voters. This is a new factor in the tactics of campaigning which political parties will have to master if they are to present an effective campaign in a general election.

*   *   *   *   *

Political parties lie at the heart of the democratic process. The extent to which they themselves are democratic is a good measure of the effectiveness of democratic institutions. The parties operate at an intermediate level between government and the people. At the same time they are formally outside the constitution since they are private and voluntary bodies which control their own internal processes. There can be no doubt that the growth of urbanization has had a bad effect on the democratic character of political party organization. When Canadian life was still essentially rural, the leading positions in political parties fell naturally into the hands of the natural leaders of the community. In small communities there was an instinctive system of selection in which people of ability almost unavoidably rose to the top in community affairs. It thus did not matter much if the actual conduct of the affairs of a local party organization was a friendly arrangement among the recognized few who made their decisions informally in whatever manner they chose. A formal apparatus of constitutional government within parties would have led in fact to the same people taking the same decisions in much the same way.

With the growth of urbanization it seems likely that this informal but essentially democratic process has been undermined. No longer does everyone know everyone else in the community. More and more of community functions fall into the hands of those in key positions who need have little direct contact with the constituents on whose behalf they run local organizations. What is true of the community chest is equally true of the political party. The consequnce of this is the growing separation between an elite group and the mass of apathetic nonparticipators who have to be herded, by the most skilful available techniques of public relations, to do their civic duty whether it be voting or donating blood. In the process the lumpen mass is being manipulated by a class of persons with whom they have no real contact. This tendency is as true of political parties as it is of other kinds of community operation.

What is happening in our politics is a part of what is happening in our whole social life. The average man is becoming more and more a spectator of life, herded by various kinds of emotional appeals into some perfunctory performance of some kind of OK activity, whether it be the act of consumption or the effort of voting. In so doing he responds to increasingly high-pressured and over-simplified appeals to overcome his apathy and the ennui which arises from his essential loneliness.

It may be that the image of the tough-minded citizen who made up his own mind and did what he felt like doing has always represented the ideal rather than the reality of Canadian life. But it is impossible to escape the feeling that in the modern social context, where no one is too unimportant to be the victim of a battery of persuasion-mechanisms, that we are on the way to producing a robot citizen. He is exposed to an enormous quantum of "information" and "education" in all sorts of media which his grandfather escaped. But it is hard to believe that his saturation point for the reception of information has not been passed, and he remains a poor thing dumbly responding to nothing at all but high-pitched emotional stimuli.

This means that he is a long way from John Stuart Mill's ideal citizen, who had enough education to read and (more important) enough time to digest what he read. The question I raise is this: can modern man retain the ability to make sensible decisions when his whole waking life is surrounded by propaganda so that he may well have never tasted the precious liquid of truth at all?

Recent elections add to one's disquiet. A provincial electorate is quite content to return sixty-one out of sixty-five candidates of a single political party. Another province produces a disparity between the majority and the minority which is great enough to reduce opposition to impotence. The modern voter is remarkably susceptible to the "bandwagon effect." If everyone else seems to be voting a particular way, he feels insecure and lost unless he can identify himself with the majority. Thus June 10, 1957 produced an election result which was perhaps politically awkward, but probably represented what the country really felt. But the election of 1958 brought out the insecurity of the other-directed voter. He felt that the Conservative Party was the party of the majority so he voted for it in overwhelming numbers—and in the process nearly destroyed the opposition, which is after all an essential part of the constitution.

Such results do not augur well for the future of constitutional government in Canada. Even those who felt that it was time that the Liberals spent a chastening period in opposition must have been dismayed at an election which almost destroyed parliamentary opposition. The thing for which we must hope is an ability which the parties in opposition can show in cultivating solid strength in the country. It is important that governments should have the majority support necessary to govern, but it is dangerous if the country is so conformity-minded that only a small percentage of the electorate will vote against a party which they think may win. Admittedly, our electoral system of single member constituencies combined with three and four concerned contests tends to exaggerate the appearance of conformity and majority-mindedness. But we have for a long time been threatened by a system in which ony one party in each generation seems capable of winning elections. Down that road we shall find arrogant and arbitrary governments, and we shall get the kind of unchecked exploitation of power which is the normal lot of animals whose instincts encourage them to huddle behind a leader.

The most important thing about Canadian politics is that they are parochial rather than national. This is at once the greatest weakness and the greatest source of strength of our national political system. It is a weakness not only because it threatens from time to time to destroy the very idea of a Canadian nation, leaving us paralyzed with dissention when we need to be united and strong to survive. It enables whole provinces to fall prey to demagogues, charlatans and grafters. Provincial autonomy covers a multitude of sins, not least of them corrupt political systems which would be unthinkable in the majority of the provinces of Canada. Should the electors of a province be gullible, easily bribed, and politically frail no one in Canada can save them—except themselves. This is a consequence of the federal system.

However, a federal system tolerates not only great variety in the standard of political morals and in the level of political intelligence, it also ensures variety and destroys the possibility of uniformity. The new engines of mass-communication which make all of our newspapers a common product of the same matrix of predigested news and features, which expose us all to the same ways of dressing and eating and thinking, can never wholly break through the essentially parochial character of

Canadian life. As long as we retain the variegated pattern of political organization that we have, it remains nearly impossible to cajole or frighten us all into the same voting pattern, meekly following the same bandwagon. There will always remain pockets of opposition to the prevailing national pattern in some provinces. As long as opposition remains we possess an insurance policy against totalitarianism, in a world where liberal values are continually in peril.

4

Recent Changes in Canadian Parties

JOHN MEISEL

*

Our concern with the transformation which has affected political parties compels us to define our terms of reference. Are we to explore the changes which have taken place *within* each of the parties or shall we examine transformations in party systems? Shall we confine our interest to Canadian parties, and if so, should we look at both federal and provincial organizations or merely at one or the other? What time-span shall we apply as we analyze party metamorphoses? In this introductory statement I shall comment both on changes affecting the party system and on changes affecting individual parties; I shall confine myself to Canada and specifically to the federal parties; and I shall deal primarily with changes dating very roughly from the end of the second World War or perhaps from the decline of the King-St. Laurent Liberal party and its aftermath.

Let us begin by assessing what is happening to the Canadian party system.

PART 1: THE PARTY SYSTEM

The most useful approach, from my point of view, is to proceed within the framework suggested by functional analysis. We shall, therefore, think of parties as performing certain functions within a political system and we shall distinguish between manifest and latent functions and dysfunctions.

There is yet no unanimity in the rapidly growing literature on political parties with respect to all the manifest functions performed by parties. In so far as I can tell, however, there is agreement on at least these points: parties are the agencies *par excellence* for the recruitment, nomination, and election of political officeholders, and it is through their medium that these officeholders are responsible to the public. It is their job, in short, to elect a government accountable to the people. In performing

*The basis of a paper delivered to the Association canadienne-française pour l'Avancement des Sciences, Montreal, November 5, 1965.

these functions, the parties meet the requirements of two of the major functions which must be performed in every society: they articulate and aggregate interests, to use the language of Gabriel Almond. The chief latent functions of parties—and here I am departing from the view usually expressed by our colleagues who have written extensively on parties—is to play a central role in the process which permits governments to formulate and apply policies which are both sound and popular, or at least acceptable. In the parliamentary system particularly, the government outputs are the result of a subtle and delicate interaction between elected and permanent officials, one group ideally keeping its eyes on public opinion, the other being more concerned with the substantive advantage of a given policy. In addition, however, to providing a vital link between technical and popular opinion, parties perform other latent functions, the chief of which is the reduction and simplification of issues into manageable proportions.[1] In Canada, an additional latent function of the parties is of the greatest importance and must, therefore, receive our special attention.

The prototype of the Canadian parliamentary system originally developed in a homogeneous community in which a high level of consensus prevailed about the ends to be sought by government. The British type of parliamentary system cannot, I believe, function effectively without such a fairly high level of underlying consensus. Since Canada is notoriously lacking in a strong sense of national cohesion and its concomitant—a high degree of consensus on the ends to be sought by society—the parliamentary system has not always performed effectively. This is particularly evident at the present time when Canadians are genuinely, and I believe seriously, divided about the nature of their country and about how it ought to be governed. For the parliamentary system to function smoothly and, consequently, for the party system which has grown up in association with it to function effectively, a high level of cohesion and consensus is required. In a country lacking a strong national political culture and the institutions fostering it, political parties have a special role to play as agencies for the creation of national symbols, experiences, memories, heroes, and villains, not to mention national favours, benefits, and concessions. When I use the term "national" I do not, of course, mean that each is associated equally and in the same way with every citizen, but rather that they apply to significant groups of the population among all sections, regions, and other important groupings of the population. An absolutely critical latent function of the party system in Canada is, therefore, the role it plays in the development and fostering of a national political culture; it must play a vital role, in fact, in generating support for the regime. So few other institutions do so and, in any event, few are as well suited for this task as the parties.[2]

Transformations in the Party System

Among the changes which have recently been affecting the Canadian party system, three seem to me to be of particular importance. They are:

(a) A decline in the importance of the parties in the political system,

(b) The solidification and normalization of a multi-party system,

(c) The emerging "regionalism" of parties.

(A) DECLINE OF PARTY IMPORTANCE

Political parties taken as a whole seem to have become less important actors in the political system than was the case in the past. This means, in effect, that their activities affect fewer aspects of the political system and/or that they are active in relatively less important sectors. In other words, they either do less or their activities are less important and are, presumably, supplemented or replaced by those of other institutions. The most fruitful way of substantiating the assertion that the party system is being downgraded and of explaining this development is to examine it under three headings: (i) Societal change, (ii) Changes in the governmental process, (iii) Changes in parties themselves.

i) *Societal Change*—All the societal factors which have led to the relative diminution of the importance of political parties can be traced to the growing industrialization and urbanization and, more particularly, to the accompanying growth of general affluence. These factors have combined to extend enormously the pluralism of West European and North American societies. Not only have the sheer numbers of voluntary associations, interest groups, and private and semi-public organizations increased on an unprecedented scale, but their wealth has grown rapidly and substantially. They are often unwilling to permit their interests to be expressed and transmitted only by parties, but wish to participate directly in making their voices heard and their influence felt. Furthermore, as the state continues to invade new fields of activity, controlling or operating ever growing numbers of enterprises affecting every facet of the life of the community, these groups have a growing stake in participating in the major decision-making processes. Their numbers and their means permit them to become rivals of political parties in many of the latter's traditional spheres of activity. These rapidly proliferating groups and institutions can gain access[3] to the decision-making process without having

---

[1]For a slightly different approach, see Frank J. Sorauf, *Political Parties in the American System* (Boston, 1964), pp. 164-6.

[2]The same can be said of the party system in the United States, although in that country there is a more viable political culture and there are probably many more agencies than in Canada fostering a sense of underlying unity. Note the illuminating discussion of this point in A. Ranney and W. Kendall, *Democracy and the American Party System* (New York, 1956), pp. 507-13 and particularly "Although many American social forces and social characteristics operate to minimize our civil-war potential, it is the party system, more than any other American institution, that consciously, actively, and directly nurtures consensus." 508.

[3]For a discussion of the importance of "access" see David B. Truman, *The Governmental Process* (New York, 1951), pp. 264-70.

recourse to parties which become bypassed in the vital area of mediation between individual and group interests and the state.

Another set of related societal changes has reduced the effectiveness of political parties. These changes are complex and somewhat similar developments are usually referred to under such broad headings as "the end of ideology" or "other-directedness."[4] A consequence of these phenomena has been the gradual diminution, in Europe and North America, of the cleavage in attitudes towards social issues. The old bitter struggles between the rich annd the poor, between the privileged and the underprivileged, have become international and, domestically, have given way to a general acceptance of what we might, for want of a better word, describe as the welfare state. Political parties, as has often been noted, have responded to this by occupying a central position permitting them to maximize their electoral support. Their policies have become extremely bland, so as to antagonize the smallest possible number of people. This tendency has been observed not only in the traditionally centre parties but even among most of the more ideologically inclined and more extreme parties. As a result, the task of formulating new ideas, creating institutional "homes" for their development and propagation is no longer being performed by the parties on the same scale as before. Innovation, in this sense, has become the business not even of minor parties but of youth groups, temporary ideological groups emerging in response to particular crises, or pressure groups pursuing a particular interest[5]. To the extent, therefore, that parties have formerly played an important role in the process of innovation, their role is being taken over by less partisan and often less permanent bodies.

ii) *Changes in the Governmental Process*—The vast increase in both the amount and complexity of knowledge which has accompanied industrialization has, of course, had a profound effect on governmental institutions. One of the most far-reaching of these has been on the legislature which, in an age of specialization, has found itself at a distinct disadvantage. Confronted by the massive and esoteric knowledge available to the executive through its control over the public service, the legislators, who are generally amateurs *vis-à-vis* the technical aspects of the problems discussed in parliaments, can merely exercise a veto power over decisions, rather than having a genuine voice in the process of decision-making. This fact has reduced the role of parties, whose theatre of operation is *par exellence* on the floor of the legislature.

Many of the most important decisions affecting the direction of economy, defence policy, foreign affairs, social services, etc., are nowadays made by inter-departmental committees of the civil service, by independent or quasi-independent administrative boards, agencies, and commissions, by so-called advisory bodies and, to some extent, even by Royal Commissions. The parties have either no contact with, and control over, most of these bodies or, if they do, it is usually of a rather tenuous and formal kind. Our lives are increasingly run by highly skilled specialists whose virtual monopoly of knowledge in certain fields reduces the efficacy of those who are supposed to control the experts on behalf of some sort of general, community interest. All of this is well known and need not be elaborated here. What we must note, however, is that the process has affected the function performed by parties who have not been notably successful in adapting themselves to the new conditions. Parties have occasionally tried to cope with this situation by themselves enrolling experts and by placing them in positions of power but, as the Liberal party has clearly shown, the entry of the specialist into politics, particularly at the cabinet level, does not necessarily make of him a politician, and certainly not an effective one.

Canada's federal system has imposed a particularly difficult task on the parties. To the extent that many of our major governmental decisions have resulted from intensive consultations between different levels of government, parties have to some measure been locked out of the most important decision-making processes. Dominion-provincial conferences, meetings of premiers, committees of experts representing the civil services of several provinces, and possibly two or three levels of government, working parties of various provincial ministers and experts, have all downgraded the role of parties who still bear considerable responsibility for the consequences of decisions but cannot always participate in their making. Canadian federalism has, therefore, been a major contributor to the decline in the importance and effectiveness of political parties.

iii) *Changes in Parties*—Our discussion so far suggests that developments which can be observed in a number of liberal democracies[6] have contributed to the decline in the importance of Canadian parties. In addition, certain purely domestic conditions have aggravated the situation in Canada. No home-made factor—not even federalism—has been as important in this respect as a number of internal changes wrought by the parties themselves. Several details will be mentioned in the second part of this paper but we must here isolate *some* of the changes, since they are directly relevant to the decline in the role of parties.

---

[4]See Daniel Bell, *The End of Ideology* (New York, 1961), particularly Part III and David Riesman,*The Lonely Crowd* (New Haven, 1950) and the considerable literature stimulated by these and similar works.

[5]For a discussion of the traditional role of inovation performed by the party system in the United States, see Theodore Lowi, "Toward Functionalism in Political Science: The Case of Innovation in Party Systems," *American Political Science Review*, LVII.

[6]Note, for example, the observations of Sorauf about the United States: ". . . the political party in the United States finds it progressively harder to monopolize its traditional political activities." and "they [ie parties] no longer control the major share of political expertise and political loyalties they once did." *op. cit.* pp. 55, 165. Samuel J. Eldersveld raises the same problem with reference to the United States at least by implication, although not explicitly, in his *Political Parties: A Behavioral Analysis* (Chicago, 1964), pp. 18-23. For data on France see Association Française de Science Politique, *La Dépolitisation—Mythe ou Réalité* (Paris, 1962), *passim*.

Each of the major parties has, oddly enough, reduced its effectiveness for quite different reasons. The Liberals' major handicap has, I think, been the party's tendency to nominate candidates with no, or only tenuous, connections with the Liberal party, and to place in positions of leadership large numbers of non-politicians. The art of politics, like any other complex skill, must be learnt, and the Liberals' continuous recruitment of high party personnel from the ranks of public service, business, universities, etc. has contributed to difficulties in arousing public enthusiasm and in performing well at the governmental level. The early ineptitude of the Pearson government and the manner in which the Liberal front bench allowed itself to be terrorized by the opposition during the twenty-sixth parliament, resulted in large part from the partisan political amateurism of the Pearson team. The process had, of course, started during the long tenure in office of the Liberal party during the King-St. Laurent era,[7] but it reached critical proportions in the sixties. In the face of admittedly extremely serious challenges, the party has failed to display the skill required of it in the Canadian political system.

If the Liberals were too little a party of politicians, the Conservatives were perhaps too much so. During the long sojourn of the Conservatives out of office, from 1935 to 1957, they found it increasingly difficult to attract able young people as candidates. Few promising and ambitious men were willing to run for a party which appeared to have little chance of election. The nucleus of Conservative MPs which survived in Parliament during the middle fifties was so accustomed to seeing the world from the viewpoint of the opposition benches that it found it difficult to adopt the posture required of members of a government party. The new leader, Mr. Diefenbaker, was not only intensely partisan but he was also inclined to play a lone hand. He completely dominated his party and ultimately caused it to become deeply divided. The consequences of these developments were that the party acted in government as if it were still in opposition, that some promising and able Conservative politicians who were originally attracted to the party during the middle fifties—the years of growing Liberal unpopularity—now lost interest in a career with the Conservatives, and the performance of the Conservative government alienated an increasing number of voters. Both major parties have, therefore, succeeded in substantially undermining the public's confidence in their capacity to provide really effective government. More serious, perhaps, both are suffering from incapacities which prevent them from coping successfully with the tasks before them. Since the so-called third parties are not considered by the general public as a viable alternative to the Liberals and the Conservatives, the whole party system is incapable at present of performing the functions required of it.

Political scandals and the disappointing behaviour of Parliament have, of course, added to the general disillusionment with the parties. They have also made the task of parties more difficult by undermining the public's support for the regime in general, and by reducing the public's interest in, and respect for, the political process in any form.

Canadian parties have also been influenced by the well known general changes affecting parties in all modern democracies. The introduction and extension of the merit system in the public service, the awarding of public contracts on the basis of competitive tenders, the governments' assumption of many social and welfare services, and the permeation of bureaucratic controls into virtually all phases of life, have combined to reduce the amount of direct patronage available to politicians. While parties can still cater to the interests of large regional or other groups through large-scale public spending, the politician, on whom the party's success must ultimately depend, has been deprived of the most effective local means of practicing his trade.

Changes in society, in the governmental process, and in the parties themselves have reduced the importance of the party system in the Canadian political system. The parties participate in a smaller proportion of public decisions than before and a number of particularly important decisions, such as those affecting Dominion-provincial relations, are reached outside the party system.

Two other transformations of the Canadian party system must be mentioned before we turn to a detailed discussion of internal changes in each of the parties.

(B) SOLIDIFICATION AND NORMALIZATION OF THE MULTI-PARTY SYSTEM

Among the many myths with which we surround ourselves for the sake of making life appear more comfortable than it really is, a special place should be reserved for the idea that Canada has a two-party system. There are, of course, many ways of classifying or defining party systems,[8] but it seems utterly unrealistic to think of Canada in terms of a two-party system. The critical evidence lies in two areas: (i) the magnitude of support obtained by the various parties, particularly the largest ones and (ii) the number of parties capable of obtaining parliamentary majorities. The two-party system fails in Canada on both scores.

Since 1935 the two major Canadian parties have failed, with only minor exceptions, to attract the support of from one-fifth to one-quarter of those actually voting.[9] Some observers have argued that this is largely irrelevant since only two parties have been anywhere near actual political power and that the real test of a party system is in the number of

---

[7]See J. E. Hodgetts, "The Liberal and the Bureaucrat," *Queen's Quarterly*, LXII, No. 2; idem, "The Civil Servant and Policy Formulation," *The Canadian Journal of Economics and Political Science*, XXII, no. 4, pp. 470-3; and John Meisel, "The Formulation of Liberal and Conservative Programmes in the 1957 Canadian General Election," *Canadian Journal of Economics and Political Science*, XXVI, no. 4, pp. 566-7, 573.

[8]A useful survey is Neil A. McDonald, *The Study of Political Parties* (New York, 1955) and, of course, Maurice Duverger's classic *Les Partis Politiques*, (Paris, 1951).

[9]For greater detail and a discussion see John Meisel, "The Stalled Omnibus: Canadian Parties in the 1960's," *Social Research*, XXX, n. 3, pp. 368-9.

parties capable of forming a government. I do not accept this view since parties perform other vital functions not directly related to forming governments.

But even if one did accept this argument one would be hard put to find the two-party system in Canada. The ability of a party to govern is clearly related to its command of a parliamentary majority and Canada has elected a majority government only once in the five most recent elections; minority governments, usually relying on the tacitly agreed support of one of the so-called third parties, have become the norm in Canada. Even if one party does win a majority in one of our future elections, I expect that this will not, in the foreseeable future, permanently re-establish the two-party system in Canada. Important regions of the country and sections of the population are, at present, totally unprepared to succumb to the blandishments of the old parties. I expect this state of affairs to continue.

The 1957 and 1958 elections have every appearance of having been "critical elections" in the sense that they produced a long-lasting realignment of party support in Canada.[10] While all the details are not yet available, there is evidence to suggest that the hold of Mr. Diefenbaker over the loyalties of prairie voters will be inherited by the party he transformed.[11] One could argue, on the basis of this evidence, that the NDP and Social Credit are losing their traditional strongholds and that their days as effective parties are, therefore, numbered. This argument overlooks the fact that the regional base of Social Credit cannot be exorcised so long as the party is firmly in control of the provincial governments of Alberta and British Columbia and support for the NDP has shifted in part into the urban centres. We shall return to this point later in the paper. Here, the important point to note is that the realignment in the prairies may have more serious consequences for the Liberals. Their *exclusion* is likely to be more permanent than that of their rivals; they are in danger of losing what has been their greatest asset for over forty years—the image of being a genuine national party. The more entrenched the Liberal party becomes in French Canada and the more effectively it espouses a dualist conception of Canada, the more likely will be this loss of at least some western support.

My argument can be put in a more general form by linking the number of parties to the number and intensity of cleavages in the country. Canada's traditional cleavage was essentially regional (although ethnic differences occasionally became acute) and the two-party system was able to contain it. During the thirties the divisions became more complex and the party system adjusted itself to the new conditions by allowing third parties to become a safety-device absorbing serious regional discontent without threatening the legitimacy of the whole system or the regime. The emergence in Canada of several powerful centres of economic life (or subeconomies) and the transformation of some regional cleavages into sharply defined ethnic cleavages, have placed new demands on the parties and have called for new kinds of inter-relationships among them.

Maurice Duverger has argued that "the multi-party system in France is a result of the non-coincidence of the main cleavages in opinion."[12] While I am not for a moment suggesting that Canada's party system is likely to resemble that of France, I do think that Duverger is right in stressing the multiplicity and *non-coincidence* of cleavages as one of the explanations for the presence and survival of more than two parties. In Canada also, the greater number and the growing non-coincidence of cleavages will make it difficult, in the foreseeable future, for the parties to return to a two-party system and it is to be expected, therefore, that the multi-party system permitting majority governments some of the time, but not always, will continue to be the norm.

(C) REGIONALISM OF PARTIES

If our assumption is correct, that the changes in voting patterns which have occurred since 1957 are likely to solidify to some extent, then we must also conclude that Canadian parties are becoming increasingly regionally based, almost to the point of becoming regional parties. The Liberals are, at present, the only genuinely national party, although their strength west of Ontario is dangerously low. The Conservatives are still suffering from their disastrous weakness in Quebec which, however, may change when the party finds a new leader. While the NDP has some strength in most parts of the country, it can hardly be called a national party in the sense of having more than merely token support in all regions. It does, however, through a mildly class appeal, have a thin stratum of consistent support in urban centres throughout the country.

None of this is particularly new but it is becoming apparent that the trend towards greater regionalism is growing more pronounced. The present state of regionalism among Canadian parties is not, in my view, so far advanced as to threaten the traditional function of our parties as brokers between sectional interests. Political scientists, particularly in the English-speaking world, have frequently pointed to the dangers to a political system of parties which are too narrowly based, particularly in a heterogeneous country like Canada.[13] While this view may be unnecessarily rigid in rejecting ways in which parties can perform vital functions in democracies—ways which differ from the classic Anglo-American model—it nevertheless contains a compelling warning of the dangers we may be confronting. An unchecked trend towards regionalism among Canadian parties might easily prevent the party system from containing and reducing internal conflict and so from performing one of its

---

[10]V. O. Key Jr., "A Theory of Critical Elections," *Journal of Politics*, XVII, and idem, "Secular Realignment and the Party System," *ibid.*, XXI.

[11]Peter Regenstreif, "Pearson Can't Break Through That 'Wall' on the Prairie," *Toronto Daily Star* (October 23, 1965).

[12]Barbara and Robert North, trans., *Polidical Parties* (London, 1954), p. 232.

[13]For a succinct expression of this view see Corry, J. A. and Hodgetts, J. E., *Democratic Government and Politics* (Toronto, 1959), pp. 277-8.

most important functions, the encouragement of consensus and cohesion. Present trends in our party development should, therefore, be read as constituting a danger sign.

PART 2: CHANGES IN EACH OF THE PARTIES

Studies of political parties have suffered from the reluctance of political scientists to examine them within an explicit analytical framework. In this paper, for example, statements have been made about Canadian parties which are virtually useless as guides towards an accurate and penetrating statement of the party viewed as a whole. The usual categories of cadre or mass parties, parties of the left or right, ideological and electoral parties, etc. are of limited usefulness when parties in their full splendour are to be compared within one or more political systems or over a reasonably short period of time. What is required, therefore, is a general descriptive schema which will permit the comparison and analysis of parties under headings which allow the major characteristics to be presented and examined in an orderly way.

A Schema for Comparing Parties

The accompanying table indicates that our particular schema seeks to distinguish six particular aspects of parties. They are:

I   Ideology
II   The locus of power
III   Structure
IV   The basis of support (social groups)
V   Personnel (activists)
VI   Modus operandi

The data placed under some of these headings will be presented under sub-headings which will differ from one political system to another. My own concern with Canadian parties, for example, prompts me to examine their ideology under four sub-headings:

1. Definition of Canada (domestic)
2. Definition of Canada (international)
3. Role of the State
4. The Game of Politics

Under the first heading we will try to identify the conception of Canada held by each of the parties. What sort of country do its leaders and spokesmen think it is? Do they, for example, assume that it is a British country, a partnership between the the two founding groups, or a multi-ethnic, pluralistic state like the United States of America, dedicated to the idea of creating a "melting pot"? The second heading permits us to compare the parties on the basis of their attitudes towards the role Canada should play in the world. Is Canada conceived of primarily as a member of the Commonwealth, a member of the North American political community, or a state defining its foreign policies within a different framework of allegiances and international "reference groups"? Is the concept of Canada one which leads to a nationalist foreign policy, or one which sees Canada primarily as playing a part in some sort of broader international system? The third subsection of the ideology heading shows whether a party assigns the state a socialist-welfare-state function, or whether it leans more to what used to be called laissez-faire. This division indicates whether a party is on the left or the right, in the sense in which these terms are usually employed. Finally, the fourth heading leads us into a consideration of the general concept of the party process. What is the party's attitude towards patronage, financing of its expenses, conforming with the existing electoral law, etc? Is it satisfied with the rules of the game or does it wish to bring about change?

Some of the other headings are similarly broken down into smaller areas permitting a reasonably realistic examination of the physiognomies of parties. The details of these subdivisions can be seen in the accompanying table and will become clarified as necessary when we apply the schema to Canadian parties.

Before we begin I must, however, issue a warning of the tentative and experimental nature of our schema. The outline has been worked out only roughly. Despite having undergone several revisions it is still only a modest beginning, and a crude beginning at that. Some of the categories overlap and others are not nearly as precise as we should wish. These qualifications notwithstanding, however, the framework provided for the comparison of parties seems to be very promising. It should not only illumine our discussion but also perhaps lead, in the long run, towards more effective comparisons of parties in different political systems, using, in some instances, simple quantitative methods of evaluating the available data.

In the table I have placed a short descriptive comment for each of the parties (except the Ralliement which is not really a national party) and, when dealing with ideology and the locus of power, I have tried to give a very rough quantitative expression of my assessment of the party's performance. Ideology (the party's attitude or posture would perhaps be a more accurate heading for what I am trying to describe) is a particularly imprecise category and I have therefore felt it necessary to refine it slightly. For each party and in each subdivision of ideology I have scored the party on a scale of from 1 (low) to 5 (high) for each of three criteria:

    A. the degree to which the party's avowed position (as expressed by the leaders, documents etc.) corresponds to its actual performance,

    B. the degree of agreement (consensus) within the party on the point under discussion,

    C. the intensity of the party's concern over this issue or, to put it differently, the importance attached by the party to it, compared with other matters.

Take, for example, the first item in the table, the concept of Canada held by the parties. The Liberals are held to think of the country as a political entity in which the French- and English-speaking people have a special position; Canada is a partnership of English and French but it also embraces a plural society in which various groups have claim at least to ethnic survival. This has been scored as follows:

	A	B	C
'65 Score	5	3	4
Trend	+	0	+

These numbers and symbols indicate that I judge (A) there is a high convergence between ideology and performance on this point,[14] (B) there is only a medium degree of concensus in the party on it and (C) the party attached considerable importance to it but that the importance was not overwhelming. The plus, minus (not used in this example) and the O symbols indicate the change or trend I detect. (A) the convergence of ideology and performance is growing; (B) there is no change in the degree of agreement within the party, (C) it is an increasingly important component of their ideology.

Under II, Locus of Power, I try to assess where the centre of power lies within the party with respect to the federal and provincial organizations. Here, obviously, the strength of the party in the provinces, is of decisive importance, particularly, the number and importance of provincial governments it controls. A score of provincial power was computed very roughly for each party by assigning it a high score for every provincial government it controls and a somewhat lower score for provinces in which it provides a substantial opposition. The scores were then totalled for each party.[15]

* A = Convergence of
    Ideology and Performance
    1 = low convergence;
    5 = high convergence

B = Degree of party *Consensus*
    1 = low consensus;
    5 = high consensus

C = Degree of *Importance*
    attached by party
    1 = little importance;
    5 = great importance

Trend   0 No change
      + increase
      − decrease

† PROVINCIAL SCALE
  3 points given party holding office
    in province
  1 point given party constituting
    important opposition

Province	Libs	Cons	NDP	SC
B.C.	0	0	1	3
Alberta	0	0	0	3
Saskatchewan	3	0	1	0
Manitoba	1	3	0	0
Ontario	1	3	1	0
Quebec	3	0	0	0
New Brunswick	3	1	0	0
Nova Scotia	1	3	0	0
P.E.I.	1	3	0	0
Newfoundland	3	0	0	0
Total	16	13	3	6

‡ 1 = Poor or very low
  2 = Fair or low
  3 = Good or medium
  4 = Very good or high
  5 = Excellent or very high

[14]This is probably too generous a score. It accurately reflects the Liberals' consistency in championing Canadian dualism but overlooks their failure to recruit into the highest party posts people whose origin is neither French nor Anglo-Saxon.

[15]The calculation is shown in the footnote, although it is so simple and rough as to make its reproduction here highly pretentious.

A SCHEMA FOR THE COMPARISON AND ANALYSIS OF PARTIES: CANADA 1965

Party Characteristic	Liberal (*)	A	B	C	Conservative (*)	A	B	C	NDP (*)	A	B	C
I IDEOLOGY												
Definition of Canada (domestic)	Dualism-pluralism				British connection-pluralism				Dualism-strong centralism			
'65 Score		5	3	4		4	4	4		3	4	2
Trend		+	0	+		+	-	+		+	-	+
Definition of Canada (international)	N. American-internationalist				Br. Commonwealth-nationalist				Internationalist-nationalist			
'65 Score		5	5	3		4	3	3		4	5	3
Trend		0	0	+		0	-	+		0	0	-
Role of State	Welfare statist-business oriented				Welfare statist-business-farm-oriented				Welfare statist-socialist oriented			
'65 Score		4	2	4		3	4	3		5	5	5
Trend		+	-	0		0	0	0		-	0	-
Game of Politics	Traditional-N. American				Traditional-N.American				Reformist-traditional			
'65 Score		3	3	1		5	5	1		5	5	4
Trend		-	-	-		0	0	0		-	-	0

Party Characteristic	Liberal	Conservative	NDP
II LOCUS OF POWER	Federal Prov'l. score: 16†	Provincial-Federal Prov'l. score: 13†	Federal Prov'l. score: 3/†
III STRUCTURE			
Organization	Centralized-decentr'd	Decentr'd-centr'd	Centralized
Locus of power (in org'n.)	Cabinet-leader	Leader-caucus-prov'l. parties	Nat'l. Exec.-leader
Internal unity (fed)	Good-fair (3-2)‡	Poor (1)‡	Very good (4)‡
Int'l unity (dom-pr.)	Good (3)	Very good (4)	Excellent (5)
Quality of election machinery	Excellent (5)	Good (3)	Good (3)
IV SUPPORT			
Electoral base	Urban (metrop'n) Catholic-Prot-other French-A-S.-other Young, university Que.-Ont.-Atlantic	Rural-farm Protestant-Cath A-S. older Prairies-Marit-rural Ont.	Urban (metrop'n.) Protestant-other A-S. older BC.-Ont. cities, Sask.
V PERSONAL	Urban (Pearson men) Business-Profession-law ex-public servant egg-head more amateurs	Rural (Dief. men) Business-law politician more professiona'l	Trade unionist-teacher "low income" profession egg-head
VI MODUS OPERANDI	Am. style, administrative politics gov'tl. expertise+ PR	Traditional-personalized politics pol. experience+ PR	"Movement"-tradit'l politics amateur+PR

The Liberal Party

The Liberals, as we have seen, stress dualism in their definition of Canada but they are also only rarely forgetful of the pluralistic nature of the country. The importance of an adequate definition of what Canadians believe their country to be, is a matter of growing concern to the Liberals, as it is to all parties. In the field of Dominion-provincial relations, there has been a growing shift from the centralist assumptions epitomized by the report of the Rowell-Sirois Commission to an attitude tolerating the highly decentralized policies dictated by co-operative federalism and the recognition of a special status for Quebec. Looking at Canada from the outside, the Liberal party is notable for its sympathies with the United States and for its willingness to accept (or perhaps for its belief in the futility of resisting) the increasing integration of Canada in the English-speaking part of the North American community.[16] This is not so much the result of a carefully thought-out and fully debated policy decision, as a reflection of the often unconsciously held economic, social, and cultural values of the party leaders. At the same time the Liberals have shown an unmistakable enthusiasm for collective security in international politics, based on vigorous participation in the United Nations and in regional pacts like NATO.

There has been little change in the Liberals' support of a powerful state apparatus which provides a minimum cushion of economic wellbeing to all citizens while at the same time fostering conditions enabling business to flourish. The party is sympathetic, therefore, not only to large-scale welfare measures, like government-operated medical insurance and pension programmes but also to providing a climate in which corporations can amass enormous resources, profits and, of course, influence.

Despite numerous protestations by the men who have come into the Liberal party in recent years that the Pearson party is developing a new politics free from some of the old blemishes, the Liberal party is deeply committed to the traditional North American style of politics. Quite aside from the notorious scandals revealed in the last year or so, and the insouciance with which the cabinet met them, the party has, since 1963, relied as heavily as before on rewarding its friends by the use of patronage and attractive appointments. The party has not been heard to complain about corporate and other large contributions to its campaign coffers but it should be noted that it has appointed a non-partisan committee to look into the problems posed by election expenses.

Despite the fact that its provincial affiliates hold office in Newfoundland, New Brunswick, Quebec, and Saskatchewan, the locus of power is very much at the centre. It is the federal leaders who dominate the party and notably, of course, Mr. Pearson and those who can influence him. This is not surprising. Anyone in command of the Ottawa governmental apparatus is likely to outweigh the power of men in command of less strategically based and less massive units within the party. The federal party is, therefore, dominated by the cabinet or, more precisely, by the most powerful members of the cabinet and by those particularly interested in the party. There is considerable unity in the federal party but, as we shall see a little later, there are many signs of impending divisions and possible schisms. The Dominion-provincial relations within the party are fairly good. The provincial parties are, of course, autonomous and so their relations with Ottawa depend largely on how much assistance they need from the centre. Mr. Smallwood is, in the party sense, a sovereign chieftain who can afford to take an independent line. The same is true even more, of course, for Mr. Lesage who negotiates with the central party (or government) virtually as one head of state with another. The national Liberal party has succeeded in maintaining amicable although not intimate, relations with its "sister" governments in the east. Relations with Mr. Thatcher have never been good and have not improved recently. The national party has, in fact, had considerable difficulty in maintaining warm or effective relations with the Liberal parties in the Western provinces.

It is perhaps dangerous to say anything about a party's election machinery. Regional differences preclude the making of safe country-wide generalizations about the fighting capacity of any party; the state of the provincial organization is a vital factor in this regard. It is my impression, however, that the Liberal party has, on the whole, an excellent electoral machinery benefitting from capable direction at the centre, from the wealth of the party, and from its long-standing ability to use every time-honoured local method of winning votes including the nomination of candidates who give it the image of a party which is above such things.

Support for the Liberal party has, in recent years, become strongly concentrated in the large metropolitan areas, among Roman Catholics, French-speaking Canadians and most so-called "other" ethnic groups except, perhaps, those who come from countries behind the iron curtain. Newfoundland, Quebec, and Ontario are the provinces in which the Liberals now thrive, and particularly in central Canada, in the largest cities. The party appeals more to the young and the middle-aged than to the old and it receives the support of a large proportion of university graduates. In recent elections it has done well in the large suburban fringes of the metropolitan areas. In a sense, therefore, the Liberals have attracted the beneficiaries of the present affluence without losing the votes of many of its earlier supporters—people, for instance, who themselves suffered, or who remember their parents suffering, from the depression, for which the Conservatives were generally blamed.

We have had occasion, earlier, to refer to the growing presence in contemporary society of the so-called "other directed" personality type. To the extent that this type has not become depoliticized, he seems, at present, to be attracted to the Liberals. This is most noticeable in eastern Canada, particularly Ontario and metropolitan Toronto.

Indeed, as we have pointed out already, the Liberal party is in some measure a sectional party strongly based in Quebec, urban

---

[16]See George Grant, *Lament for a Nation* (Toronto, 1965).

Ontario and some areas in the Atlantic provinces. In the west it is still weak and quite unpopular.

Nowhere, in talking about political parties, is one likely to do more violence to the facts than when generalizing about their personnel, their activists. Thousands of people become involved with each party in a Canadian election and they obviously represent a large cross-section of the public. In distinguishing between the personnel of the parties I am particularly concerned with the people who seek the nominations, the leading members in the constituency and provincial parties, and the rather small group at the top who almost give it its personality. Both Canadian major parties appeal to many similar types but their committee rooms, and particularly their inner councils, tend to have a somewhat different atmosphere and to be peopled by somewhat different personality types.

Subject to numerous exceptions, one can say that, on the whole, the Liberals have attracted more urban, well-to-do activists, men from the professions, and probably a larger proportion from the newer occupations, such as the communication industries. Among the Liberal leaders there is a larger proportion of academics than among the Conservatives, very few trade unionists, a noticeable number of former public servants and generally a sizable number of people who have come to be known as "eggheads." Among the candidates there are quite a few who have previously had only a slight interest in politics and also many who were not previously active Liberals, or even very interested in politics, but who were persuaded to run by the local Liberal organization because they were well known in the community. Many of the Liberal elite, therefore, are political amateurs whose interest in the Liberal party is probably not passionately felt and may be of only recent origin.

The composition of a party's leading personnel affects its method of operation. For reasons which should now be obvious, the Liberal party has become a highly rationalized, bureaucratic organization. It uses more opinion polls than anyone else, its campaigns are strongly influenced by public relations specialists and advertising agencies. The Liberal party has learnt much from John F. Kennedy's campaign and is, in fact, Canada's most American party in the organizational sense. The point I have just made should not be exaggerated; other parties use PR techniques and the Liberals still rely heavily on all the traditional campaign techniques. However, the particular flavour of the Liberal party's method of operation stems from its combination of considerable political (party) amateurism with the highly professional services of specialists in various branches of the communications industry.

This is not the place to explore the historical reasons for the emergence of the Liberal physiognomy which I have just described. Suffice it to say that the combination of Mr. Diefenbaker as the Conservative Prime Minister, and the way in which he conducted his government, and the presence of Mr. Pearson at the head of the Liberals, explains a great deal about the recent changes and present state of our parties. The Liberals have become an administrative party, i.e., a party which thinks it is uniquely suited to run the country and a party, furthermore, which seeks power not so much because of the spoils of office but because many of its leaders believe that they genuinely have a special gift for running public affairs. Many of the leading Liberals became intensely disillusioned with the Diefenbaker government and found in Mr. Pearson an ideal alternative. They entered politics not because they were Liberals but because they wanted to help run the country "properly" according to their scheme of things. This partly explains the large numbers of ex-civil servants and eggheads among the people now dominating the Liberal party.

The Conservative Party

If Mr. Diefenbaker's influence on the Liberals was strong, how much greater would one expect his impact to have been on the changes in his own party? I have described these changes elsewhere[17] and will not go into any detail here except to underline that virtually every change which has recently occurred in the Conservative party can only be explained in relation to the personality and activities of the leader. And since the leader is almost certainly going to retire in the foreseeable future we must consider not only recent changes in the Conservative party but also the turn of events likely to take place when Mr. Diefenbaker gives up his present position.

Under Mr. Diefenbaker's leadership the party retained much of its former attachment to the British connection, as was evident in the flag debate. Mr. Diefenbaker promulgated his view of Canada as a country composed of unhyphenated citizens—Canadians, plain and simple. In effect, this concept of Canada gave a greater place to "new Canadians" than had formerly been recognized in the Conservative party and also to some degree in governmental policies. The concept of Canada developed by the Conservatives therefore assumed the existence of a pluralistic society with strong symbolic attachments to the British connection. Any approach to Canada based on dualism is rejected because it overlooks not only the rights of groups other than the British and the French but also because it does not accord a special position to the British past and to its traditions. The rights accorded French Canada at the time of Confederation must be protected and maintained but the French group is just one of the various elements composing the country. To hold it together, a fairly strong central government is required and, consequently, any policies or administrative arrangements likely to weaken unduly the welfare of the whole country must be rejected. There is, thus, in the party's official position, little predisposition to grant Quebec special status.

The scores given the Conservative party under the heading Definition of Canada (domestic) suggest that the party is reasonably consistent on this point, that it has been reasonably united on the issue

---

[17]See particularly *The Canadian General Election of 1957* (Toronto, 1962), "The Stalled Omnibus," (cited already) and "The June 1962 Election: Break-up of Our Party System?" *Queen's Quarterly*, LXIX, no. 3 (1962).

but that the consensus is lessening (a minus sign under the B in the Trend Line), and that the party is attaching increasing importance to this aspect of its ideology. We shall see that this is a position which is likely to change under a different leader.

The Conservatives are more nationalistic than the Liberals, particularly insofar as Canadian relations with the United States are concerned. There is somewhat less support for a vigorous role in the United Nations than among Liberals and the party is probably still a little more inclined to consider Canada's external position in relation to the United Kingdom and the Commonwealth. But this part of the Conservative ideology is disappearing.

There is very little difference between the Conservatives and the Liberals with regard to their attitudes towards the welfare state and towards the role of free enterprise in the Canadian economy. As for the game of politics, the Conservative party adheres to the traditional North American pattern. In this sense it has fewer reformers than the Liberals, but then its period in office was free of major scandals.

Four provincial governments are in Conservative hands and Ontario, Canada's most populous province, is one of them. The position of the party in the federal House has been declining and it is not surprising therefore that the locus of power in the national party cannot be ascribed simply to the federal party. The problem is complicated by the serious divisions which have occurred over the leadership of Mr. Diefenbaker. While he is at present [1965] the undisputed leader of the party, the situation is certain to continue to be quite unsettled for a long time as the struggle for the succession develops fully.

After the serious divisions which rent the party after 1962, and after the loss of power in 1963, the party underwent a change which, not unnaturally, led to a decentralization of the party structure. The national organization then fulfilled a co-ordinating function and one which was designed to assist the party organization in provinces where it was weak. The 1965 election temporarily reduced the intensity of a long-standing power struggle involving the leader, the Parliamentary caucus, the national association leaders, various elements in the provincial associations and some influential individuals associated with the business community and the mass media. This struggle was complicated by a number of the participants being seriously interested in succeeding Mr. Diefenbaker as party leader. The locus of power in the organization cannot, therefore, be identified or at least it is impossible to say where it is going to rest in the future. Much will depend on the date on which Mr. Diefenbaker will retire and, even more, on the person who will succeed him.

The degree of unity in the federal party has, as we have seen, been exceedingly low. Relations between the national organization and the provinces have not been too bad, although even here the controversial figure of Mr. Diefenbaker has created problems. When discussing relations between Ottawa and the provincial organizations one must not forget that in Quebec the provincial party has, to all intents and purposes, disappeared. This has had a serious effect on their electoral chances, not only in Quebec but elsewhere as well. Where the Conservatives are strong provincially their electoral organization has not been bad; elsewhere the general lack of funds and, even more important, the inability to find good candidates, have made it difficult to wage an effective campaign.

Much electoral support for the Conservative party has recently come from rural areas, Protestants, people whose ancestors came from the British Isles, older citizens, and from non-university graduates. Regionally, the Conservatives' greatest strength has been in the prairies and they have solid strongholds also in the Maritimes and in the rural parts of Ontario and Manitoba.

A party's activists inevitably reflect its bases of party support. Westerners, for example, are little in evidence among the Liberal hierarchy and one is hard pressed to find a French-speaking Canadian of any stature among the top Conservatives. Generally, the party's leading personnel fall into several groups: the old Tories who have been with the party for a lifetime; the new men brought in by the Diefenbaker sweep in the late fifties; party activists who have become involved in politics at the provincial level, particularly where the Conservatives form the government, and who have developed an interest in strengthening the federal party; and finally those who have become disillusioned with the Liberals and the other parties and who have found in the Conservative party the only alternative to eternal Liberal rule. Some of these men were alienated from the Conservatives during its 1961 and 1962 crises but they have been drifting back. Which of these groups becomes dominant will depend on who becomes the leader and the various groupings will not, of course, be idle during the final stages of the leadership contest.

Compared with the Liberals, the Conservative top personnel consist of a larger proportion of professional politicians and a much smaller contingent of eggheads. The business community is well represented but probably no more so than among the Liberals.

The modus operandi of the party in the recent period was dominated completely by Mr. Diefenbaker. A highly personalized political style, dependent on the leaders's views and interests, marked virtually every aspect of the national Conservative party. At the local level the traditional way of conducting party affairs survived, but the closer one came to the top of the party the more visible became the influence of Mr. Diefenbaker. The party has been less given to using the latest American methods of electioneering and of conducting its business but it has, of course, also had recourse to the services of the advertising and public relations specialists, some of whom are among the influential members of the party's high command.

In assessing the changes affecting the Conservative party, one must recall that Mr. Diefenbaker started a transformation which will probably go through several stages. His major contribution was to make the Conservative party, which had been associated with eastern interests and wealth, into a champion of the lower income groups, the neglected minorities, and the elderly. Mr. Diefenbaker has undoubtedly moved the party a long way towards the left, in the traditional sense of that term. But at the same time he has also alienated some extremely important groups, notably French Canada and the eggheads. The party will either become a sectional spokesman, forced to renounce all claim to being a national organism, or it will have to make a strong comeback among those whose support and respect it has lost in the early sixties. An interesting development recently has been the growing awareness of many leading Conservatives of the peril and dilemma they are facing. There is some evidence that an impressive group of leaders is available and will emerge to play an active role in the second phase of the party's transformation. Whether they succeed will depend on the outcome of the leadership question.

The New Democratic Party

The NDP is, I think, an extremely important actor on the Canadian political scene and our neglect of it should not be construed as indicating a lack of interest or a failure to recognize the degree to which it may affect the future course of Canadian politics. But the NDP is smaller and in many ways simpler than the older parties and it has changed relatively little in recent years, even when one compares it with its parent, the CCF, except that it has become much more urban.

Two fundamental changes in the NDP have to be noted if we are to assess the party's likely role in the Canadian party system. (i) It is becoming increasingly an "electoral" party in that its ideological commitment to democratic socialism is giving way to a greater concern with winning office and instituting welfare policies not necessarily rooted in the doctrine of a planned society. A growing degree of opportunism (flexibility?) is to be expected in its performance. This flexibility has not, however, affected its basic rejection of the method of financing parties encouraged by the older parties. (ii) The party has traditionally been an Anglo-Saxon, Protestant party, at least in so far as its main electoral appeal was concerned. Recently it has made significant attempts to broaden its base and particularly to find some popular support in Quebec. If these efforts bring encouraging results, the NDP may be transformed quite substantially and may become a much more national political group than it has ever been before.

Conclusion

Parties in the liberal democracies have been declining in importance; other agencies—either at the level of associations or that of the machinery of government—have gradually usurped some of the functions formerly performed by them. But there are latent functions of parties for which they are particularly well suited and in which they cannot easily be replaced. The main function of the Canadian party system, in this sense, is to contribute to the development of a national political culture, or to foster a degree of cohesion permitting the effective functioning of the parliamentary system.

Does our examination of the changes and trends in the individual parties suggest that they will be able to discharge successfully this latent function of "nation-building"?

To answer this question we must distinguish between our expectations of the party system as a whole and of the individual parties. Taking the system as a whole, we have found that there is a strong likelihood of the survival of the multi-party system. But Canadian politicians and, naturally enough, those in the major parties, have been reluctant to come to terms with the idea that Canada might have a permanent multi-party system. They have consequently been reluctant to adapt parliamentary institutions and practices to allow for a multiplicity of parties. We are still assuming that our system is a two-party system and our machinery of government is not geared, therefore, to functioning effectively when no party has a majority. It appears that neither the politicians, nor members of the general public, are prepared to revise the conduct of parliamentary business so as to function better when a multiplicity of parties competes for office. In the future, therefore, as minority governments are likely to alternate with majority ones, the performance of the party politicians may disappoint the public further and the decline of parties may continue unchecked. If this happens, they will become less able to perform their latent function.

Our examination of the individual parties has revealed that each faces the tasks it confronts under certain handicaps arising from important internal characteristics. Most important among these is the regional base of the major parties. Neither of them can claim to be a genuinely national party although the Liberals come much closer to it than the Conservatives. The usual pattern in Canada has been for the necessary regional compromises to take place *within* national parties. If the parties cannot check the trend towards regionalism this method will no longer be available. In that event the parties will have to revise the rules of the political game in such a way as to permit the compromises required between regions to be arrived at through the bargaining of various regional parties. This is difficult and may well be beyond the skill of the parties and their leaders.

The Liberals, who look at present like the party which might find it least difficult to become a genuinely national force, are weakened by two features: (i) the lack of political skill among its leading members and (ii) potential disunity. The party, as I have argued, is dominated at the top by men who have come to politics late and who do not think primarily as party politicians. Many of them have had more experience in public service or in private business than in politics and they are likely to seek solutions through means normally employed outside parties. Their possible continued poor performance as politicians and their adoption of solutions outside the world of parties, therefore, may lead to a further diminution in the importance of parties in Canada.

The second weakness of the Liberals concerns the degree of unity which can be expected to prevail in the party. Our table shows that under three of the four headings in the section dealing with Ideology their score under B (cohesion) is 3, and 3. This suggests that there is anything but unanimity on some of the positions adopted by the party. There was a good deal of difference on questions of social and economic policy in the first Pearson cabinet. The advent of men such as Winters and Marchand is certain to sharpen these controversies. It is also very likely that on questions concerning the relations between English- and French-speaking Canada and the place of Quebec in Confederation, the reasonable harmony of the past may give way to serious divisions. From now on the voice of Quebec is almost certain to be heard in harsher tones in the cabinet chamber, and the response from some of the English-speaking ministers may become correspondingly tougher. Should the Liberals increase their representation in the west, the latter tendency would probably become particularly pronounced.

Finally, Mr. Pearson is not much younger than Mr. Diefenbaker. He too will soon wish to retire from the party leadership. The struggle for the succession may exacerbate the divisions likely to develop between the doves and the hawks in the cabinet, whether the ornithological distinction refers to economic policy, ethnic relations, or the nature of Confederation.

The Conservatives, as we have seen, are divided now and may fail in the tasks before them. There are some among them who will find it difficult not to exploit the short-run advantage of making a strong appeal to the public on an only thinly veiled anti-French and anti-Quebec platform. The party has, so far, resisted this temptation, but the balance of power may shift away from the moderates. At any rate, the party faces a serious trial in its leadership crisis. It may emerge as a stronger and more effective political instrument, in which case it may improve the functioning of the party system. But it may also take the wrong turn and so contribute to the ineffectual operation of the Canadian party system.

The NDP, as a third party, should, theoretically, offer a corrective to the inadequacies of the others. But it has had too little support so far to be a serious alternative to either of the old parties. If it attracts a respectable level of support in all parts of the country, it may reach the take-off position from which it may become a vital factor in the party system of the future. At present this is unlikely.

We see, therefore, that the future is highly uncertain. It is, of course, possible that the parties will overcome their present or incipient problems and that they will improve their general performance. The ideas presented in this paper suggest, however, that this is unlikely. We are almost certain to witness a substantial transformation in the operation of the Canadian party system and its further weakening. It is therefore probable that other structures will emerge, performing some of the functions heretofore expected of the parties. The other possibility is that these functions will not be performed at all. In that event, the Canadian political system will enter a period of acute danger.

5

Conservatism, Liberalism, and Socialism in Canada: An Interpretation

G. HOROWITZ

*

1 / INTRODUCTION: THE HARTZIAN APPROACH

In the United States, organized socialism is dead; in Canada, socialism, though far from national power, is a significant political force. Why this striking difference in the fortunes of socialism in two very similar societies?

. . . It will be shown that the relative strength of socialism in Canada is related to the relative strength of toryism, and to the different position and character of liberalism in the two countries.

In North America, Canada is unique. Yet there is a tendency in Canadian historical and political studies to explain Canadian phenomena not by contrasting them with American phenomena but by identifying them as variations on a basic North American theme. I grant that Canada and the United States are similar, and that the similarities should be pointed out. But the pan-North American approach, since it searches out and concentrates on similarities, cannot help us to understand Canadian uniqueness. When this approach is applied to the study of English-Canadian socialism, one discovers, first, that like the American variety it is weak, and second, that it is weak for much the same reasons. These discoveries perhaps explain why Canadian socialism is weak in comparison to European socialism; they do not explain why Canadian socialism is so much stronger than American socialism.

The explanatory technique used in this study is that developed by Louis Hartz in *The Liberal Tradition in America*[1] and *The Founding of New Societies*.[2] It is applied to Canada in a mildly pan-North

*Reprinted from the *Canadian Journal of Economics and Political Science*, XXXII, no. 2, May, 1966.

[1]Louis Hartz, *The Liberal Tradition in America* (New York: Harcourt, Brace and World [Toronto: Longmans], 1955).

[2]Louis Hartz, *The Founding of New Societies* (New York: Harcourt, Brace and World [Toronto: Longmans], 1964).

American way by Kenneth McRae in "The Structure of Canadian History," a contribution to the latter book.

The Hartzian approach is to study the new societies founded by Europeans (the United States, English Canada, French Canada, Latin America, Dutch South Africa, Australia) as "fragments" thrown off from Europe. The key to the understanding of ideological development in a new society is its "point of departure" from Europe: the ideologies borne by the founders of the new society are not representative of the historic ideological spectrum of the mother country. The settlers represent only a fragment of that spectrum. The complete ideological spectrum ranges—in chronological order, and from right to left—from feudal or tory through liberal whig to liberal democrat to socialist. French Canada and Latin America are "feudal fragments." They were founded by bearers of the feudal or tory values of the organic, corporate, hierarchical community; their point of departure from Europe was before the liberal revolution. The United States, English Canada, and Dutch South Africa are "bourgeois fragments," founded by bearers of liberal individualism who have left the tory end of the spectrum behind them.

The significance of the fragmentation process is that the new society, having been thrown off from Europe, "loses the stimulus to change that the whole provides."[3] The full ideological spectrum of Europe develops only out of the continued confrontation and interaction of its four elements; they are related to one another, not only as enemies, but as parents and children. A new society which leaves part of the past behind it cannot develop the future ideologies which need the continued presence of the past in order to come into being. In escaping the past, the fragment escapes the future, for "the very seeds of the later ideas are contained in the parts of the old world that have been left behind."[4] The ideology of the founders is thus frozen, congealed at the point of origin.

Socialism is an ideology which combines the corporate-organic-collectivist ideas of toryism with the rationalist-egalitarian ideas of liberalism. Both the feudal and the bourgeois fragments escape socialism, but in different ways. A feudal fragment such as French Canada develops no whig (undemocratic) liberalism; therefore it does not develop the democractic liberalism which arises out of and as a reaction against whiggery; therefore it does not develop the socialism which arises out of and as a reaction against liberal democracy. The corporate-organic-collectivist component of socialism is present in the feudal fragment—it is part of the feudal ethos—but the radical—rationalist-egalitarian component of socialism is missing. It can be provided only by whiggery and liberal democracy, and these have not come into being.

In the bourgeois fragment, the situation is the reverse: the radical-rationalist-egalitarian component of socialism is present, but the corporate-organic-collectivist component is missing, because toryism has been left behind. In the bourgeois fragments "Marx dies because there is no sense of class, no yearning for the corporate past."[5] The absence of socialism is related to the absence of toryism.

It is *because* socialists have a conception of society as more than an agglomeration of competing individuals—a conception close to the tory view of society as an organic community—that they find the liberal idea of equality (equality of opportunity) inadequate. Socialists disagree with liberals about the essential meaning of equality because socialists have a tory conception of society.

In a liberal bourgeois society which has never known toryism the demand for equality will express itself as left-wing or democratic liberalism as opposed to whiggery. The left will point out that all are not equal in the competitive pursuit of individual happiness. The government will be required to assure greater equality of opportunity—in the nineteenth century by destroying monopolistic privileges; in the twentieth century by providing a welfare "floor" so that no one will fall out of the race for success, and by regulating the economy so that the race can continue without periodic crises.

In a society which thinks of itself as a community of classes rather than an aggregation of individuals, the demand for equality will take a socialist form: for equality of condition rather than mere equality of opportunity; for cooperation rather than competition; for a community that does more than provide a context within which individuals can pursue happiness in a purely self-regarding way. At its most "extreme," socialism is a demand for the *abolition* of classes so that the good of the community can truly be realized. This is a demand which cannot be made by people who can hardly see class and community; the individual fills their eyes.

2 / THE APPLICATION TO CANADA

It is a simple matter to apply the Hartzian approach to English Canada in a pan-North American way. English Canada can be viewed as a fragment of the American liberal society, lacking a feudal or tory heritage and therefore lacking the socialist ideology which grows out of it. Canadian domestic struggles, from this point of view, are a northern version of the American struggle between big-propertied liberals on the right and *petit bourgeois* and working-class liberals on the left; the struggle goes on within a broad liberal consensus, and the voice of the tory or the socialist is not heard in the land. This pan-North American approach, with important qualifications, is adopted by Hartz and McRae in *The Founding of New Societies*. English Canada, like the United States, is a bourgeois fragment. No toryism in the past, therefore no socialism in the present.

But Hartz notes that the liberal society of English Canada has a "tory touch," that it is etched with a tory streak coming out of the American revolution."[6]

* * * * *

---

[3]*Ibid.*, p. 3.   [4]*Ibid.*, p. 25.   [5]*Ibid.*, p. 7.
[6]*Ibid.*, p. 34.

Take as an example the central concern of this study—the differing weights of Canadian and American socialism. . . The CCF failed to become a major party in urban Canada, but it succeded in becoming a significant minor party—a success denied to the American socialists . . .

*   *   *   *   *

The most important un-American characteristics of English Canada, all related to the presence of toryism, are: (a) the presence of tory ideology in the founding of English Canada by the Loyalists, and its continuing influence on English Canadian political culture; (b) the persistent power of whiggery or right-wing liberalism in Canada (the Family Compacts) as contrasted with the rapid and easy victory of liberal democracy (Jefferson, Jackson) in the United States; (c) the ambivalent centrist character of left-wing liberalism in Canada as contrasted with the unambiguously leftist position of left-wing liberalism in the United States; (d) the presence of an influential and legitimate socialist movement in English Canada as contrasted with the illegitimacy and early death of American socialism; (e) the failure of English Canadian liberalism to develop into the one true myth, the nationalist cult, and the parallel failure to exclude toryism and socialism as "un-Canadian"; in other words, the legitimacy of ideological diversity in English Canada.

*   *   *   *   *

3 / THE PRESENCE OF TORYISM AND ITS CONSEQUENCES

Many students have noted that English-Canadian society has been powerfully shaped by tory values that are "alien" to the American mind. The latest of these is Seymour Martin Lipset, who stresses the relative strength in Canada of the tory values of "ascription" and "elitism" (the tendency to defer to authority), and the relative weakness of the liberal values of "achievement" and "egalitarianism."[7] He points to such well-known features of Canadian history as the absence of a lawless, individualistic-egalitarian American frontier, the preference for Britain rather than the United States as a social model, and generally, the weaker emphasis on social equality, the greater acceptance by individuals of the facts of economic inequality, social stratification, and hierarchy, . . . belief in monarchy and empire unity, greater stress on "law and order," revulsion against American populistic excesses, different frontier experiences, and so on. One tory touch in English Canada . . . is the far greater willingness of English Canadian political and business elites to use the power of the state for the purpose of developing and controlling the economy. . . . Canada is not a feudal (tory) fragment but a bourgeois (liberal) fragment touched with toryism. . . .

Let us put it this way: pre-revolutionary America was a liberal fragment with insignificant traces of toryism, extremely weak feudal survivals. But they were insignificant in the *American* setting; they were far overshadowed by the liberalism of that setting. The Revolution did not have to struggle against them; it swept them away easily and painlessly, leaving no trace of them in the American memory. But these traces of toryism were expelled into a *new* setting, and in this setting they were no longer insignificant. In this new setting, where there was no pre-established overpowering liberalism to force them into insignificance, they played a large part in shaping a new political culture, significantly different from the American. As Nelson wrote in *The American Tory,* "the Tories' organic conservatism represented a current of thought that failed to reappear in America after the revolution. A substantial part of the whole spectrum of European . . . philosophy seemed to slip outside the American perspective."[8] But it *reappeared* in Canada. Here the sway of liberalism has proved to be not total, but considerably mitigated by a tory presence initially and a socialist presence subsequently. . . . In Canada, the Family Compacts were able to maintain ascendancy and delay the coming of democracy because of the tory touch "inherited in part from American Loyalism, which restrained egalitarian feeling in Canada."[9] The early power of whiggery serves to emphasize the importance of the Tory touch in English Canada. . . .

In the United States, the masses could not be swayed by the Federalist-Whig appeals to anti-egalitarian sentiments. In Canada the masses *were* swayed by these appeals; the role of the Compacts was to save "the colonial masses from the spectre of republicanism and democracy."[10] What accounts for this is the tory presence in English-Canadian political culture—the "greater acceptance of limitation, of hierarchical patterns."[11]

The next step in tracing the development of the English-Canadian political culture must be to take account of the tremendous waves of British immigration which soon engulfed the original American Loyalist fragment. . . . These British immigrants had undoubtedly been heavily infected with non-liberal ideas, and these ideas were undoubtedly in their heads as they settled in Canada. The political culture of a new nation is not necessarily fixed at the point of origin or departure; the founding of a new nation can go on for generations. If the later waves of immigration arrived before the *point of congealment* of the political culture, they must have participated actively in the process of culture formation. . . .

Between 1815 and 1850 almost one million Britons emigrated to Canada. The population of English Canada doubled in twenty

---

[7]Seymour Martin Lipset, *The First New Nation* (New York, 1963), esp. chap. 7.

[8]William Nelson, *The American Tory* (New York, 1961), pp. 189-90.

[9]Hartz, *New Societies,* p. 91.

[10]*Ibid.,* p. 243.

[11]Lipset, p. 251.

years and quadrupled in forty. The population of Ontario increased ten-fold in the same period—from about 95,000 in 1814 to about 950,000 in 1851.[12]. . . . Is it not possible that the immigrants, while they were no doubt considerably liberalized by their new environment, also brought to it non-liberal ideas which entered into the political culture mix, and which perhaps even reinforced the non-liberal elements present in the original fragment? If the million immigrants had come from the United States rather than Britain, would English Canada not be "significantly" different today?

The difficulty in applying the Hartzian approach to English Canada is that although the point of departure is reasonably clear, it is difficult to put one's finger on the point of congealment. Perhaps it was the Loyalist period; perhaps it was close to the mid-century mark; there are grounds for arguing that it was in the more recent past. But the important point is this: no matter where the point of congealment is located in time, the tory streak is present before the solidification of the political culture, and it is strong *enough* to produce *significant* "imperfec-tions," or non-liberal, un-American attributes of English-Canadian soci-ety. My own opinion is that the point of congealment came later than the Loyalists. . . .

The indeterminate location of the point of congealment makes it difficult to account in any *precise* way for the presence of socialism in the English-Canadian political culture mix, though the pres-ence itself is indisputable. If the point of congealment came *before* the arrival of the first radical or socialist-minded immigrants, the presence of socialism must be ascribed primarily to the earlier presence of toryism. Since toryism is a significant part of the political culture, at least part of the leftist reaction against it will sooner or later be expressed in its own terms, that is, in terms of *class* interests and the good of the community as a corporate entity (socialism) rather than in terms of the individual and his vicissitudes in the competitive pursuit of happiness (liberalism). If the point of congealment is very early, socialism appears at a later point not primarily because it is imported by British immigrants, but because it is contained as a potential in the original political culture. The immigrants then find that they do not have to give it up—that it is not un-Canadian—because it "fits" to a certain extent with the tory ideas already present. If the point of congealment is very late, the presence of socialism must be explained as a result of *both* the presence of toryism and the introduction of socialism into the cultural mix before congealment. The immigrant retains his socialism not only because it "fits" but also because nothing really *has* to fit. He finds that his socialism is not un-Canadian partly because "Canadian" has not yet been defined.

Canadian liberals cannot be expected to wax enthusiastic about the non-liberal traits of their country. They are likely to condemn the tory touch as anachronistic, stifling, undemocratic, out of tune with the essentially American ("free," "classless") spirit of English Canada. They dismiss the socialist touch as an "old-fashioned" protest, no longer necessary (if it ever was) in this best (liberal) of all possible worlds in which the "end of ideology" has been achieved. The secret dream of the Canadian liberal is the removal of English Canada's "imperfections"—in other words, the total assimilation of English Canada into the larger North American culture. But there is a flaw in this dream which might give pause even to the liberal. Hartz places special emphasis on one very unappetizing characteristic of the new societies—intolerance—which is strikingly absent in English Canada. Because the new societies other than Canada are unfamiliar with legitimate ideological diversity, they are unable to accept it and deal with it in a rational manner, either internally or on the level of international relations.

The European nation has an "identity which transcends any ideologist and a mechanism in which each plays only a part."[13] Neither the tory, nor the liberal, nor the socialist, has a monopoly of the expression of the "spirit" of the nation. But the new societies, the fragments, contain only one of the ideologies of Europe; they are one-myth cultures. In the new setting, freed from its historic enemies past and future, ideology transforms itself into nationalism. It claims to be a moral absolute, "the great spirit of a nation."[14] In the United States, liberalism becomes "Americanism"; a political philosophy becomes a civil religion, a nationalist cult. The American attachment to Locke is "absolutist and irrational."[15] Democratic capitalism is the American way of life; to oppose it is to be un-American.

To be an American is to be a bourgeois liberal. To be a French Canadian is to be a pre-Enlightenment Catholic; to be an Australian is to be a prisoner of the radical myth of "mateship"; to be a Boer is to be a pre-Enlightenment bourgeois Calvinist. The fragments escape the need for philosophy, for thought about values, for "where perspectives shrink to a single value, and that value becomes the universe, how can value itself be considered?"[16] The fragment demands solidarity. Ideologies which diverge from the national myth make no impact; they are not understood, and their proponents are not granted legitimacy. They are denounced as aliens, and treated as aliens, because they *are* aliens. The fragments cannot understand or deal with the fact that *all* men are *not* bourgeois Americans, or radical Australians, or Catholic French Canadians, or Calvinist South Africans. They cannot make peace with the loss of ideological certainty.

The specific weakness of the United States is its "inability to understand the appeal of socialism" to the third world.[17] Because the United States has "buried" the memory of the organic medieval community "beneath new liberal absolutisms and nationalisms"[18] it cannot

[12]L. Hartz, *New Societies*, p. 245.
[13]*Ibid.*, p. 15.
[14]*Ibid.*, p. 10.
[15]Hartz, *Liberal Tradition*, p. 11.
[16]Hartz, *New Societies*, p. 23 .
[17]*Ibid.*, p. 119.
[18]*Ibid.*, p. 35.

understand that the appeal of socialism to nations with a predominantly non-liberal past (including French Canada) consists precisely in the promise of "continuing the corporate ethos in the very process" of modernization.[19] The American reacts with isolationism, messianism, and hysteria.

English Canada, because it is the most "imperfect" of the fragments, is not a one-myth culture. In English Canada ideological diversity has not been buried beneath an absolutist liberal nationalism. Here Locke is not the one true god; he must tolerate lesser tory and socialist deities at his side. The result is that English Canada does not direct an uncomprehending intolerance at heterodoxy, either within its borders or beyond them. (What a "backlash" Parti-Pris or PSQ-type separatists would be getting if Quebec were in the United States!) In English Canada it has been possible to consider values without arousing the all-silencing cry of treason. Hartz observes that "if history had chosen English Canada for the American role" of directing the Western response to the world revolution, "the international scene would probably have witnessed less McCarthyite hysteria, less Wilsonian messianism."[20]

Americanizing liberals might consider that the Pearsonian rationality and calmness which Canada displays on the world stage—the "mediating" and "peace-keeping" role of which Canadians are so proud—is related to the un-American (tory and socialist) characteristics which they consider to be unnecessary imperfections in English-Canadian wholeness. The tolerance of English-Canadian domestic politics is also linked with the presence of these imperfections. If the price of Americanization is the surrender of legitimate ideological diversity, even the liberal might think twice before paying it. . . .

Non-liberal British elements have entered into English-Canadian society *together* with American liberal elements at the foundations. The fact is that Canada has been greatly influenced by both the United States and Britain. This is not to deny that liberalism is the dominant element in the English-Canadian political culture; it is to stress that it is not the sole element, that it is accompanied by vital and legitimate streams of toryism and socialism which have as close a relation to English Canada's "essence" or "foundations" as does liberalism. English Canada's "essence" is both liberal and non-liberal. Neither the British nor the American elements can be explained away as "superstructural" excrescences.

4 / UN-AMERICAN ASPECTS OF CANADIAN CONSERVATISM

So far, I have been discussing the presence of toryism in Canada without referring to the Conservative party. This party can be seen as a party of right-wing or business liberalism, but such an interpretation would be far from the whole truth; the Canadian Conservative party, like the British Conservative party and unlike the Republican party, is not monolithically liberal. If there is a touch of toryism in English Canada, its primary carrier has been the Conservative party. It would not be correct to say that toryism is *the* ideology of the party, or even that some Conservatives are tories. These statements would not be true even of the British Conservative party. The primary component of the ideology of business-oriented parties is liberalism; but there are powerful traces of the old pre-liberal outlook in the British Conservative party, and less powerful but still perceptible traces of it in the Canadian party. A Republican is always a liberal. A Conservative may be at one moment a liberal, at the next moment a tory, and is usually something of both.

If it is true that the Canadian Conservatives can be seen from some angles as right-wing liberals, it is also true that figures such as R. B. Bennett, Arthur Meighen, and George Drew cannot be understood simply as Canadian versions of William McKinley, Herbert Hoover, and Robert Taft. Canadian Conservatives have something British about them that American Republicans do not. It is not simply their emphasis on loyalty to the crown and to the British connection, but a touch of the authentic tory aura—traditionalism, elitism, the strong state, and so on. The Canadian Conservatives lack the American aura of rugged individualism. Theirs is not the characteristically American conservatism which conserves only *liberal* values.

It is possible to perceive in Canadian conservatism not only the elements of business liberalism and orthodox toryism, but also an element of "tory democracy"—the paternalistic concern for the "condition of the people," and the emphasis on the tory party as their champion —which, in Britain, was expressed by such figures as Disraeli and Lord Randolph Churchill. John A. Macdonald's approach to the emergent Canadian working class was in some respects similar to that of Disraeli. Later Conservatives acquired the image of arch reactionaries and arch enemies of the workers, but let us not forget that "Iron Heel" Bennett was also the Bennett of the Canadian New Deal.

The question arises: why is it that in Canada the *Conservative* leader proposes a New Deal? Why is it that the Canadian counterpart of Hoover apes *Roosevelt*? This phenomenon is usually interpreted as sheer historical accident, a product of Bennett's desperation and opportunism. But the answer may be that Bennett was not Hoover. Even in his "orthodox" days Bennett's views on the state's role in the economy were far from similar to Hoover's; Bennett's attitude was that of Canadian, not American, conservatism. Once this is recognized, it is possible to entertain the suggestion that Bennett's sudden radicalism, his sudden concern for the people, may not have been mere opportunism. It may have been a manifestation, a sudden activation under pressure, of a latent tory-democratic streak. Let it be noted also that the depression produced two Conservative splinter parties, both with "radical" welfare state programmes, and both led by former subordinates of Bennett: H. H. Stevens' Reconstruction party and W. D. Herridge's New Democracy.

---

[19]*Ibid.*, p. 119.
[20]Ibid., p. 120.

The Bennett New Deal is only the most extreme instance of what is usually considered to be an accident or an aberration—the occasional manifestation of "radicalism" or "leftism" by otherwise orthodox Conservative leaders in the face of opposition from their "followers" in the business community. Meighen, for example, was constantly embroiled with the "Montreal interests" who objected to his railway policies. On one occasion he received a note of congratulation from William Irvine: "The man who dares to offend the Montreal interests is the sort of man that the people are going to vote for."[21] This same Meighen expressed on certain occasions, particularly after his retirement, an antagonism to big government and creeping socialism that would have warmed the heart of Robert Taft; but he combined his business liberalism with gloomy musings about the evil of universal suffrage[22]—musings which Taft would have rejected as un-American. Meighen is far easier to understand from a British than from an American perspective, for he combined, in different proportions at different times, attitudes deriving from all three Conservative ideological streams: right-wing liberalism, orthodox toryism, and tory democracy.

The Western or agrarian Conservatives of the contemporary period, John Diefenbaker and Alvin Hamilton, who are usually dismissed as "prairie radicals" of the American type, might represent not only anti-Bay Street agrarianism but *also* the same type of tory democracy which was expressed before their time by orthodox business-sponsored Conservatives like Meighen and Bennett. The populism (anti-elitism) of Diefenbaker and Hamilton is a genuinely foreign element in Canadian conservatism, but their stress on the Tory party as champion of the people and their advocacy of welfare state policies are in the tory democratic tradition. Their attitudes to the monarchy, the British connection, and the danger of American domination are entirely orthodox Conservative attitudes. Diefenbaker Conservatism is therefore to be understood not simply as a Western populist phenomenon, but as an odd *combination* of traditional Conservative views with attitudes absorbed from the Western Progressive tradition.

Another aberration which may be worthy of investigation is the Canadian phenomenon of the red tory. At the simplest level, he is a Conservative who prefers the CCF-NDP to the Liberals, or a socialist who prefers the Conservatives to the Liberals, without really knowing why. At a higher level, he is a conscious ideological Conservative with some "odd" socialist notions (W. L. Morton) or a conscious ideological socialist with some "odd" tory notions (Eugene Forsey). The very suggestion that such affinities might exist between Republicans and Socialists in the United States is ludicrous enough to make some kind of a point.

Red toryism is, of course, one of the results of the relationship between toryism and socialism which has already been elucidated. The tory and socialist minds have some crucial assumptions, orientations, and values in common, so that from certain angles they may appear not as enemies, but as two different expressions of the same basic ideological outlook. Thus, at the very highest level, the red tory is a philosopher who combines elements of socialism and toryism so thoroughly in a single integrated *Weltanschauung* that it is impossible to say that he is a proponent of either one as *against* the other. Such a red tory is George Grant, who has associations with both the Conservative party and the NDP, and who has recently published a book which defends Diefenbaker, laments the death of "true" British conservatism in Canada, attacks the Liberals as individualists and Americanizers, and defines socialism as a variant of conservatism (each "protects the public good against private freedom").[23]

5 / THE CHARACTER OF CANADIAN SOCIALISM

Canadian socialism is un-American in two distinct ways. It is un-American in the sense that it is a significant and legitimate political force in Canada, insignificant and alien in the United States. But Canadian socialism is also un-American in the sense that it does not speak the same language as American socialism. In Canada, socialism is British, non-Marxist, and wordly; in the United States it is German, Marxist, and other-worldly.

I have argued that the socialist ideas of British immigrants to Canada were not sloughed off because they "fit" with a political culture which already contained non-liberal components, and probably also because they were introduced into the political culture mix before the point of congealment. Thus socialism was not alien here. But it was not alien in yet another way; it was not borne by foreigners. The personnel and the ideology of the Canadian labour and socialist movements have been primarily British. Many of those who built these movements were British immigrants with past experience in the British labour movement; many others were Canadian-born children of such immigrants. And in British North America, Britons could not be treated as foreigners.

When socialism was brought to the United States, it found itself in an ideological environment in which it could not survive because Lockean individualism had long since achieved the status of a national religion; the political culture had already congealed, and socialism did not fit. American socialism was alien not only in this ideological sense, but in the ethnic sense as well; it was borne by foreigners from Germany and other continental European countries. These foreigners sloughed off their socialist ideas not simply because such ideas did not "fit" ideologically, but because as foreigners they were going through a general process of Americanization; socialism was only one of many ethnically alien characteristics which had to be abandoned. The immigrant's ideological change was only one incident among many others in the general process of changing his entire way of life. According to David Saposs, "the factor that contributed most tellingly to the decline of the socialist movement

[21]Roger Graham, *Arthur Meighen*, vol. II (Toronto, 1963), p. 269.
[22]*Ibid.*, vol. III (Toronto, 1965), pp. 71-4.
[23]George Grant, *Lament for a Nation* (Toronto, 1965), p. 71.

was that its chief following, the immigrant workers, . . . had become Americanized."[24]

A British socialist immigrant to Canada had a far different experience. The British immigrant was not an "alien" in British North America. The English Canadian culture not only granted legitimacy to his political ideas and absorbed them into its wholeness; it absorbed him as a person into the English-Canadian community, with relatively little strain, without demanding that he change his entire way of life before being granted full citizenship. He was acceptable to begin with, by virtue of being British. It is impossible to understand the differences between American and Canadian socialism without taking into account this immense difference between the ethnic contexts of socialism in the two countries.

The ethnic handicap of American socialism consisted not only in the fact that its personnel was heavily European. Equally important was the fact that it was a *brand* of socialism—Marxism—which found survival difficult not only in the United States but in all English-speaking countries. Marx has not found the going easy in the United States; but neither has he found the going easy in Britain, Canada, Australia, or New Zealand. The socialism of the United States, the socialism of De Leon, Berger, Hillquit, and Debs, is predominantly Marxist and doctrinaire, because it is European. The socialism of English Canada, the socialism of Simpson, Woodsworth, and Coldwell, is predominantly Protestant, labourist, and Fabian, because it is British.

*   *   *   *   *

The CCF has not been without its otherwordly tendencies: there have been doctrinal disagreements, and the party has always had a left wing interested more in "socialist education" than in practical political work. But this left wing has been a constantly declining minority. The party has expelled individuals and small groups—mostly Communists and Trotskyites—but it has never split. Its life has never been threatened by disagreement over doctrinal matters. It is no more preoccupied with theory than the British Labour party. It sees itself, and is seen by the public, not as a coterie of ideologists but as a party like the others, second to none in its avidity for office. If it has been attacked from the right for socialist "utopianism" and "impracticality," it has also been attacked from the right for abandoning the "true" socialist faith in an unprincipled drive for power.

*   *   *   *   *

6 / CANADIAN LIBERALISM: THE TRIUMPHANT CENTRE

Canadian Conservatives are not American Republicans; Canadian socialists are not American socialists; Canadian Liberals are not American liberal Democrats.

The un-American elements in English Canada's political culture are most evident in Canadian conservatism and socialism. But

Canadian liberalism has a British colour too. The liberalism of Canada's Liberty party should not be identified with the liberalism of the American Democratic party. In many respects they stand in sharp contrast to one another.

The three components of the English-Canadian political culture have not developed in isolation from one another; each has developed in interaction with the others. Our toryism and our socialism have been moderated by liberalism. But by the same token, our liberalism has been rendered "impure," in American terms, through its contacts with toryism and socialism. If English-Canadian liberalism is less individualistic, less ardently populistic-democratic, more inclined to state intervention in the economy, and more tolerant of "feudal survivals" such as monarchy, this is due to the uninterrupted influence of toryism upon liberalism, an influence wielded in and through the conflict between the two. If English-Canadian liberalism has tended since the depression to merge at its leftist edge with the democratic socialism of the CCF-NDP, this is due to the influence which socialism has exerted upon liberalism, in and through the conflict between them. The key to understanding the Liberal party in Canada is to see it as a *centre* party, with *influential* enemies on both right and left.

*   *   *   *   *

In English Canada Liberal Reform, represented by King's Liberal party, has had to face the socialist challenge. Under socialist influence, it abandoned its early devotion to "the lofty principles of Gladstone, the sound economics of Adam Smith, and the glories of laissez faire."[25] King's *Industry and Humanity* and the Liberal platform of 1919 mark the transition of English-Canadian Liberalism from the old individualism to the new Liberal Reform.

King's Liberal Reform, since it had to answer attacks from the left as well as from the right, projected a notoriously ambivalent conservative-radical image:

> *Truly he will be remembered*
> *Wherever men honor ingenuity*
> *Ambiguity, inactivity, and political longevity.*

When he faced Bennett and Meighen, King was the radical warrior, the champion of the little people against the interests. When he turned to face Woodsworth and Coldwell, he was the cautious conservative, the protector of the *status quo*. He

> *. . . never let his on the one hand*
> *Know what his on the other hand was doing.*[26]

*   *   *   *   *

[24]David Saposs, *Communism in American Unions* (New York, 1959), p. 7.
[25]Bruce Hutchison, *The Incredible Canadian* (Toronto, 1952), Longman's, Green and Co., p. 6.
[26]F. R. Scott, "W.L.M.K.," *The Blasted Pine*, ed. F. R. Scott and A. J. M. Smith (Toronto, 1962), p. 28.

Hartz points out that [the] "pragmatism" of the New Deal enabled it to go farther, to get more things done, than European Liberal Reform. "The freewheeling inventiveness typified by the TVA, the NRA, the WPA, the SEC"[27] was nowhere to be found in Europe. Defending itself against socialism, European Liberal Reform could not submerge questions of theory; it had to justify innovations on the basis of a revised liberal ideology; it had to stop short of socialism openly. The New Deal, since it was not threatened by socialism, could ignore theory; it "did not need to stop short of Marx openly"; hence it could accomplish more than European Liberal Reform.

King had to face the socialist challenge. He did so in the manner of European Liberal Reform. . . . The similarity of socialism and Liberal Reform could be acknowledged; indeed it could be emphasized and used to attract the socialist vote. At the same time, King had to answer the arguments of socialism, and in doing so he had to spell out his liberalism. He had to stop short of socialism openly. Social reform, yes; extension of public ownership, yes; the welfare state, yes; increased state control of the economy, yes; but not too much. Not socialism. The result was that King, like the European liberals, could not go as far as Roosevelt. . . . Like the Europeans, and unlike Roosevelt, he had to defend private property, he had to attack excessive reliance on the state, he had to criticize socialism as "impracticality" and "utopianism." "Half radical and half conservative—a tired man who could not make up his mind"—is this not the living image of Mackenzie King?

"In America, instead of being a champion of property, Roosevelt became the big antagonist of it; his liberalism was blocked by his radicalism."[28] In Canada, since King had to worry not only about Bennett and Meighen and Drew, but also about Woodsworth and Coldwell and Douglas, King had to embark upon a defence of private property. *He* was no traitor to his class. Instead of becoming the antagonist of property, he became its champion; his radicalism was blocked by his liberalism.

An emphasis on the solidarity of the nation as against divisive "class parties" of right and left was "of the very essence of the Reformist Liberal position in Europe." "Who," asks Hartz, "would think of Roosevelt as a philosopher of class solidarity?"[29] Yet that is precisely what Roosevelt would have been if he had had to respond to a socialist presence in the American political culture. And that is precisely what King was in fact in Canada. His party was "the party of national unity." One of the most repeated charges against the CCF was that it was a divisive "class party"; the purpose of the Liberal party, on the other hand, was to preserve the solidarity of the Canadian people—the solidarity of its classes as well as the solidarity of French and English. . . .

The Liberal party has continued to speak the language of King: ambiguous and ambivalent, presenting first its radical face and then its conservative face, urging reform and warning against hasty, ill-considered change, calling for increased state responsibility but stopping short of socialism openly, speaking for the common people but preaching the solidarity of classes.

In the United States, the liberal Democrats are on the left. There is no doubt about that. In Canada, the Liberals are a party of the centre, appearing at times leftist and at times rightist. As such, they are much closer to European, especially British, Liberal Reform than to the American New Deal type of liberalism.

In the United States, the liberal Democrats are the party of organized labour. The new men of power, the labour leaders, have arrived politically; their vehicle is the Democratic party. In English Canada, if the labour leaders have arrived politically, they have done so in the CCF-NDP. They are nowhere to be found in the Liberal party. The rank and file, in the United States, are predominantly Democrats; in Canada at least a quarter are New Democrats, and the remainder show only a relatively slight, and by no means consistent, preference for the Liberals as against the Conservatives.

In the United States, left-wing "liberalism," as opposed to right-wing "liberalism," has always meant opposition to the domination of American life by big business, and has expressed itself in and through the Democratic party; the party of business is the Republican party. In Canada, business is close to both the Conservatives and the Liberals. The business community donates to the campaign funds of both and is represented in the leadership circles of both.

*   *   *   *   *

The Liberal party in Canada does not represent the opposition of society to domination by organized business. It claims to be based on no particular groups, but on *all*. It is not against any particular group; it is for *all*. The idea that there is any real conflict between groups is dismissed, and the very terms "right" and "left" are rejected. "The terms 'right' and 'left' belong to those who regard politics as a class struggle. . . . The Liberal view is that true political progress is marked by . . . the reconciliation of classes, and the promotion of the general interest above all particular interests."[30]

A party of the left can be distinguished from parties of the centre and right according to two interrelated criteria: its policy approach, and its electoral support.

Policy Approach

The policy approach of a left party is to introduce innovations on behalf of the lower strata. The Liberals, unlike the liberal Democrats, have not

---

[27]Hartz, *Liberal Tradition*, p. 271.
[28]*Ibid.*, p. 267.   [29]*Ibid.*
[30]Pickersgill, *The Liberal Party* (Toronto: McClelland and Stewart, 1962), p. 68.

been a party of innovation. As a centre party, they have allowed the CCF-NDP to introduce innovations; they have then waited for signs of substantial acceptance by all strata of the population, and for signs of reassurance against possible electoral reprisals, before actually proceeding to implement the innovations. By this time, of course, they are strictly speaking no longer innovations. The centre party recoils from the fight for controversial measures; it loves to implement a consensus. Roosevelt was the innovator *par excellence*. King, though he was in his own mind in favour of reform, stalled until public demand for innovation was so great and so clear that he could respond to it without antagonizing his business-sponsored right wing. He rationalized his caution into a theory of democratic leadership far different from Roosevelt's conception of the strong presidency:

> *Mackenzie King's conception of political leadership, which he often expressed, was that a leader should make his objectives clear, but that leadership was neither liberal nor democratic which tried to force new policies . . . on a public that did not consent to them.*[31]
> *He believed that nothing was so likely to set back a good cause as premature action.*[32]

This was the official Liberal explanation of King's failure to embark on any far reaching programme of reform until 1943. King himself undoubtedly believed that his caution was based at least in part on a "democratic" theory of leadership. But his diaries suggest that the reforms came when they did because CCF pressure became so threatening that it could no longer be ignored by King's right-wing colleagues, so threatening that King felt able to surrender to it without jeopardizing the unity of his party. The bare facts are these: In August, 1943, the CCF became the official opposition in Ontario. In September, 1943, the CCF overtook the Liberals in the Gallup poll (Canada: CCF 29%, Liberals 28%; Ontario: CCF 32%, Liberals 26%; The West: CCF 41%, Liberals 23%). [33] King's reaction is summed up in the following quotation from his diary: "In my heart, I am not sorry to see the mass of the people coming a little more into their own, but I do regret that it is not the Liberal party that is winning that position for them. . . . It can still be that our people will learn their lesson in time. What I fear is we will begin to have defections from our own ranks in the House of the CCF."[34] Almost immediately after the release of the September Gallup Poll, the Advisory Council of the National Liberal Federation, meeting at King's request, adopted fourteen resolutions "constituting a programme of reform . . . of far reaching consequences."[35] King wrote in his diary: "I have succeeded in making declarations which will improve the lot of . . . farmers and working people. . . . I think I have cut the ground in large part from under the CCF. . . ."[36]

The Liberal slogan in the campaign of 1945 was "A New Social Order for Canada." The election of June 11 returned King to power with a drastically reduced majority. The CCF vote rose from 8.5

per cent to 15.6 per cent, and its representation in the Commons from 8 to 29. But King's swing to the left had defeated the CCF's bid for major party status. The CCF's success was much smaller than it had expected. The success was actually a defeat, a disappointing shock from which socialism in Canada has not yet recovered.

The Liberal-CCF relationship in 1943-1945 is only the sharpest and clearest instance of the permanent interdependence forced upon each by the presence of the other, a relationship which one student describes as "antagonistic symbiosis." The Liberals depend on the CCF-NDP for innovations; the CCF-NDP depends upon the Liberals for implementation of the innovations. When the left is weak, as before and after the Second World War, the centre party moves right to deal with the Conservative challenge; when the left is strengthened, as during the war and after the formation of the NDP, the centre moves left to deal with that callenge.

In a conversation between King and Coldwell shortly before King's death, King expressed his regrets that Coldwell had not joined him. With Coldwell at his side, he would have been able to implement reforms which were close to his heart; reforms which had either been postponed until the end of the war or not introduced at all. He said the CCF had performed the valuable function of popularizing reforms so that he could introduce them when public opinion was ripe. Coldwell replied that it was impossible for him to join King, especially in view of the people who surrounded King.[37] There, in a nutshell, is the story of the relationship between the Liberal party and the CCF-NDP. The Liberals, says King, are too conservative because the left has not joined them. The left has not joined them, replies Coldwell, because they are too conservative.

King wanted to show the people that he was "true to them." He was saddened that the CCF and not the Liberals were fighting the people's battles. But he could not move from dead centre until CCF power became so great that the necessity of moving was clear, not only to himself but to all realistic politicians. King's best self wanted to innovate; yet he saw the Liberal party not as a great innovating force but as the party which would implement reforms once they had been popularized by the CCF. Yet he wanted to absorb the CCF. The lot of the centrist politician is not a happy one.

*　*　*　*　*

[31]*Ibid.*, pp. 26-27.

[32]J. W. Pickersgill, *The Mackenzie King Record* (Toronto: University of Toronto Press, 1960), p. 10.

[33]*Globe and Mail* (Sept. 29, 1943).

[34]Pickersgill, *Record*, p. 571.

[35]National Liberal Federation, *The Liberal Party*, p. 53.

[36]Pickersgill, *Record*. p. 601.

[37]Interview with M. J. Coldwell, March 28, 1962.

The absence of Lockean "monotheism" strengthened socialism in Canada. Socialism was present in the political culture when liberalism began to concern itself with the problems of the industrial age; liberalism was therefore forced to react to the socialist challenge. In doing so, it was cast in the mould of European Liberal Reform (centre) parties —ambivalent, radical and conservative, alternating attacks on the *status quo* with defence of the *status quo*. Socialism had sufficient strength in English Canada to force liberalism into the European rather than the American position—centre rather than left. King's liberalism was therefore not capable of reacting to the depression in a Rooseveltian manner. As a result, socialist power grew.

Socialism was not powerless, so there was no New Deal. There was no New Deal, so socialism grew more powerful. Socialism grew more powerful, so King reacted with "A New Social Order for Canada." The centre and the left dance around one another, frustrating one another and living off the frustration; each is locked into the dance by the existence of the other.

I have been stressing the strength of Canadian socialism in order to make clear the differences between the Canadian and the American situations. Of course this does not mean that the differences between Canada and Europe can be ignored. Canadian socialism has been strong enough to challenge liberalism, to force liberalism to explain itself, and thus to evoke from it the same sort of centrist response as was evoked in Europe. But socialism in Canada has not been strong enough to match or overshadow liberalism. The CCF became a significant political force but, except for the years 1942-45, it never knocked on the gates of national power.

In Europe, the workingman could not be appeased by the concessions of Liberal Reform. The centre was squeezed out of existence between its enemies on the right and on the left. In Canada, the centre party's concessions were sufficient to keep the lower strata from flocking en masse to the left. The concessions were not sufficient to *dispose* of the socialist threat, but they were sufficient to draw the socialists' sharpest teeth. In Canada the centre party emerged triumphant over its enemies on the right and on the left. Here, then, is another aspect of English Canada's uniqueness: it is the only society in which Liberal Reform faces the challenge of socialism *and* emerges victorious. The English Canadian fragment *is* bourgeois. The toryism and the socialism, though significant, *are* "touches."

Electoral Support

There is a dearth of information about the influence of class on voting behaviour in Canada, but there are strong indications that the higher strata are more likely than the lower to vote Conservative, the lower strata are more likely than the higher to vote CCF-NDP, and that both groups are about *equally* attracted to the Liberals. This would, of course, confirm the picture of Conservatives as the right, NDP as the left, and Liberals as the "classless" centre. This is in sharp contrast to the situation in the

United States, where the lower strata prefer the Democrats, the higher prefer the Republicans, and there is no centre party.

Although this picture of the relationship between class and voting is broadly true, it is also true that class voting in Canada is, generally speaking, over-shadowed by regional and religious-ethnic voting. In some parts of Canada, e.g. Ontario, class voting is as high as in the United States or higher. Nevertheless, in Canada considered as a whole class voting is lower than in the United States; non-class motivations appear to be very strong.[38] Peter Regenstrief suggests that one factor accounting for this is the persistent cultivation by the Liberal party of its classless image, its "abhorrence of anything remotely associated with class politics,"[39] its refusal to appeal to any class against any other class.

What this points to again is the unique character of English Canada as the only society in which the centre triumphs over left and right. In Europe the classless appeal of Liberal Reform does not work; the centre is decimated by the defection of high-status adherents to the right and of low-status adherents to the left. In Canada, the classless appeal of King centrism is the winning strategy, drawing lower-class support to the Liberals away from the left parties, and higher-class support away from the right parties. This forces the left and right parties themselves to emulate (to a certain extent) the Liberals' classless strategy. The Conservatives transform themselves into Progressive Conservatives. The CCF transforms itself from a "farmer-labour" party into an NDP calling for the support of "all liberally minded Canadians." The Liberal refusal to appear as a class party forces both right and left to mitigate their class appeals and to become themselves, in a sense, centre parties.

Class voting in Canada may be lower than in the United States not entirely because regional-religious-ethnic factors are "objectively" stronger here, but also because King Liberalism, by resolutely avoiding class symbols, has made other symbols more important.

> He blunted us.
> We had no shape
> Because he never took sides,
> And no sides,
> Because he never allowed them to take shape.[40]

---

[38]R. Alford, *Party and Society* (Chicago, 1963), chap. 9.
[39]"Group Perceptions and the Vote," in Meisel, ed., *Papers on the 1962 Election*, p. 249.
[40]Scott, *The Blasted Pine*, p. 27.

The Two Old Parties

*

In recent years party platforms have become less important. The parties have concentrated on cultivating a favourable emotional attitude towards them among the public and, because of virtually instantaneous national coverage in press, radio, and television, it has become dangerous for a party to make specific promises to one particular region. Since radio and television lend themselves to the communication of feeling, a new style of politics has emerged to exploit the emotions of the electorate. Campaign planners are eager to develop for the party an image that will appeal to the mood of the country—but to do this is expensive.

The result of this process is the development of a peculiarly Canadian style of political leadership, in which top priority goes to the avoidance of public controversy over real issues and stress is placed upon success in covering over the basic differences among regions and among the various regional interests. Do recent election results suggest that this system is breaking down?

6

Party Images In Canada

J. M. BECK and D. J. DOOLEY

*

. . . For a party to be successful, it must be skilful in performing the
brokerage function; through compromise, it must seek to adjust the differences between the significant interest groups in the country. The successful party leaders have been the ones most adept at minimizing the
differences between Canadians and emphasizing what Canadians have in
common. Sometimes they have persuaded the people that their party is the
instrument through which the economic expansion of the country is to be
secured; such an image involves little danger, since Canadians are generally agreed on accelerated material development through governmental
paternalism. But sometimes the successful leader has not built up a clear
image of his party; he has concentrated on avoiding offense to any significant interest group, keeping his fences mended, and creating the impression
of efficient, business-like government, while relying on the unfavourable
images associated with his opponents to assist him to victory. Sometimes,
again, the party leader possesses such a commanding personality that
his image supersedes that of his party; sometimes, in fact, it is to the
party's advantage to call as little attention as possible to its traditional
policies and to put as much emphasis as possible upon its leaders.

These three kinds of images are of course not the only ones
which we can distinguish in Canadian political history; but perhaps they
are the predominant ones. Our analysis of them cannot be exhaustive
here; but we can give some indication of how they have been produced
and employed. We can observe how each of the two major parties has
tried at various times to present itself as the party of economic expansion,
the party of national unity, or the party which rejoices in a leader whose
greatness dwarfs all other considerations.

Under John A. Macdonald, says Professor Creighton, the
Conservatives pictured themselves as the nation-building party: "They
kept their original conception of a strong Dominion, which would be
economically integrated and politically united. They stood by their national
policies, political and economic." Politically, they used the power of disal-
lowance to protect the interests of the Dominion. Economically, they
relied on three policies: the protective tariff under the resounding title of

*Reprinted from *Queen's Quarterly*, LXVII, No. 3, 1960.

the "National Policy," western settlement, and all-Canadian transportation. They had few scruples about giving capitalists a free hand to exploit the country's natural resources.

Blake and the Liberals, for their part, were fearful of the moral as well as the economic costs of such a programme. Professor Underhill shows that "this attitude of sober and rather mournful criticism made it easy for Government leaders to taunt the Liberals with lack of faith in their country. . . ." The party became stamped, as a result, with "little Canadianism," and the repellent image was in no small measure responsible for its being relegated to opposition until 1896. Yet the Conservative vision of a nation integrated politically and economically could not be realized, as depression, the reappearance of racial and sectional strife, and unfavourable court decisions thwarted their intentions. The Rowell-Sirois Commission reported that in 1896 "it was by no means clear . . . that the equilibrium necessary to a working federalism could be reached."

The sequel is an interesting one. After 1896 Laurier and the Liberals took over the three national economic policies of the Conservatives, and, in the altered circumstances of world-wide prosperity, the Macdonald dream became a reality. "Canadians became conscious of themselves as a nation," says the report of the Commission. "The growing sense of community was accompanied by increasing interdependence." Under these conditions Laurier had no trouble convincing the people that Canada was to be "the country of the twentieth century." The Liberal experiment in face lifting paid large political dividends—victories at four successive general elections.

The techniques of Macdonald and Laurier, however, were unsuited to Mackenzie King. When he came to office in 1921, he was the evangelist of a forward-looking liberalism. But by the fall of 1923, the *Canadian Forum* was suggesting that the leaders of the two major parties should switch; while Mr. Meighen was a bit too radical for the Conservative financial magnates, Mr. King had the outlook on life of a comfortable Tory Clubman: "he will never willingly venture upon untrodden paths or blaze new trails of economic innovation." It was frequently observed that he was reluctant to stimulate public discussion of economic and other issues, and that he preferred to await events rather than to force them. Indeed, a major criticism of him by Professor Underhill at the end of his long career was that he had presented to the country no positive, constructive nation-building policy: "Liberalism in his day has not meant any concrete positive programme which could stir the enthusiasm of the young and the energetic."

In the war years and after, however, under King and St. Laurent, the Liberals were able to create an image of themselves as the party which was bringing the material prosperity of Canada to undreamt-of levels through good management. The remarkable development of Canadian industry during the war and the skilful transition to peace-time prosperity were almost entirely due, it was widely felt, to one man—C. D.

Howe. The nation shared his own image of himself as a builder, a plain-speaking, two-fisted business executive who was interested in getting a job done. He was the kind of person, wrote J. B. McGeachy in May 1957, about whom it can be asked, "How could the country have managed without him?" The Liberals, for most voters, were the party which had the executive ability and the personal contacts in Washington and London to keep that prosperity going.

And then, in 1958, the Conservatives turned again to the nation-building image. John Diefenbaker, never so happy as when he is re-enacting the rôle of Sir John A. Macdonald, conjured up "the vision." Arthur Blakely described it in this way:

A vision of Canada's future. A great future. A future which is all bound up with Canada's great northland and its untapped riches. It is a vision which contemplates the building of roads, the construction of rail lines, the building of dams, the establishment of great new cities, the creation of new wealth. And all of this in our generation. Oh yes, he admits, with a fine scorn, there are the scoffers, the cynics, the unbelievers. Those who suggest, among other things, that roads in the north will run "from igloo to igloo." But those imaginative Canadians, those who make this a land flowing in milk and honey in our own time, they will have a chance to deal with the scoffers on March 31[1].

Most of Mr. Diefenbaker's audiences must have felt that they too had seen the promised land; they proceeded to mete out to Lester Pearson the same kind of treatment they had accorded to Edward Blake in the 1880's.

Only when conditions are right can a party resort to the nation-building image; at all times it must attempt to appear as the party of national unity, the party of all Canadians. It can do this only if its leaders are skilful group diplomats; they must be adept in the brokerage function of reconciling the disparate elements within the community. This way involves, instead of a positive course of action, a policy of avoiding offence to any significant group.

The modern master of this technique was, of course, Mackenzie King. He came to power after a period unique in Canadian history, because during it an attempt had been made to govern Canada without Quebec's cooperation ."Mr. King's life," wrote Professor A. R. M. Lower, "has been devoted to the restoration of a working national harmony of the two races through a revived Liberal party." He came on the scene as a crusading liberal, but the image quickly faded. The Liberal platform of 1919 emphasized policies of social welfare; when it became apparent that these had little appeal to Sir Lomer Gouin and the other Quebec Liberals, they were quietly dropped. However, Mr. King had to conciliate Quebec while not offending other sections of the country; in time, he arranged the growth of Canadian autonomy so cleverly that he did not antagonize even the Anglo-Saxon element in Ontario. The *Canadian Forum* complained in 1944 that he succeeded because of the Canadian preference for living in a mental haze: "We never make issues clear

to ourselves. We never define our differences so that they can be understood clearly or resolved." In Mr. King's view, a Canadian political leader
could not be doctrinaire; he had to balance one pressure group against
another, and he had to prevent issues becoming so clearly defined that
they caused deep divisions. No clarion calls to action from him, but
instead pronouncements so complicated and qualified that no one knew
exactly what they meant. Consequently, in J. R. Mallory's opinion, he
made the party system a subtle and sensitive instrument: "Under him the
Liberal party became the master pattern for a Canadian political party. It
became an instrument for the accommodation of reconcilable differences
rather than a vehicle for a coherent set of ideas." And he restored Quebec's confidence in the system; as Professor Lower points out, the image
which French Canadians had of Mr. King was that of a reasonable man,
a man who would hold the balance even between the two jealous, suspi-
cious peoples, a man who could be trusted to act in the interests of the
whole country and not of his race alone.

He was helped, of course, by the mistakes of his opponents:

> *First there was Meighen, the lean and hungry Cassius, the
> bitter fanatic who lost votes all across the country every time he won a
> debate in the House. . . . Then there was the preposterous Bennett of the
> booming voice and the beetling brows, the lord of the iron heel. Mr. King
> had only to sit back quietly in opposition for five years and let Bennett
> hang himself. Then there was the lightweight Manion, followed quickly
> by the old muzzle-loading blunderbuss from New Brunswick. . . . and just
> when the strain of a long war seemed to make it certain that even a
> government of archangels could not survive the next election, along came
> the two Georges from Toronto.*[2]

Meighen, described by the *Canadian Forum* in 1923 as
"the most arresting and capable personality in our public life," and by
Grattan O'Leary as an orator in a class beyond even Lloyd George,
Roosevelt, and Churchill, never could overcome the public impression of
him as a cold and austere man whose spiritual home was Toronto. His
stand on conscription enabled the Quebec Liberals to picture him as a
man who had filled the cemeteries of Flanders with Canadians, and the
picture of him as a fanatical imperialist was reinforced by his statement
that Canada should have said "Ready, aye ready" when Britain became
involved in the Chanak dispute with Turkey in 1922 and asked for Canada's support. At the same time his inflexible support of protection went a
long way to alienate western Canada.

Bennett, who succeeded him as Conservative leader, did not
evoke the same initial feelings in Quebec, and the party won twenty-four
seats in that province in 1930. However, the Conservative success

---

[1] Arthur Blakely in the *Montreal Gazette*, March 25, 1958.
[2] Arthur Lower, "The Close of an Era," *Canadian Forum*, XXIV
(September, 1944), 126.

throughout Canada in that year was clearly attributable to the depression, which dwarfed all other issues.

By the time Mr. Bennett was through, the fortunes of the Conservative party had sunk to a new low. Canadians have never exhibited the same fascination with the millionaire in politics as have their American cousins; it was easy, therefore, for the Liberals to picture the prime minister as a rich, intolerant despot. Mr. Bennett made a desperate effort to blot out the unfavourable picture, but his proposed reform of capitalism through a so-called "New Deal" was regarded by many Conservatives as unbelievably radical and by many others as a form of death-bed repentance in the face of defeat. His government's failure, understandable though it may have been, to deal effectively with unemployment created an impression among Canadians generally that the Conservatives were bumbling incompetents. That image took years to erase.

In the next two decades, the Conservatives sought by a variety of devices to broaden their appeal. At their leadership convention in 1938, they even changed their name to "National Conservatives." At the same time a group headed by Georges Héon insisted that the party must make an all-out effort to appeal to Quebec; this group had its way in the choice of Dr. R. J. Manion to succeed Mr. Bennett. To expect that Mrs. Manion's being a French Canadian would help the party's chances in Quebec is understandable; to consider that her husband—an Irish Catholic who had deserted Laurier on the conscription issue in 1917—would be equally acceptable is inconceivable. The fact that the next election came when Canada was at war made the miscalculation particularly disastrous. Also, Mr. Manion's campaigning for a "National Government" in that election reinforced a popular opinion that the Conservatives did not have enough men of calibre to form a ministry.

Under King, the Liberals experienced none of the same difficulties in appealing to Canadians generally. At their leadership convention in 1948, the basic question which the delegates asked themselves was: "Who can maintain the Liberal tradition of a truly national party, the party of Canadian unity?" The answer they found, of course, was Mr. St. Laurent; but even they were astonished at his success as a vote-getter outside the province of Quebec. Like Mr. King before him, he made few pledges and promises; when Mr. Drew promised to cut taxes by five hundred million dollars in 1953, Mr. St. Laurent's simple reply was, in effect, "We shall do as well for you in the future as in the past." J. A. Stevenson wrote that in the 1953 campaign, Mr. St. Laurent was the image of a "benevolent elder statesman, who has shed all personal ambitions for himself and is anxious to spend his closing years in improving the lot of all classes in our community." "It may be," wrote *The Economist* after the 1949 election, "that Canada has found a man who can really unify and lead her. . . ." This was a tribute to Mr. St. Laurent's ability to convince even independent observers that he was a reasonable man who would never attempt to impose upon any section of the Canadian nation policies which were offensive to it.

George Drew, Mr. St. Laurent's opponent in 1949 and 1953, found it impossible to soften the repellent image which his party conjured up for many Canadians. Orthodox Conservative he was, pro-British and pro-Imperialistic, and this outlook was of doubtful value in a country whose proportion of Anglo-Saxons was shrinking. He had other disabilities. Even before he had assumed the federal leadership of his party, the Toronto *Daily Star* had stereotyped him as in favour of big business and against labour. In contrast with the corporation lawyer who was his opponent, Mr. Drew had never had any ties with big business; but the label stuck.

In one respect, Mr. Drew led his party to unaccustomed channels with disastrous results. The Conservatives took over the old Liberal rôle of defender of provincial rights. They alleged that the tax-sharing agreements with the provinces destroyed provincial autonomy and weakened Canadian federalism. But this new direction of the Conservative party was badly taken in the have-not provinces, where the agreements enabled a higher standard of provincial services than would otherwise have been possible.

Theoretically this new orientation ought to have improved the popularity of the Conservatives in Quebec; in this and other ways Mr. Drew sought the support of Mr. Duplessis and his Union Nationale machine. But both in 1949 and in 1953, his efforts produced anything but the desired effect. It would have required something more substantial than the provincial rights issue to make Quebec abandon its compatriot, Mr. St. Laurent. Mr. Duplessis, not willing to risk his prestige for a hopeless cause, took no part in either election, although he allowed his supporters to participate as they pleased. Nevertheless, Mr. Drew's opponents were able to express moral indignation over a Drew-Duplessis alliance, and all observers agree that this hurt the Conservatives in Ontario. Mr. Drew's campaign shows clearly how an attempt to create a favourable image in one section of Canada may create an unfavourable one elsewhere.

After Mr. Drew, it was again the turn of the unorthodox; in December 1956, John Diefenbaker became the Conservative leader. To some observers the choice appeared to be a mistake, because Mr. Diefenbaker, despite his name, gave "every indication of possessing the annoying Anglo-Saxon faculty of being oblivious to any other group." The Conservative party, A. Vixen alleged, was still "by nature intuitively Anglo-Saxon. Its reflex actions are automatically British . . . [Its] tragedy is that it cannot free itself from its inherent Anglo-Saxon personality, try as it will, and this inhibition is slowly fossilising it in a country becoming less Anglo-Saxon all the time." The conclusion was that until the party could "branch out beyond its present inhibited character and develop a personality that grows and changes with the times, it is unlikely that it will be able to attract anything better than a second class leader." Thus the party was still thought of as a sectional one, based primarily on Ontario.

The Conservatives realized that they could not contend successfully with "Uncle Louis" in Quebec in 1957; hence they allocated a minimum of their resources to it. But, as Michel Brunet has pointed out, Mr. Diefenbaker possessed all the qualities required of a "principal interpreter" for English-speaking Canada. His Dutch origin won favour among many of the New Canadians. His deep British convictions appealed to citizens of Anglo-Saxon descent. His modest beginnings were admired by the mass of little people. He had served in the armed forces, and could appeal to the veterans of two wars. He had lived in Ontario, and he was a westerner. He possessed a vitality which could impress youth. His evangelistic eloquence awakened familiar echoes among many Protestants. Mr. Brunet considers that still another factor may have been at work: English Canada—without being fully aware of it—may have been looking for a leader belonging entirely to itself. Mr. Diefenbaker's detachment from French Canada would have rendered him acceptable in this respect.

On June 11, 1957, the Liberal party, which had long considered itself Canada's only national party, awoke to the fact that, if representation in the Commons was the criterion, it had become largely a French Canadian party. The Conservatives were equally surprised to discover that their representation made them a party of all the races. Their ranks included a Jung, a Jorgenson, a Mandziuk, a Kucherepa, and a Martini; they had a larger number of non-French Catholics than for many years past; and they had more French Canadians from Quebec— even if they numbered only eight—than they had elected since 1930.

By appointing a Ukrainian to the cabinet, elevating an Indian to the Senate, and choosing a Canadian of Chinese descent as president of their young people's organization, the Conservatives reinforced the idea that they were the party of a united Canada. The repellent image of the party collapsed even in Quebec in the 1958 election. As usual, the Liberals painted the Conservatives as enemies of the French Canadian race; they brought out all the allegations they had been making since 1917. But they could accuse Mr. Diefenbaker of no specific anti-French actions or policies. The Conservative newspaper advertisements had their effect; they forecast a shattering triumph for Diefenbaker and they pleaded, "Let us not isolate Quebec." And so Quebec climbed on the bandwagon too.

If the successful Canadian party is sometimes the party with a national policy and usually the party which reconciles differences, it is also at times the party which is distinguished chiefly by the personality of its leader. This is to be expected when the parties and hence the voters are not divided on basic principles; the absence of principles tends to exalt the leader. In the case of Macdonald, the "Old Man" and the "Old Party" became one and the same thing; Conservatives never thought of separating the two. In time, the same development occurred in the case of Laurier and the Liberal party.

Mackenzie King re-created the Liberal party in his own image, which was hardly that of Macdonald or Laurier. Surprisingly, we read, on the authority of such a good judge of oratory as Grattan O'Leary, that there was something of Byran's "Cross of Gold" impact to

King's final salute to Laurier. The early King pictured himself as a liberator and unifier; he had come to free Canadians from the black night of Conservative oppression, from "an unholy combination of political autocracy and industrial plutocracy," and he had come to put an end to the period in which Canada was ruled without the effective cooperation of Quebec. This image of a decisive and positive figure did not last for long. By 1923 there had arisen an image which never faded from some people's minds—that of King the opportunist, the conciliator, the bargainer, the man who was willing to compromise as long as he could stay in office. "The truth is," declared the *Canadian Forum's* political correspondent in 1924, "that our present Prime Minister has less qualifications for the very complicated task of governing Canada than any of his predecessors since Confederation, and whenever two or three Liberals are gathered together they proceed to lament his deficiencies and quarrel about the allocation of responsibility for his selection." In 1926, the same journal reported that Ottawa teemed with tales of King's vanity and pomposity, his predilection for strange and unworthy favourites, and his old-maidish obsession with petty problems of etiquette. The Liberals were delighted at the coming of Charles Dunning to the national scene, and it was expected that he would soon assume the leadership; never again would the anti-Conservative forces in the country be asked to rally around this "absurd and preposterous person...."

The image of King as an absurd and preposterous figure never left some people's minds—even some of those who voted for Liberal candidates in election after election. Yet a number of political commentators have ascribed his success to his presenting an image of mediocrity with which Canadians could identify themselves. Only the national mental haze, wrote the *Canadian Forum*, could explain him: "Mr. King is obviously the most complete personification of this national Canadian characteristic who has ever appeared in our public life. He is the typical Canadian, the essential Canadian, the ideal Canadian, the Canadian as he exists in the mind of God." Professor Lower wrote, "His appeal was consciously to the head, rather than to the heart. And the qualities of 'head' to which he appealed were those of the average man of good, plain intelligence. There was nothing fancy about his electorate. He spoke as the plain man did—with all the repetitions, the painful elaboration of the obvious, the turgidity of the ordinary man—only more so!" He was "the ordinary man projected and modified."

It is to be doubted, however, that the ordinary man identified himself with Mr. King. The Prime Minister was thought of as a frosty bachelor, neither a man's man nor a lady's man, surrounded by ceremonial etiquette, a man of mystery. In fact, it was often necessary for his followers to protest that the public image was not really correct; Norman Rogers, in the biographical account of King which he wrote in 1935, went to some lengths to stress his boyishness, willingness to listen, and charm of manner. But, in the view of most Canadians, he remained an aloof and inscrutable personality.

Yet the associations his name summoned up were sufficiently favourable for his party to secure election time and again. If he was not a great orator, if he did not summon up visions of Canada's national destiny, if he could not give friendly fireside chats like Roosevelt, if he did not in any way fulfill the popular image of a democratic politician, he was still felt to be the right man for the job. What the political commentators with greater sophistication call his awareness of, or identification with, the inarticulate feelings of the people, or his concept of a national destiny which most Canadians could accept, was probably part of the image of King seen by the average voter: probably the general public would have agreed that he had a remarkable flair for assessing how far the Canadian people were willing to see a particular course of action pursued at a given time. Perhaps the picture of him which was generally held was that of a man who, by methods far from clear, did succeed in giving Canada the kind of government it wanted.

Mr. St. Laurent is a noteworthy example of how quickly a man can come to represent a party. A remarkable change took place within ten months of his selection as Liberal leader at the convention in August, 1948. At that time, he was still an unknown quantity; he was described as an able corporation lawyer, though a bit hard and a bit sharp-tempered; as quiet, scholarly, and courteous; and as a man with "a cold look in his eyes, for all their Irish-French sparkle." Less than a year later he had won a decisive victory in an election which was clearly a personal triumph for him; he was being credited with qualities of leadership such as Mr. King had never possessed; and "Uncle Louis" had been born.

Ian Scanders has related in *Maclean's* how the austere image was replaced by the benevolent one. As Mr. St. Laurent travelled westwards on his election campaign, he began to shed his starchy formality; he still gave uninspired speeches which drew only polite applause, but, remembering his boyhood days in a Quebec village, he began to chat easily with the voters about the crops and the weather. Then at Eden, Alberta, he faced an audience in which schoolchildren outnumbered adults; he talked to the schoolchildren, in a grandfatherly way—and the adults applauded. After this he spoke extemporaneously and familiarly; on one occasion, he said, "After all, I am among friends, and, well, I can speak to them as I can speak to members of my own family." By the end of his tour, he had become a kind of universal father image. Finally when his train was stopped at Field, B..C, Norman Campbell, a reporter for the Toronto *Telegram,* made the remark "I'm afraid Uncle Louis will be a hard one to beat" and Mr. St. Laurent had received the nickname which was to cling to him.

Saturday Night described this campaign as more like a presidential election in the United States than a parliamentary election in 262 separate constituencies: the new methods of advertising and publicity made the party leader all-important and the individual candidate in the constitutency relatively insignificant. In the 1949 election, it was the Conservatives who brought up issues; Mr. St. Laurent said there were no major political or economic issues, the voters agreed with him, and the contest became one concerned with the personalities of the two leaders. The same was true of the 1953 election, in which Mr. St. Laurent proved himself the greatest vote-getter since Confederation. The *Globe and Mail* said that "the Liberal platform is Louis St. Laurent." The Liberal strategy was simply to display their leader as the image of a kindly father of a family. As *Saturday Night* found by making a survey, the image did not have to be precise or filled in; few people could say more about Mr. St. Laurent than that "He's a fine gentleman" or "He was born in Quebec, he used to be a lawyer, and he's got a large family." The image, however, had its effect even in the House of Commons; in 1955, when Mr. Fulton delivered an attack upon the Prime Minister, the Liberals treated it almost as *lèse-majesté*, and the *Ottawa Journal* had to protest that there was no parliamentary tradition by which Prime Ministers were regarded as immune from criticism and that even Sir Wilfred Laurier had not been treated with such deference.

Sometimes a party seeks to abandon its own identity and even its name in favour of an "attractive" leader, hoping thereby to get rid of a repellent image. In 1942, under Mr. Meighen's urging, the Conservatives tried another of their experiments at face lifting. In an obvious effort to woo the West, where the party had almost disappeared, they turned to a man who had never been identified with the Conservative party—John Bracken, Premier of Manitoba. He exacted his own pound of flesh for accepting the thankless job, and the party became the Progressive Conservative Party. The *Canadian Forum* was not impressed: "So the old lady has gone and had her face lifted again! The Canadian Tory party changes its name as often and as easily as the Canadian Communist party changes its line. *Plus ça change. . . .*"[3]

Once again, the result was failure: the local factors which made Bracken a success in Manitoba could not be translated to the federal sphere, and Bracken's attempt to sell the Conservatives as a progressive party was unsuccessful. The McKim advertising agency's attempt to touch up "the pale personality of their leader in a series of advertisements that treated him 'like a new breakfast food' " (as Mackenzie King put it) got nowhere. And so in 1948, the party turned back to orthodox Conservatism and George Drew.

Mr. Drew was the image of typical Conservatism, and the Liberals were delighted. The convention which chose Mr. Drew as leader ought perhaps to have thought a little more of his past history. In the provincial campaign in Ontario in 1948, the Conservatives had used the slogan, "Make Ontario strong with George Drew." Later in the campaign, they became doubtful of the popularity of their leader and made less use of the slogan; the Conservatives were elected, but Drew was defeated in his own riding. *The Round Table* was probably correct in an estimate it made in 1953 ". . . in the eyes of the numerous plain folk, who live on the farms and in the small towns of Canada, Mr. Drew is the perfect pattern

[3]"The Pro and Con Party," *Canadian Forum*, XXII (January, 1943), 293.

of the prosperous urban citizen, who in their view gets too large a share of the national income, and they look askance at him as a Curzonian type of 'most superior person'." This image he was never able to efface.

It was not clear, when John Diefenbaker succeeded Mr. Drew, that he would have any greater success in winning over the Canadian voter. His opponents were, of course, suffering from continued success, and their high-handed treatment of Parliament made them vulnerable to attack by the Diefenbaker platform method. "He is reminiscent sometimes," said *The Economist*, "of a Hollywood small-town lawyer, with a smile of bitter sarcasm, a wagging forefinger of accusation and a short scornful laugh. But he does it all rather well, and it is proving effective."

In these circumstances, Mr. St. Laurent was unable to captivate his audiences to the same extent as in 1949 and 1953: "Like many fading actors, Uncle Louis started overdoing the act. He kissed too many babies, patted too many little heads, propounded too many platitudes. The press and the crowds began to complain that a prime minister should have something positive to say about current problems. Latterly, Mr. St. Laurent has been trying to use more arguments about specific policy, but it is hard to elbow Uncle Louis's soothing platitudes off the stage." So wrote *The Economist* in the middle of the campaign.

When Mr. St. Laurent complained that the Conservative party was concentrating on selling its leader rather than itself, the complaint backfired: it convinced the high command of the Tory party that they were on the right track. By the admission of Allister Grosart, the party's national director, they concentrated on this technique. The Conservative party became, in fact, the Diefenbaker party. The Liberals charged that it was the height of deception for a party to seek to increase its chances of success by looking as little as possible like itself. But their criticism was all in vain: the Diefenbaker party won.

From this survey, it would appear that certain types of party images have had profound effects on Canadian politics. The exact kinds of political images which obtain in Britain are not to be found in Canada; a North American political party is by nature considerably different from a European political party, and the image a Canadian party conjures up must respond to the peculiar needs of the Canadian nation. As in Britain, however, once a party has created a bad impression upon a significant interest group it may take years for the repellent picture to disappear. Yet the evidence of recent Canadian elections is that the change can take place with astonishing rapidity. This is particularly true when the third type of image, that in which the personality of the leader overshadows or supplants the traditional concept of his party, is dominant. We have observed a trend towards greater emphasis on the party leader, and, if the influence of the professional manipulators of images becomes more important, this trend is likely to continue. But we can only speculate on the role which the admen are going to play in future elections—and on the function as well of that seemingly all-pervasive projector of images, the television set.

7

The Economic Elite and Political Leadership in Canada

JOHN PORTER

*

There is no clear alignment between the economic elite and the two major political parties. In fact, political affiliation is, in the majority of cases, omitted from biographical reference material, but this political anonymity does not mean a sinister concealment of political loyalty. In the corporate world both major political parties, the Liberals and the Conservatives, are seen as being favourable to the interests of corporate power. There would seem to be operating the same formula that Samuel Gompers applied to the political behaviour of trade unions in the United States: that corporation leaders, in the main, keep themselves detached from a particular political party so that they can shift their support from one to the other when it is in their interests to do so. There are some dramatic examples of such shifting on the part of earlier economic elites. A group of Toronto finance and business men deserted the Liberal party over reciprocity, just as the compensation for the nationalization of the Mackenzie and Mann railways created a long-standing breach between the Conservative party and financial interests in Montreal.[1]

In the long years that the Liberal party held power until 1957 there was no doubt a close association between the corporate world and the party in power. If there was any change over to the Conservatives after 1958 it was a change that involved little if any ideological strains. Judgments about which political party is "best" are more often in terms of the men in them and their ability to stabilize the field for corporate activity. This criterion can lead the corporate world to support one party provincially and another federally. Thus Social Credit in Alberta and British Columbia, and the Union Nationale in Quebec all have made acceptable governments for the corporation. It was a Liberal federal government which gave a large temporary subsidy to the Trans-Canada Pipe

*Reprinted from *The Vertical Mosaic*, Toronto: University of Toronto Press, 1965.
[1]See the discussion of these shifts in Roger Graham, *Arthur Meighen: The Door of Opportunity* (Toronto: Clarke, Irwin and Co., 1960).

Lines Ltd., the President of which was a former cabinet minister in the Social Credit government in Alberta. . . .

Although the proportion of the economic elite being considered here was small, a few general statements can be made. It is clear, for example, that no industry stood out as favouring one of the parties. Liberals and Conservatives were found on the boards in all types of industries. Similarly the board of a single corporation would include members of both parties. The popular image of the Conservative party as representing the "Bay Street crowd" is not accurate because men of the financial world find themselves at home in the Liberal party too. This fact became very apparent with the return of the Pearson Liberals to power in 1963.

Only a very few of the economic elite, thirty-seven Liberals and nineteen Conservatives, had been politicians at some stage of their careers. Thus it would seem that the two functional areas of economic and political power tend, on the whole, to be separate as far as career systems are concerned. Those links which did exist were through the legal profession, particularly through the corporation lawyer. There were also a few cases of the graduated politician of national status who picked up directorships when he left political life. After the Liberal defeats of 1957 and 1958 many former Liberal cabinet ministers picked up numerous directorships in the corporate world as did several of the public servants who had been closely associated with them. However, it is very clear that the opposite movement does not take place; that is, corporate leaders do not go into politics (except the Senate) from the corporate board rooms. The Senate is perhaps the main institutional link between economic and political power. There were seventeen senators (all Liberal), or about one-fourth of the membership of the Upper House (1952), in the economic elite. Altogether twenty-six of the dominant corporations, four banks, and three of the life insurance companies had this direct "representation" in Parliament. Thus "business" probably had larger representation than any other functional group. It is to be expected, of course, considering the long period that Liberal administrations controlled appointments, that Liberal rather than Conservative senators would be found on boards of directors.

*   *   *   *   *

MAJOR PARTIES: THE CONSERVATIVE TONE

The most significant characteristic of the two parties which have held power at the national level in Canada is the fact that they share the same conservative values. Both have at times been responsible for reform legislation which might suggest progressive values, but these steps to the left have been taken more with a spirit of opportunism than from a basic orientation to social progress and change. The Progressive Conservative party has been ingenious enough to incorporate the political dynamic within its name. As some of its opponents have suggested it is neither conservative nor progressive, but has remained opportunistic. Both parties have produced successive contingents of administrative politicians. The political dialogue, if it can be called such, in which they participate is not related to any basic class difference in the society from which the conservative-progressive dynamic might arise. It is not that Canadian social structure is so static that it has no immanent potential for dynamic politics; it is rather that Canada's basically opportunistic parties have not harnessed this potential in the political system. They have either ignored these basic social differences or covered them up in the pretence that they do not exist.

*   *   *   *   *

POLITICAL CAREERS

The Entrances

In Canada the political career can begin at the municipal or county level, in the provincial legislature, or in the federal Parliament. It can proceed through all three levels. It can also begin at the very top, in the federal cabinet. Ward has shown that a considerable proportion, about one-third, of members of Parliament between 1867 and 1945 went directly from local to federal politics, and that about one-third of new members entering Parliament had had only local experience.[2] About one-quarter of M.P.'s had had experience in provincial legislatures. When both municipal and provincial experience was combined about one-half of M.P.'s had had some previous political experience before going to Ottawa.

Such pre-parliamentary experience seems to be less of a prerequisite for the highest political offices. Of eighty-eight federal cabinet ministers only sixteen per cent had had experience at the municipal level of politics, and only twenty per cent had been in provincial legislatures. The fact that more cabinet ministers had had experience at the provincial than at the municipal level is partly the result of the custom of co-opting provincial cabinet ministers (including provincial premiers or ex-premiers) into the federal cabinet as provincial "representatives." Five of the eighteen federal cabinet ministers who had had experience in provincial legislatures (J. B. M. Baxter, J. Gardiner, A. L. Macdonald, S. Garson, and H. J. Flemming) were co-opted from provincial premierships or, because some of their governments had been defeated, party leaderships in their provinces. A further five of the eighteen (I. A. Mackenzie, J. H. King, F. G. Bradley, H. F. G. Bridges, and G. C. Marler) were also co-opted because of their experience either as provincial cabinet ministers or as opposition leaders. In most cases, the appointment of these ten to the federal cabinet preceded their election to the House of Commons. A further two among the eighteen with provincial experience never did sit in the House of Commons; they were government leaders in the Senate.

---

[2] Norman Ward, *Canadian House of Commons* (Toronto: University of Toronto Press, 1950), chap. VII.

Only six of the eighteen had political careers which progressed by stages from a provincial legislature, to the House of Commons, and finally to the federal cabinet.

This co-opting of provincial politicians to make up provincial representation in the cabinet does not seem to be necessary to achieve representation for the central provinces of Quebec and Ontario. (One exception was G. C. Marler.) Because between them both these provinces have a large proportion of the total seats, the party which forms the government is likely to have a sufficient reservoir, among members elected, from which cabinet ministers can be drawn. Other provinces not only have fewer seats, but the western ones also tend to support minor parties. Thus if there is to be provincial representation for these other provinces, co-opting becomes necessary.

With the exception of Baxter, who served briefly in the Meighen ministry of 1921 and H. J. Flemming, the former premier of New Brunswick brought into the Diefenbaker ministry, all of the co-opted provincial politicians have been Liberals. Both those provincial politicians who are in provincial office at the time of their appointment to the federal cabinet and those who have been defeated by their provincial electorates can fill the need for provincial representation.

With provincial party leaders going directly into the federal cabinet provincial and national politics become interwoven. Provincial leaders often are not known outside their provinces. They rarely achieve national stature as federal political leaders and, because they have been co-opted without a political following in Parliament and sometimes with a shattered one in their home province, they do not constitute threats to the prime ministers who bring them in. These co-opted provincial politicians can be considered outsiders as far as the national political system is concerned.

In the recruitment of the political elite there has been a second type of co-opting, that is, bringing in the real political outsider who has never had a political career. Nine of the eighty-eight were recruited in this fashion. All but one of these outsiders, Sydney Smith, were brought into Liberal governments. After the resurgence of the Conservative party at the federal level, Flemming and Smith, as noted above, were the only ones until 1962 co-opted into the political elite.

Another way of looking at the relationship between parliamentary experience and cabinet office is to distribute the eighty-eight cabinet ministers by their parliamentary experience before going into the cabinet. Thirty-five (forty per cent) entered during their first parliamentary term. Included in this number are the political outsiders and provincial politicians previously discussed, as well as some, like C. D. Howe, who were brought into the cabinet immediately after their election. A further three cabinet ministers were never in the House of Commons, but came to the cabinet through the Senate, so that in all forty-three per cent of cabinet ministers had very limited parliamentary experience before becoming cabinet ministers. (Of the thirty-five "first termers" only nine had had previous experience in provincial legislatures.) During the period for which the elite was selected, more men were appointed to the cabinet in their first parliamentary term than in any other term. An additional fourteen of the eighty-eight were appointed during their second parliamentary term, in some cases immediately after the general election which started their second term. The short session of 1957-58 has been included as a parliamentary term so that some who were appointed during their second term would have had little more experience than those appointed in their first term. Thus, altogether, fifty-nine per cent could be said to have had a minimum of parliamentary experience before reaching high office. Nineteen of the eighty-eight (twenty-two per cent) were appointed during their third parliamentary term and seventeen (twenty per cent) had served more than three terms. Among the seventeen old-timers were nine front-bench Conservative members who went into Mr. Diefenbaker's first cabinet. These men probably experienced acute frustration at seeing the procession of outsiders that went through Liberal cabinets. There may well have been some substance to their claims that Parliament had become a relatively unimportant institution during the long administrative regime of the Liberal party.

Of the thirty Conservatives who served in the federal cabinet between 1957 and 1960, seven were brought in during their first parliamentary term. Of these, two were the outsiders previously mentioned, and all but one of the remainder were from Quebec where previous Conservative representation had been sparse. Five were brought in during their second parliamentary term, seven during their third, and eleven served more than three. Thus, for the recent Conservative ministry, there is a closer relationship between parliamentary career and cabinet office than was the case with previous Liberal ministries.

Among the thirty-eight provincial premiers there is a smaller proportion than with the federal cabinet ministers who had had only a slight experience of politics before becoming provincial premiers. Eight of them became premiers during their first term. Three of these were political outsiders in that their first term in the legislature was their first venture into politics. A further four became premiers during their second term in the legislature. Almost two-thirds of these provincial premiers, however, had reached provincial cabinets during the second term in their legislatures. This latter observation suggests that the relationship between provincial cabinets and their legislatures is similar to that between the federal cabinet and Parliament.

Federal cabinet office is reached at a relatively early age. More were appointed between the ages of forty and forty-nine than in any other ten-year age range. One-half of the eighty-eight were in the cabinet before they were fifty years old. All but thirteen were appointed before they were sixty years old. It is not quite correct then to suggest, as Professor Underhill has, that the late age of politicians is an important reason why Canadian politicians as a class are "dull and fatuous" and why "nothing imaginative or creative is to be hoped from them."[3] He notes that the "fathers" of Confederation, the "genuinely creative" politicians, were much younger than the Liberal ministry and the opposition leaders in 1956. In an even earlier period of Canadian politics, Underhill points out, Robert Baldwin retired at forty-seven and Louis LaFontaine at forty-four. Nevertheless, although it is true that at the end of the Liberal era some of the leaders were old, life expectancy was much greater than it was a century earlier. In any case, Canadian cabinets of the 1950's had young men in them as well as old. Brooke Claxton was in the cabinet at the age of forty-six and left at fifty-six to become vice-president of the Metropolitan Life Insurance Company. Douglas Abbott was in at the age of forty-four and out again to the Supreme Court of Canada by the time he was fifty-five. Winters, Lapointe (the younger), and Hellyer were in the cabinet when they were in their thirties. Lesage, Harris, Pinard, Rinfret (the younger), Sinclair, and Pickersgill were all in during their forties. The cabinet was being regenerated with young men.

Thus if Canadian politicians are dull and fatuous (as politicians, presumably Professor Underhill meant) it is not so much because of their age as because of the practice of avocational politics, where a stint in politics is an interstitial stage in a career devoted to something else. It is also unlikely that a political system which lacks the dynamic element of polarization will provide much scope for creative men.

*   *   *   *   *

The Exits

The political career has its peculiar exits as well as its entrances. Cabinet ministers remain in office relatively few years even though, on the average, they are young when appointed. In order to gain an accurate picture of how long they do hold cabinet positions, we must remove, from the total of eight-eight, the twenty who were still in office in 1960. Of the sixty-eight remaining, thirty-two were in office for less than five years, twenty-two for six to ten years, seven for eleven to fifteen years, and seven for more than fifteen years. Those who stayed in office for a long time were the dominant men within Liberal cabinets such as Mackenzie King, C. D. Howe, and Ernest Lapointe. They stayed, while lesser people did a stint of administrative politics or served time as provincial representatives.

There are various exits from cabinet office including appointments to the bench, the Senate, lieutenant-governorships, resignations, deaths, and of course, defeat at the polls. Once again we must remove the twenty of the eighty-eight cabinet ministers who were still in office in 1960. Of the remaining sixty-eight, ten went to the bench, seven to the Senate, and two to lieutenant-governorships. These patronage appointments made up about twenty-eight per cent of the exits. Eight died in office; fourteen resigned their cabinet positions; twenty were personally defeated at the polls; and a further seven went out of office with their governments' defeat. Thus electoral defeat (in forty per cent of the cases) is the most frequent reason for leaving the cabinet. If defeats and resignations are combined as non-patronage exits they make up forty-one cases. Of these forty-one, seventeen retired from politics; three went to the federal bureaucracy; three went into provincial politics; and thirteen remained in federal politics, four going to the Senate to which they were appointed after their defeat and nine remaining in the House of Commons after their resignations from the cabinet or after the defeat of their governments. (Five ministers were defeated in 1962 but it is not possible yet to tell whether or not they have closed the door on political life.) Of the seventeen who retired from politics either after defeat or after resignation from the cabinet, six were over seventy years old. The remaining eleven abandoned politics to return to private law practices or to business.

Where the political career is unstable and taken up for an interstitial period only, during a career devoted to something else, the political system will probably be strong in administration and weak in creativity. There is, of course, always an element of uncertainty in the political career, at least uncertainty about being in office, but because opposition is as important to the functioning of the system as government, men should be as much available for opposition as for office. Where there is an aristocratic and financially secure class willing to assume political roles, career uncertainty is less significant in avoiding politics as a career. But, as noted above, Canada's financially secure class has, by and large, kept out of politics, and political leaders have been unable or unwilling to control safe seats as a means of removing some of the uncertainty.

. . . If we divide the eighty-eight cabinet ministers into those who had, or appeared to have, left elected political roles for good, and those who were still in such roles, we can see what proportion of their working lives were spent in politics. These calculations are based on their ages when first elected to any legislature and their ages when they left elected political office through any of the exits previously discussed. Of the first group, those who had made their political exits, almost two-thirds (sixty-five per cent) had spent less than half their working lives in politics. Of the second group, almost the same proportion (sixty-four per cent) had spent less than half their working lives in politics, although some, no doubt, would spend more than half before they were finished. Provincial premiers devote more of their working lives to politics than do federal cabinet ministers. For those premiers who had left office the proportions were equal between those who had spent half or more of their working lives in politics (fifty per cent) and those who had spent less than half (fifty per cent). Seven of the ten still in office in 1960 had spent more than half their lives in politics.

* * * * *

The pattern of instability which can be seen in this collective portrait of political careers in Canada has been the result in part of

---

[8]F. H. Underhill, *In Search of Canadian Liberalism* (Toronto, 1960), 248ff.

the long period in office, from 1935 to 1957, of the Liberal party, and in part of the fact that our political elite includes men in office during World War II, when perhaps different qualities were needed in the political elite. These two factors combined resulted in the depoliticizing of the political system by the recruitment of political outsiders. These administrative politicians were almost indistinguishable from the leaders of the federal bureaucracy which the Liberal administration built up at the same time. In the process of taking politics out of the political system there developed a detachment of the executive branch of government, that is cabinet ministers and their senior officials, from Parliament, an informal separation of powers not unlike the more formal separation of powers in the United States government. Howe, Rogers, St. Laurent, Gibson, McNaughton, Lafleche, and Mitchell were not parliamentary men before going into the cabinet. Ralston, MacKinnon, McLarty, Abbott, and Claxton had only a short acquaintance with political life before King brought them into his government. Nor had the co-opted provincial politicians much of a role on the national scene. Some never did acquire such a role, but rather remained provincial representatives within the cabinets in which they served.

After the war the recruitment of the political outsider continued. Pearson and Pickersgill came directly from the bureaucracy into the cabinet. Campney, Winters, Prudham, and Gregg had the minimum of a political career. When Mr. St. Laurent's government was defeated in 1957 he and many of his colleagues retired from politics, never to return. Some, such as Abbott and Claxton, had left before the *débâcle*. Only nine of the ministers defeated in 1957 entered the election of 1958, and only five were in the House of Commons after it. The depoliticized Liberal party chose Mr. Pearson, the ex-bureaucrat, as leader over Mr. Martin, the professional politician. The depoliticizing went through to the 1962 and 1963 elections when Mr. Pearson fielded his "team." Prominent in this team and generally considered to be Mr. Pearson's close advisers and prospective cabinet colleagues, were men, such as Walter Gordon, Mitchell Sharp, C. M. Drury, and Maurice Lamontagne, who had never been in Parliament. Thus, when the Liberal party formed a minority government in 1963 political outsiders received immediate cabinet positions. Several of these men were former civil servants.

In his analysis of politics as a vocation Max Weber emphasized the inability of civil servants to become satisfactory political leaders.

According to his proper vocation, the genuine official . . . will not engage in politics. Rather he should engage in impartial "administration". . . . Sine ira et studio, "without scorn and bias" he shall administer his office. Hence he shall not do precisely what the politician, the leader as well as his following, must always and necessarily do, namely, fight.

To take a stand, to be passionate—ira et studium—is the politician's element, and above all the element of the political leader.

His conduct is subject to quite a different, indeed, exactly the opposite, principle of responsibility from that of the civil servant.[4]

The responsibility of the civil servant, Max Weber continues, is to carry out to the best of his ability the instructions of his superior officials. The responsibility of the political leader is a personal responsibility which cannot be transferred to anyone else. A career devoted to the first type of responsibility cannot be easily transformed into the second type of responsibility. Consequently, Max Weber argued, civil servants become politically "irresponsible" politicians.

The separation of bureaucratic and political careers with their two types of responsibility has come about during the evolution of the British type of parliamentary government. Among Liberal politicians in Canada, however, the two careers have become mixed, probably because Mackenzie King, who dominated the party for so long, was himself a civil servant before he was a politician. When he appointed Mr. Pearson to the cabinet he made the curious observation that the civil service was "the stepping stone to the ministry." This demotion of Parliament was at least consistent with administrative politics.

* * * * *

Avocational and administrative politics leaves the political system relatively weak as a system of institutional power. With a political elite of substantially middle class origins the dynamics of social class which give rise to conservative and progressive social forces have never worked themselves out within the political system. Perhaps it is from looking at their politicians that Canadians get the impression that their society is a middle class one. Neither the corporate elite, nor the very wealthy, have much to fear from middle class politicians. It is more likely that the politicians hold the corporate elite in awe. It would certainly seem that these middle class men are dependent on the corporate world to keep their political parties in funds.

The instability of the political career reduces the number of national political leaders to a mere handful because each cabinet has within it a relatively large number who have never been heard of, and whose claim on office is that they represent particular provinces. All governments require men of ability, but able men are less likely to be attracted to political life when the course is so uncertain. There is no way in which to measure the ability of members of Parliament, but perhaps the problem is not so much the absence of ability as the high rate of turnover in each Parliament. There is a vicious circle operating. Prime ministers frequently co-opt outsiders to "strengthen the government." But the practice of co-opting does not enhance the stature of the House of Commons, either as the forum of debate on national issues, or as the training ground for political leadership at the national level.

* * * * *

---

[4]Gerth and Mills, eds. and trans., *From Max Weber*, p. 95.

8

The Liberals In Convention

NORMAN WARD

*

On January 16, 1958, for the third consecutive time, the Liberal party chose as its national leader a man who had not worked his way upwards through the party ranks, but instead had originally moved in close to the top. Mr. King was Deputy Minister of Labour when he resigned to contest a seat for the House of Commons in 1908, and shortly thereafter was Minister of Labour. The three men who opposed him for the party leadership in 1919 had a combined record in the party's service of over seventy-five years, and all three had begun their political careers in the provincial arena.

Mr. King at least entered politics as a young man, but his two successors did not. Mr. St. Laurent and Mr. Pearson were both cabinet ministers before they were elected to Parliament, and had to wait a number of years before they could enjoy the experience of sitting elsewhere than on the Treasury benches; they too defeated rivals who had served apprenticeships as ordinary members. Since Laurier, indeed, the only serious candidates for the party leadership who have not taken at least a youthful fling at provincial politics before attempting to enter the federal field have been Messrs. King, St. Laurent, Pearson, and Power—and Mr. Power, when he contested the leadership in 1948, had been a member of parliament for thirty-one years. Whatever the validity of the tradition that alternates the Liberal leadership between French and English Canada (and that was briskly challenged in 1958), it would appear to be established that one excellent way of ensuring that one will not rise to the top of the Liberal party is to start at the bottom.

In other important respects, the 1958 convention was featured by departure from ancient ways and submission to new ones. The party has never met before under so recent or unexpected a defeat as that of 1957, nor in the full knowledge that, partly because Parliament and a convention were meeting concurrently for the first time, and partly because of the party's strength in Parliament, the party could almost certainly precipitate another general election any time it chose. With the possible exception of Alexander Mackenzie, who called no caucus meeting during his last session as leader and first announced his resignation in

*Reprinted from *Queen's Quarterly*, LXV, No. 1, 1958.

the House of Commons, no departing leader has ever been less specific than Mr. St. Laurent about his choice of successor. Such open campaigning for the leadership as that of Mr. Martin and Mr. Pearson has not been seen before in Liberal affairs, nor has the party previously been favoured by would-be leaders who admitted frankly and frequently that they considered one of their rivals to be not merely unbeatable, but the best man anyway.

It is significant too that for the first time while convening when in opposition, the party had nothing to say about such matters of liberal interest as responsible government and the rôle of parliament. Considerable eloquence was devoted to these items in 1893 and 1919 (when Mr. King urged that control of the executive be restored to Parliament), but in 1958 one could kill a private conversation with a delegate by bringing the subject up. For the first time in any of the Liberal national conventions, signs of potentially divisive forces appeared, which could gather strength under the right circumstances. This is a point of historical as well as immediate interest, for previous Liberal conventions (most notably those of 1893 and 1919, with which one can justifi ably couple the Reform conventions of 1859 and 1867) made positive and lasting contributions towards party strength and unity.

Finally in this catalogue of real and suspected "firsts," the Liberals in 1958 met for the first time under glass. The all-seeing eyes of the Canadian Broadcasting Corporation's television cameras, so placed that no corners and no faces were beyond reach, undoubtedly helped produce some of the most self-conscious spontaneity yet seen in Canadian politics. (At that, the television coverage did not include everything that the party might have wished, for during the pre-convention planning at least one organizer showed an interest in having the cameras show a well-rehearsed fragment of convention procedure that would have demonstrated nicely how democratic the whole thing was.) The scheduled periods of telecasting were all prominently marked on the convention programmes, though the radio broadcasts were not mentioned, and before the first performances the delegates were admonished from the chair to be in their seats early "so that when television starts at eight o'clock we will be in good shape to be observed by the people of Canada."

The party naturally sought to put its best foot forward for the televised parts of the convention, and it is no coincidence that the daily highlights—the departing leader's farewell, the speeches of his potential successors, and the announcement of the results of the ballot— were seen from coast to coast. All these results would have taken place in any event, but not necessarily either at the times chosen, nor under all the pressures of rigid time limits, had they not been selected for broadcast. Undoubtedly the use of television, combined with the party's decision to use the televised periods for set "programmes" instead of random and unplanned hours, added some inflexibility to the convention's procedure. (The number of minutes allotted to each candidate for his speech for the leadership, for example, depended on a mathematical calculation of the

number of minutes available, divided by the number of candidates.) At
the same time, the preparations for television added something to the
convention, for to most of the delegates the programmes were ordinarily
the most interesting parts of each day, and they were interesting partly
because they were telecast.

It may be objected that television distorts a gathering such
as a convention, for on the one hand the broadcasts are not truly representative of the convention as a whole, with its milling groups of noisy
delegates, and the large amount of work that is done behind closed doors;
on the other hand the temptation to put on a show is too readily indulged
in. The disorder that often marked the proceedings is attested to by the
frequency with which the chairmen and other speakers requested attention, as well as by the number of times when, to an interested observer,
there appeared to be nobody at all listening to what was going on; in this
regard the Liberals' 1958 meeting was like any other large party meeting.
To blame television for converting the convention into a show, however,
ignores the obvious fact that a leadership convention *is* a show, and is
carefully arranged to be as good a show as possible.

As is customary with large modern party meetings, preparations for the Liberals' fourth national convention began months before
January of 1958, under the guidance of a committee that was top heavy
with senators, M.P.'s and former M.P.'s. (Some of the preparations are
necessitated by the absence of a constitution for the Liberal national
convention, which means that not only must each convention begin by
adopting its own rules, but that part of the first day must be given over to
setting up the various convention committees; this consumes considerable
time, but it also gives several people a chance to move and second mo-
tions.) The committee had subcommittees to deal with major matters
relevant to the convention, ranging from Accommodation and Hospitality
to Resolutions (the subcommittee chairman was Hon. George Marler),
Political Organization (Senator Power), and Programme (Senator Con-
nolly). The work of the subcommittees on Resolutions and Political Organization profoundly influenced the work of similar committees on those
subjects later set up by the convention itself, and it is no exaggeration to
say that one of the main tasks of the convention committees was to decide
whether or not to adopt as their own the reports of the pre-convention subcommittees. In a striking number of cases the answer appears to have
been in the affirmative.

Some time during the pre-convention preparations two extremely important decisions were made, whether consciously or not. The
first was that the convention was to be partly a parade of the party's
"brass" (a word rubbed thin with use in January), and not merely of
survivors of the June 10th débâcle, but also of those popularly held to
have been largely responsible for it. (As in 1948, but not as in 1893 and
1919, federal leaders clearly overshadowed their provincial counterparts
at the convention.) The second decision was that the convention must
look as democratic as possible, and elaborate plans were laid for the

moving of spontaneous resolutions from the floor. Paradoxically, since not all the delegates were consummate actors, some of the actual presentations from the floor, instead of looking spontaneous, looked contrived.

There was a further paradox in that the crowded agenda and the way in which it was handled (both of which set many delegates grumbling) obscured many of the genuinely democratic aspects of the convention. Though the brass was present in quantity, for example, a majority of the delegates were representatives of the local constituency associations, three from each. For weeks before the convention, the local associations and other groups affiliated with the party (the women's organization, and those of the university and young Liberals) were not merely asked but urged to send in resolutions and suggestions for the platform. Mr. Marler's subcommittee dealt with over three hundred and sixty proposals, and care was taken to ensure that each major element in the party had its turn at the convention, not only in presenting resolutions but also in speeches and in the chair. The delegates, though they did not at first appear to be so, were free to reject any resolution or proposal presented to them, and vociferously did so with the report of the committee on party organization.

Yet it may be questioned whether it was the original intention of the convention planners that the gathering should become the free-speaking forum that it occasionally did. The rebels who turned down the first draft of the report on party organization did so through proposing amendments to it, but there was nothing in the convention rules about amendments. Theoretically any delegate was free to propose a resolution for inclusion in the platform, but under the rules all resolutions had to be cleared through the Resolutions Committee; this meant, as the Canadian Press noted, that some "policy resolutions presented from the floor . . . vanished without trace." Further, "resolutions to be submitted from the floor must be sponsored either by a National Liberal organization which has delegates accredited to the Convention or by the official Liberal organization of any Province, and such resolutions must be introduced by delegates designated by such organizations at the floor microphones provided." The four microphones available to delegates on the floor were under the control of a convention whip who could, and on two occasions did, switch off a delegate with whose remarks he was out of sympathy.

A variety of other straws in the wind suggested that the party's leaders had not found defeat at the polls in 1957 a wholly chastening experience. References in speeches to the party's having won the largest total vote in June of 1957 were never accompanied by mention of the actual provinces in which the Liberals had been more popular than all other parties. The convention had no keynote speaker, and one of the several reasons for this was interesting: the most logical choice of keynote speaker, Senator Power, had given the party a shrewd scolding in 1948, and it was feared by some that he might do it again. The first report of the committee on party organization (which was not merely drafted, but mimeographed, before the committee met) recommended "no alteration

in the basic constitutional structure of the National Liberal Federation,"
and was amended only after vigorous protests from delegates on the floor.
Remarks by Mr. Howe on the pipeline, during a prepared speech, were
well received. Shortly after the convention Mr. Pearson announced that
he planned no changes in the Liberal shadow cabinet in the House of
Commons. Taking together all the more obvious signs of self-satisfaction,
a casual bystander could be forgiven if he concluded that he was attending the convention of a party that had recently won, not lost, a general
election.

Yet the platform adopted at the convention contains some
indications of at least a desired, if not yet a real, change in direction for
the party, and this was by design. Mr. Claxton, when addressing the
convention of 1948, observed that "a party in power cannot pass resolutions with that fine free careless irresponsible rapture which is characteristic of the opposition," and while nobody quoted this passage in 1958, the
possibilities inherent in it seem to have occurred to a number of citizens
at the Coliseum. A party that has just gone out of power after prolonged
political prosperity can hardly draft a wholly new platform without tacitly
admitting it has left many important things undone, and much energy
went into the drafting of statements (some of them quite long) about
such topics as liberalism, a vigorous economy, and a fighting faith, all
intended to show that Liberalism was still fundamentally the same comfortable thing it had always been. Inevitably parts of these, because they
dealt with familiar topics and because the vocabulary of politics is limited,
sounded platitudinous; but how many mortals could draft a simple statement about (say) liberalism which, however true, did *not* sound platitudinous? There are, too, the usual types of proposals (not confined in
Canada to Liberal platforms) to attract the Maritimes, the West, and so
on. There are the customary contradictions we have come to expect of
our major parties: the Liberals appear to be in favour of both free trade
and protection, both free enterprise and a substantial increase in government activity, both larger expenditures and reduced (or "modified")
taxes.

In fairness to the new platform, however, it must be added
that, at the convention, little if any emphasis was placed on lower taxation as a catch-all for electors, and no specific resolution embodying such
a proposal was suggested, partly because the three hundred and sixty
proposed resolutions sent in to Mr. Marler's subcommittee reflected little
demand for it. Where the platform can be said to be new at all, it leans
leftward, and was apparently intended to. The leaning was readily contrived through employment of the services of a small committee of writers
and intellectuals, the most active of whom were Mr. Tom Kent, the editor
of the Winnipeg *Free Press,* and Mr. Maurice Lamontagne. This group
sifted through the proposals submitted, and drafted the original texts of
resolutions embodying all the acceptable notions. Most of these resolutions were passed by the convention without change. (An incidental benefit worth mentioning is that the practice followed in regard to resolutions

brought together in prolonged and serious discussion men like Messrs. Kent and Lamontagne.) The Liberals thus stand committed to a considerable range of policies concerning, among other things, labour, fishing, agriculture, education and social welfare, many of the details of which they either openly opposed or failed to accept when in power. And for the second consecutive time, though the period from 1948 to 1958 strongly resembles a decade, the party has agreed to hold a national convention (or a "National Policy Conference") every four years.

While possibly important changes in Liberal policy are thus discernible, it cannot be said nearly so convincingly that the campaigns for the leadership, and the final choice, also reflect a real alteration. A remark commonly passed around by delegates at the convention was that the party was fortunate to have two potential leaders of the calibre of Mr. Martin and Mr. Pearson. (Nobody at any time, so far as one could discover in conversation, took seriously the candidature of either Mr. Mackay or Mr. Henderson, who flashed across the convention sky like meteorites, and almost as mysteriously.) But what was equally striking was that after twenty-two years in power, there were in the party only two serious candidates for the leadership, both of them identified with the "old guard." Neither of them, except in an extremely general and inconclusive way, offered the convention any leadership in regard to the drafting of the party's platform, and each refrained from telling the party whether or not he would, if chosen, take steps to force an immediate general election. In a literal sense, one of the distinguishing characteristics of the convention was that it was itself clearly leaderless.

The battle for leadership, virtually stripped of references to "I will, if elected . . ." perforce became largely a popularity contest in which the candidates held court in hotel suites, hotel lobbies, the railway station, the parliamentary restaurant, the convention floor, and any other place where delegates were gathered. Both candidates had made extended trips in the months before the convention, and both had been prominent in the House of Commons. Mr. Pearson with the inertia of his great international reputation behind him got his campaign off to an appreciably slower start than Mr. Martin, but once on the convention hustings produced some pleasant surprises for his warmest (and occasionally worried) supporters. Mr. Martin, obviously seeking to demonstrate by campaigning that he was a great campaigner, worked tirelessly among the delegates (many of whom he had approached by long distance telephone before the convention began), while his supporters turned out signs, stickers, hat-band favours, and a small daily paper. Probably the oddest tactic in the Martin campaign concerned a short-lived attempt by his supporters to hold the balloting for the leadership on the second day of the convention, immediately following the candidates' speeches. The reasoning behind this apparently ran as follows: (a) Mr. King made a great speech in 1919 and was chosen leader; (b) Mr. Martin is a better speaker than Mr. Pearson; (c) therefore Mr. Martin's chances of being elected will be greatest immediately after he has spoken. But since Mr. King in

1919 had spoken the day before he was chosen, and since the party found at its 1948 convention that nobody stays around after the leadership is settled, the original plans to have the new leader's choice announced on television, as the last important item of business on the convention's third day, were left unchanged.

Two other elements in the candidates' campaigns (in addition to the full indulgence in campaigns and demonstrations) were of more than passing interest, for the Liberal party may not have heard the last of them. Mr. Martin's supporters were anxious to establish that the demand for Mr. Martin had a broad democratic basis, and as convention week wore on, sought increasingly to identify Mr. Pearson with the brass, which could be assumed to be to his discredit provided that the brass could be held exclusively responsible for last year's election result and the attempts to control the convention. This strategem produced sufficient ill-feeling to have observers wondering whether Mr. Martin's position in the party might not have been seriously damaged through the zeal of his workers, regardless of the choice of leader. It was in any event a failure, for the majority of the delegates had no quarrel with the party leaders, and those who had were more inclined to link Mr. Martin rather than Mr. Pearson with the old guard. Mr. Pearson, because of the nature of his career, was more or less considered to have escaped contamination in a manner somewhat reminiscent of that in which Mr. King in 1919 escaped identification with the Liberal Unionists.

The second issue raised, also on Mr. Martin's behalf, concerned the alternation of the party leadership between French-speaking Catholics from Quebec and English-speaking Protestants from elswhere. If it were conceded that the alternation had become an established party tradition, then anyone like Mr. Martin, a Catholic from English-speaking Canada, would be permanently disqualified from the Liberal leadership. Mr. Pearson's forces were of course not averse to having the tradition favourably spoken of, but were not disposed to make too much of it, largely because of the two and a half million Canadian Catholics who live outside Quebec, and the half million Protestants who live within it. Mr. Martin's supporters, facing the inescapable facts of party history, had to cope with the alternations that have already occurred. Although the convention as a whole presented an admirably united picture as far as the two great language groups were concerned, English-speaking delegates supporting both candidates tended to assume that Mr. Pearson's English-speaking Protestantism was the sole reason why delegates from Quebec would support him, in order not to lose Quebec's turn at the leadership after Mr. Pearson. Intelligent French Canadians not unnaturally found this cynical and patronizing, particularly since it was patently untrue. As one French-speaking commentator remarked, Mr. Pearson's background was not irrelevant, but in general French Canadian delegates favoured Mr. Pearson for the same reasons as English.

While it would probably not be difficult to exaggerate the importance of these issues raised by the campaigns for the leadership, they cannot be ignored. Whether they become potentially dangerous will depend largely on the party's fortunes in the immediate future, for presumably they will be forgotten, along with the grumbling about the management of the convention, if Mr. Pearson's leadership is successful and the party flourishes. If the party is in for a bad time, however, its 1958 convention has provided some fruitful possibilities for afterthoughts and recriminations.

But this is to speculate about a future that was far from apparent at the gathering's closing session. The Liberal convention of 1958 ended on a note of triumph, with words from such old warriors as C. D. Howe, a touching farewell to the departing leader, a belligerent speech from the winner of the leadership race, and a graceful and conciliatory gesture from the loser. No delegate, on that final night, was asking for more than that; few were asking if it was enough.

9

The Sources and Uses of
Party Funds

*

I. LIBERAL PARTY FINANCE 1920-1965

A. Raising Money for Campaigns

The national Liberal Party has traditionally raised the great bulk of its campaign funds from a relatively small number of donors, both individual and corporate. This has meant that fund-raising efforts have been concentrated in a few major urban centres, with most of the Party's funds coming from Ontario and Quebec. The whole fund-raising process has been markedly informal and *ad hoc*. Small committees of fund raisers have worked in the few months before an election to collect enough money for the campaign. These committees have come to be more and more distinct from both the national party association and the parliamentary members of the Party.

This pattern became more evident in the twenties. Although the Liberal Party's convention in 1919 had established a highly decentralized finance committee to provide for the Party's needs, this committee was purely formal.[1] A scheme of financing the Party by the annual collection of dues "had been forgotten in the urgency of the election of 1921."[2] The formal party association, then, provided little financial help.

Nor did the Liberal leader, Prime Minister W. L. Mackenzie King, do much fund raising.[3] Fund-raising activities centered around one man, the late Senator Haydon.[4] Senator Haydon held an official position in the formal structure from 1919, when he had been appointed Executive Director of the Party, until his resignation in 1922, when he dropped this official position and became the main treasurer and fund raiser for election compaigns. Another Senator, Donat Raymond, acted as a "trustee" for party funds for the Province of Quebec.

The inquiries into the Beauharnois Power Project carried on by the House of Commons and the Senate in 1931 and 1932 provided a glimpse of the procedures used to raise campaign funds. Mr. R. O.

---

*Reprinted from *Report of the Committee on Election Expenses,* Ottawa, Queen's Printer, 1966.

Sweezey, a promoter of the Beauharnois Power Corporation which was interested in obtaining the rights to develop water power resources on the St. Lawrence River, had donated between $600,000 and $700,000 to the Liberal Party prior to the election of 1930.[5] Senator Haydon had collected much of this money in several approaches to Mr. Sweezey. Sweezey had, according to Senator Haydon, also given at Haydon's request about $200,000 to Senator Donat Raymond, the Liberal "trustee" for the Province of Quebec, to whom Senator Haydon had already turned over some of the funds he had collected from Mr. Sweezey.[6]

From the foregoing, the importance of the role played by Senator Haydon is evident in the soliciting of funds and the large amounts obtained from the Beauharnois Company. It is also evident that the Party had in existence at least two major compaign funds, one for Quebec and one for the rest of the country. As in other aspects of party organization, Quebec was a "special case."[7]

The Beauharnois Affair also indicated how convenient it could be, from the point of view of a party leader, that responsibility for fund raising should appear to rest with someone else. Prime Minister King was able to claim that he had nothing at all to do with the raising of campaign funds, and thus to escape some of the notoriety which clung to Senator Haydon. Senator Haydon's statements during the investigations corroborated Mr. King's claims:

I made no explanations or disclosures regarding campaign funds to Mr. King, or to any of his ministers or to anyone else.[8]

The Affair demonstrated the effects of the long-term evolution of specialization in the party structure. Unlike Sir John A. Macdonald in 1873, Mr. King could largely dissociate himself from the charges, simply by asserting that as party leader he had remained ignorant about all matters concerning party finances. Speaking of the general election of 1921, he stated that he "had no knowledge whatever of how that

---

[1]Harrill, Ernest Eugene, *The Structure of Organization and Power in Canadian Political Parties* (Unpublished Ph.D. dissertation, Chapel Hill, University of North Carolina, 1956), p. 256.

[2]Neatby, H. Blair, *William Lyon Mackenzie King 1924-1932: The Lonely Heights* (Toronto: University of Toronto Press, 1963), p. 327.

[3]*Ibid.*, p. 331.

[4]Regenstreif, Samuel Peter, *The Liberal Party of Canada: A Political Analysis* (unpublished Ph.D. Dissertation, Cornell, 1963), p. 136.

[5]Canada, House of Commons, Special Committee on Beauharnois Power Project, *Minutes of Proceedings and Evidence* (1931), p. XX.

[6]Canada, Senate, Special Committee on Beauharnois Power Project, *Report and Proceedings* (1932), p. 243.

[7]For more details of these other aspects, see Neatby, *op. cit.*, pp. 328-329.

[8]Canada, Senate p. 189.

campaign was managed. I went where I was told to go to speak by those who had direction of the campaign."[9] His argument was:

There must be a division of labour in a political party . . . it is the duty of the political head of the party to see to matters of policy, to be able to discuss questions on the floor of parliament, and throughout the country; but . . . it is not his business to get out the literature of the party, nor is it his business to organize political campaigns. Such work belongs to the rank and file of the party and to those who will act on their behalf.[10]

It is clear that a dramatic change had taken place in party organization and structure since the days of the Pacific Scandal. By 1930 parties were no longer loose, ill-defined, largely unstructured bodies of candidates rallying around a leader or small group of leaders for a variety of motives and in return expecting from them financial support toward the costs of their election campaigns. National parties had become clearly established organizations with various parts or personnel thereof devoting themselves to specialized tasks, of which fund raising was probably one of the most important. Parties had become more or less concrete entities which were based on that simple but fruitful principle of economy, the division of labour. One very important part of, or group in, the Party had come to be those persons concerned with the raising and spending of money both for election campaigns and for the work of the Party between elections. Prominent and respected persons. often with seats in the Senate, and usually with extensive business connections were now soliciting the funds. The position of a party leader in regard to such funds and their sources was a matter of some moment, about which Mr. King and Mr. Bennett in 1931 offered widely differing interpretations.

Mr. King maintained that the division of labour, in addition to helping him avoid the taint of scandal, had other important advantages for the party leader.

I would not care to have to deal with the questions with which this house has to deal and be possessed of an inventory of those who had contributed to the party funds. All the time that I have been the leader of the party I have never asked a single individual to make a contribution to a political campaign. I have had no knowledge of what the political campaign funds were.[11]

If, as Conservatives insisted, Mr. Bennett had turned down $200,000 from Beauharnois, then he must, Mr. King argued, have known all the details of the Tory campaign fund. What must the country think of Mr. Bennett's tariff increases on textiles, etc., when Canadian companies involved in their manufacture were contributors to the Conservative campaign fund?

It was an ingenious argument, calculated to embarrass Mr. Bennett. Mr. Bennett took a different view. To Mr. King's statement that British party leaders knew nothing about organization and fund raising, Mr. Bennett replied that on the contrary they had a "most intimate knowledge." When Mr. King put the following question:

I take the position that it is not part of the duty or obligation of a leader of a political party to have to do with the organization of political campaigns or to possess an inventory of those who make contributions to party funds. That is my view; does my right hon. friend hold a different view?[12]

Mr. Bennett forcefully rejected this argument.[13]

Those who disagreed with Mr. King said that it was impossible for any party leader to discharge his duties without some knowledge of the party's financial resources, a knowledge which would inevitably include the source of funds. How could a leader plan the scope of a campaign without knowing the limitations imposed by campaign funds? Some projection had to be made of what money could be brought in during the course of a campaign. The policies advocated by the party leadership would have some bearing on this.

Indeed, could the party leader have no knowledge whatever of how a general election campaign was managed?; could the leader have gone simply where he was told to go to speak by "those who had direction of the campaign?" And if so, what about those who did have control? What was the responsibility of the party leader, when the actions of the fund raisers could involve the party in relationships like the Beauharnois Affair? Was not the leader's plea of innocence in itself an admission of negligence? Who, after all, could the fund raisers be responsible to if not the party leadership?

Mr. J. S. Woodsworth advanced a critique of Mr. King's position in the House:

Would the leader of the opposition himself be very happy in the enjoymen of the position secured through doubtful means, even though he himself was personally ignorant of them? . . .

We all know that every member of parliament is required to certify the statement of his agent with regard to contributions and expenses and thus if the contentions of the leader of the opposition were correct every private member must have moral difficulties as great as those which the leader would have."[14]

Mr. King had blazed a path for party leaders to justify their conduct in the new era of specialized fund raising. The debate among the party leaders had posed a real dilemma. Can a party leader, who has in his pocket a list of contributors, make decisions affecting those contributors with full objectivity? On the other hand, can a party leader remain ignorant of finances in fact, and should he in theory? Experience

---

[9]Canada, *House of Commons Debates* (July 30, 1931), pp. 4379-4380.

[10]*Ibid.*, p. 4380.

[11]*Ibid.*, p. 4384.

[12]*Ibid.*, p. 4382.

[13]*Loc. cit.*

[14]*Ibid.* (July 31, 1931), p. 4391.

and common sense seem to inform us that ignorance is not an attainable state, yet we must admit that knowledge also has its dangers. This dilemma remains one of the unsolved problems of Canadian politics. The Beauharnois Affair is important not as an exercise in historical fault finding but because it points up the basic issues at stake in the modern era of fund raising.

In an effort to clarify the distinction between the party leader and the fund-raising apparatus, Mr. King "imposed a central office with a permanent staff on the Liberal party."[15] This office was to take over the organizational and fund-raising duties formerly performed by Senator Haydon. In 1933, Hon. Vincent Massey was named President of the National Liberal Federation and Mr. Norman Lambert its Secretary.

Little was changed, however, in the actual methods of campaign fund raising. For the 1935 campaign, "informal Montreal and Toronto finance committees . . . to make collections" were appointed. Certain individuals were designated as collectors by "the National President, or the national organizer with advice from the party leader" and made their collections during the few months before the election.[16]

*   *   *   *   *

In theory, then, the changes of the thirties created a fund-raising apparatus outside the parliamentary membership of the Party. There is some evidence, however, that Mr. King and his Cabinet were still involved in fund raising. In 1939 Mr. King circulated a memorandum to all members of his Cabinet asking their opinions as to the advisability of holding an autumn election and the availability of campaign funds within their respective provinces and in the country as a whole. Mr. King added:

I am, of course, aware that the National Liberal Federation is expected to have to do with . . . finances, but . . . the federation is in a position to effect but little without the cooperation of the Members of the Government.[17]

Mr. King is also said to have written letters of appreciation to donors of large amounts.[18] One of Mr. King's Cabinet Ministers even raised money for a provincial campaign before the provincial election of 1939; in Quebec James G. Gardiner "was a key figure in raising money from the Toronto area for the Quebec Liberals."[19]

Throughout the thirties, forties and fifties the pattern of Liberal campaign fund raising tended to develop rather than change: the structure became more refined, but the basic patterns of organization and the basic sources of funds remained the same. Business sources continued to supply the great bulk of the campaign funds. Harrill, after detailed study of the Party's finances, reported in 1953 that 50 per cent of the national Liberal Party's income came from industrial or commercial firms, 40 per cent from businessmen closely associated with particular companies, and only 10 per cent from individuals.[20]

Conversations with fund raisers indicate that funds raised

for the 1957 campaign came largely from 300-400 donors, the donations ranging in amounts up to $75,000.[21] On occasion, Liberal supporters have been known to donate services, rather than funds. In 1958, for example, one owner of a television station produced Hon. L. B. Pearson's video tapes, and a Liberal sympathizer in the radio business helped with radio broadcasts in a certain area. During campaigns, many other individuals donate services of various kinds whose value, in the aggregate, is substantial. Such donations, however, in no way match the importance of money contributions.

Information from fund raisers active in the 1965 campaign indicates that the role of business in the Party's finances is at least as strong as it ever was. One fund raiser said that hardly any money came into the national fund from individuals, Members of Parliament or Senators, and nothing at all from trade unions, although individual candidates received funds from all of these sources. The donations received from businesses tend to be substantial.

The Liberal Party's collection structure is adapted to suit the type of source to which the Party appeals for funds.

The traditional practice has been to have standing Finance Committees, staffed by trusted party supporters in the corporate and business world, in the major cities—Montreal, Toronto, Winnipeg and Vancouver. The Montreal and Toronto Committees are the most important because these cities are in the areas which are the sources of most of the party's funds.[22]

These committees work under the national treasurer, appointed by the party leader. There are usually two key men in each of Montreal and Toronto, one in Winnipeg and Vancouver, and often one in Calgary or Edmonton. These men comprise the "first-string" fund raisers. Under these men are the "second-string" collectors, the many more workers who try to cover the network of contacts in the business world. In the 1965 campaign, for example, about twenty men collected funds in Ontario.[23]

---

[15]Neatby, p. 385.

[16]Heppe, P. H., *The Liberal Party of Canada.* (Unpublished Ph.D. dissertation, University of Wisconsin, 1957), p. 145; see also Lederle, J. W., *National Organization of Liberal and Conservative Parties in Canada.* (Unpublished Ph.D. dissertation, Ann Arbor, University of Michigan, 1942), *passim.*

[17]Regenstreif, p. 198.

[18]Harrill, p. 262.

[19]J. L. Granatstein, *Conservative Party Finance,* A Study prepared for the Committee on Election Expenses, 1965. Mimeographed, p. 19.

[20]Harrill, pp. 251-252.

[21]Confidential source. Meisel asserts that Liberal campaign costs were between $6-10 million at all levels. See Meisel, John, *The Canadian General Election of 1957* (Toronto: University of Toronto Press, 1962), p. 173.

[22]Regenstreif, p. 211.

[23]*Globe and Mail* (Oct. 11, 1965), 7.

Fund raising in Quebec has recently become slightly more formalized. Under the new Quebec wing of the Liberal Federation of Canada which has set about a "democratization" of the Party in Quebec[24] a four-man finance committee, under the chairmanship of a prominent Montreal stockbroker, has replaced the traditional fund raisers. This committee will be responsible to the leader of the Party through the leader of the Quebec wing.[25]

Clearly, in this method of party fund raising, the most useful men to use as collectors are those who have good contacts in business circles. This means that for the most part the men recruited as collectors are businessmen themselves. Sometimes they are also prominent in the formal party structure. Sometimes they are also prominent in the Cabinet and parliamentary party. This overlap between the formal party structure or the membership of the party in Parliament on the one hand, and the fund-raising structure on the other, appears to be coincidental. The operative qualification seems to be being well-known among businessmen.[26]

The method of recruitment of fund raisers shows clearly the independence of the fund-raising structure. New collectors are recruited by already active collectors. A known Liberal who is a rising young businessman will be approached very informally about collecting some money for the Party. Family ties are occasionally a factor.[27] The fact that established contacts in business circles explain success in this aspect of party activity may also account for the apparent tendency toward continuity and autonomy of the fund-raising structure.

B. Fund Raising in the Constituencies

Few generalizations can be made about the fund-raising practices of the Liberal Party at the constituency level during federal campaigns. Practices vary widely between rural, urban and metropolitan constituencies and between constituencies in different geographic areas of the country. There are also great variations over time within single constituencies depending upon the personalities of those active in the Party's organization.[28] Every candidate in a federal election is, of course, required by law to appoint an official agent to whom all campaign contributions must be made.[29] But there is a wide variation in the actual sources of funds available in constituencies.

Usually the sources tapped in a constituency are more diversified than those used by the national Party, but rarely are they adequate for a campaign.

More often than not, the candidate is forced to spend a great deal of his own money in order to get elected . . . The candidate may have local sources such as personal friends or some area business establishments to which he can appeal but it is a certainty that his constituency association (if there is one) is usually unable to help very much[30].

The candidate must therefore turn for assistance to the provincial and national party organizations. In fact, a substantial portion of the national campaign budget is allocated to "aid to constituencies." The money is distributed to the candidates through the campaign committee for each province. A former national organizer for the Liberal Party has been quoted as saying that in the 1953 campaign the national campaign chairman tried to provide a basic $3,000 for each constituency. More money was sent to key areas[31] such as Quebec constituencies where it was reported that in the 1953 campaign many candidates received $10,000 each from the national fund.[32]

In addition to the national Party, there are other local sources available to the candidate for his constituency campaign. In some urban ridings, contributions can be obtained from the business interests located there. Some large businesses even ear-mark part of their contribution to the national Party for use in the constituency where their plant is located. In urban ridings, too, contributions are often collected from trade union locals. One former Liberal organizer said that Liberal candidates get contributions from union locals in virtually every riding where there is organized labour.[33] Some ridings have been able to build up campaign funds from the annual collection of membership dues and the holding of special fund-raising events once or twice a year. However, most ridings are not highly enough organized to raise campaign funds in this way. Many set no membership fees.

*   *   *   *   *

Clearly the donations given to candidates in most ridings are smaller than those given to the national Party. The sources in the ridings are more varied than those used by the national Party, and include small businesses, union locals and personal friends of the candidate. In many cases the grant from the central Party is the largest single source of funds. In the great majority of cases constituency fund-raising activities are concentrated in the campaign period, since so much of the organization centres

[24]*Montreal Star* (June 7, 1965), 3.

[25]*La Presse* (Sept. 1, 1965), 28. See also Fournier, Jean-Pierre, "La Vieille Garde Libérale Croule," *Le Magazine Maclean* (Oct. 1965), 56.

[26]Regenstreif, p. 175.

[27]*La Presse, Loc. cit.*

[28]Some details about the practices of individual constituencies were obtained in a study of the results of a questionnaire sent out by the Committee on Election Expenses to all candidates running in the 1965 federal general election. See study No. 11 "Canadian Spending Patterns and Attitudes" in Part II of the Report.

[29]This requirement was first made in 1874. *Dominion Elections Act*, Statutes of Canada 1874, 37 Vict. c. 9, secs. 121-5.

[30]Regenstreif, pp. 164-165.

[31]Torrence, Lois E., *The National Party System in Canada 1945-1960*. (Unpublished Ph.D. dissertation, Washington, The American University, 1961), p. 453.

[32]Harrill, p. 189.

[33]Confidential source.

on the candidate, who may not be nominated until near the opening of the campaign.

C. Budgeting for Campaigns

. . . By the time of the campaigns of 1940 and 1945, there was a National Campaign Committee in charge of the overall direction of the campaign. This Committee consisted of "one or two cabinet ministers, together with the President of the Federation and the General-Secretaries."[34] The 1945 Campaign Committee was headed by Hon. James G. Gardiner and included Hon. C. D. Howe, and Ernest Bertrand, all members of the House, and Senators Campbell, Daigle and Robertson.[35]

[The Committee] began serious planning in January 1945. The National Liberal Federation's offices were turned over to the Campaign Committee for the duration, and a draft budget was prepared.[36]

It was during the forties that advertising agencies began to participate in the planning of campaigns. The Liberal Party hired Cockfield, Brown and Company, of Montreal.

Often, Ministers would by-pass the Central Office and deal directly with the agency both during election campaigns and whenever they embarked upon speaking tours. There are many within the party who claim that Cockfield, Brown was the central office of the party, particularly around election time.[37]

The pattern of overall planning and budgeting by a central campaign committee has continued to the present:

A National Campaign Chairman is appointed by the Leader. Through this National chairman, and in consultation with the provincial association concerned, ten provincial chairmen are chosen to round out a National Campaign Committee. These ten provincial chairmen then gather provincial committees in their own provinces. . . . The provincial chairmen report constantly to Ottawa and the National Federation.[38]

At the beginning of the campaign, the financial needs and resources of the National Committee are discussed by part of the Committee: the National Campaign Chairman, the National Organizer, the National Treasurer, and a representative of the Quebec campaign committee. The National Office draws up an estimate of its needs, as does each of the provincial campaign committees. The Party's national advertising agency (MacLaren's since 1958) draws up suggested advertising programs. The National Campaign Committee then decides upon allocations for national advertising, grants to constituencies and provincial offices. Since the Party's financial resources are never entirely predictable, the budgets must be flexible. Usually three alternative spending programs are drawn up.

The Quebec Campaign Committee is slightly more autonomous than those of the other provinces. At present it is said to consist of nine members, three named by the Quebec caucus, three by the Quebec wing of the Liberal Federation of Canada, and three by the organization for the Quebec City region.[39] Although the National Campaign Committee decides the general direction of the campaign in Quebec, funds are collected and expended on the approval of the Quebec Campaign Committee; even transfers to the national fund are subject to its approval. The Quebec Committee alone is responsible for national Party advertising within the Province.

Once the overall budget decisions have been made, one man is appointed to be responsible for the distribution of funds within each province. Through him, the grants to the constituencies are made. Disbursements are made by cheques written on trust accounts. Payments are usually made in instalments as the campaign funds come in. The campaign committee in each province, and the fund distributor or distributors there, have the responsibility for the spending of the budget on their level both as to allocations to constituencies in their province and as to all other expenditures on their provincial level.

The National Campaign Committee's budget covers national advertising (except for Quebec), surveys, speakers' and leaders' tours, special events, radio and television production costs, and the extra administrative costs of the national office (extra telephones, staff, etc.)

Provincial committees are shown the national advertising program and may decide to take on supplementary advertising. In the 1965 campaign, for example, all the provincial committees except Ontario's, hired advertising agencies themselves. In addition to doing this advertising, the provincial committees distribute subsidies to the candidates, provide professional public relations advice and factual information, provide a speaker's bureau, and arrange the leader's tour in the province. In arranging the tour, the provincial committee schedules special events *en route,* rents space for these events, and pays for any extra advertising connected with the tour.

In all of this process, the influence of the leader appears to be indirect. He names the National Campaign Chairman, the National Organizer and the National Treasurer and is consulted on the appointment of the provincial chairmen.[40]

*   *   *   *   *

---

[34]Regenstreif, p. 199.
[35]Granatstein, p. 58.
[36]*Ibid.*
[37]Regenstreif, p. 197.
[38]*Ibid.,* p. 234. Advertising agencies still participate in planning. "By late 1956 and early 1957, four members of the agency [Cockfield Brown] sat in on the Federation Liaison Committee in order to prepare for the coming election." (*Ibid.,* p. 197.)
[39]Jean-Pierre Fournier, "La Vielle Garde Libéral Croule, *Le Magazine Maclean*" (October, 1965), p. 57.
[40]Regenstreif, pp. 411-412.

D. Liberal Party Campaign Expenditures

According to Harrill, the Liberal Party (and the Conservative Party, too) in the fifties usually allocated their total expenditures at the national level roughly as follows.[41]

tours of party leaders 10%
headquarters organization (rent, salaries, supplies) 10%
national advertising (radio, pamphlets, newspapers,
magazines) 40%
individual candidates 40%

Harrill also made an attempt to assess the costs facing a Liberal constituency organization during the first half of the fifties as follows, in descending order of importance:[42]

1. payments to party workers
2. local advertising
3. rent and office expenses
4. cars
5. travel
6. refreshments

During the 1957 election, according to one source, the Liberal Party as a whole raised and spent an estimated $7.5 million.[48] Subsidies to candidates comprised about 33 per cent of the national Party's total budget, according to a party official active in the campaign. This was a considerably smaller percentage of the budget than the 40 per cent estimated by Harrill.

While Harrill's figure may have been correct for earlier elections, by 1957 the Party was devoting an increased proportion of its budget to national advertising. The national office staff arranged national newspaper, poster and billboard publicity; it circulated draft radio speeches and radio and television schedules; it operated a news service for weekly newspapers. The national office also employed a man experienced in television, who set up a studio to coach Liberal Members of Parliament on television technique. The studio also produced radio tapes and some television films which candidates could use on payment of a fee.[44]

In addition, the national office provided extensive aid to candidates in the form of materials and services: campaign manuals, pamphlets, leaflets, a 384-page *Speaker's Handbook* entitled *Liberal Action for a Greater Canada,* speeches by leaders, news clippings, and proofs of advertisements suitable for candidates' use.[45]

All this activity required extra staff. The staff at the national office increased from between 14 and 16 to between 50 and 60. In addition, approximately 40 people worked on the election for the Party's advertising agency, Cockfield, Brown.[46]

The 1957 election saw few significant changes in constituency expenditure patterns.[47] Meetings were still a very popular form of campaigning. However, coffee parties in private homes were becoming increasingly common. Monster rallies were also tried by constituency organizations in large population centres in addition to newspaper, radio and television publicity. Printed material such as poll cards, verandah cards, car cards, bumper stickers, banners, favours (such as blotters and match books) letters and "where you vote at" cards were also much used by Liberal candidates.

Payments to party workers and office rentals remain expensive items at the constituency level.

Rates of pay vary from region to region, but it is probably not misleading to assume that drivers with cars cost from $10 to $30 per day . . . . Canvassers, scrutineers, and baby sitters are somewhat less expensive, costing about $6 to $8. But in some constituencies very large numbers of these may have to be hired.[48]

Meisel, in his study of the 1957 election, estimated the usual cost of campaigning at the constituency level as follows:

A normal election campaign in a rural constituency probably costs the Liberals or the Conservatives from $7,500 to $12,500. It is difficult to conduct a satisfactory urban campaign for less than $15,000 and a reasonably conducted fight in a metropolitan constituency can hardly be attempted for much under $25,000.[49]

Liberal campaign expenditures since 1957 do not seem to have reached the heights achieved in that election when the Liberals enjoyed the advantages of 22 years of uninterrupted incumbency. Loss of office and the frequency of elections appear to have led to a closer rationing of funds from traditional sources.

*   *   *   *   *

II. PROGRESSIVE CONSERVATIVE PARTY FINANCE

A. Fund Raising to 1945

The financial history of the Conservative Party between 1930 and 1945 throws some light on the impact of money on Canadian

---

[41]Harrill, pp. 202-203.

[42]*Ibid.*, pp. 212-213.

[43]Confidential source. Cf. Meisel, p. 173, estimates Liberal Party national, provincial and constituency expenditures as having been between $6-10 million in the 1957 election.

[44]Meisel, pp. 67-72.

[45]*Ibid.*, p. 68.

[46]*Ibid.*, p. 65.

[47]*Ibid.*, pp. 86-119, contains a full description of constituency-level campaigning during this election.

[48]*Ibid.*, p. 116.

[49]*Loc. cit.*

politics, especially the interrelationship of policy, leadership and finance. Dr. Manion's disastrous 1940 election campaign is an excellent example. Because he was believed to hold radical views and because he was known to be an opponent of railway unification, Manion and his fund raisers faced great difficulties. The opposition was strongest in circles close to the Canadian Pacific Railway, but through various ramifications the financial channels right across the country were blocked. Manion's fate illustrates the vulnerability of a leader to a financial blockade.

By 1943, the political situation which had defeated Manion had passed. The threat of the CCF so frightened business and industry that some of the same forces that had destroyed Dr. Manion for his "radicalism" brought in Mr. Bracken as leader of the renamed Progressive Conservative Party. It was hoped that Mr. Bracken would appeal to progressive-minded Canadians not yet ready to go all out and support the CCF. Many believed that he could form the next government. In these circumstances and despite Bracken's doubtful political antecedents, the Conservatives received substantial financial support. The Party's campaign theme of free enterprise was doubtless a reassurance.

The collapse of the Popular Finance Campaign made it impossible for the Conservatives to develop an alternative to their traditional sources of campaign funds. In the end, then, the Progressive Conservative Party was dependent on funds raised with the same methods used by the Conservative Party prior to 1943. Even the provincial financial representatives did not change despite the considerable difference in outlook between the Manion-Meighen-Hanson Party and the Bracken Party. Presumably the continuity resulted from necessity rather than choice. Very few men in any party are likely to have an entrée to business and finance.

B. Postwar Fund Raising and Financial Organization

The available evidence indicates that the fund-raising structure of the Conservative Party in the postwar period exhibited the following pattern. Toronto replaced Montreal as the financial base in the reconstruction of the Party during the Second World War, after the defection of its traditional supporters. The present financial structure of the Conservative Party reflects this shift. The senior finance chairman is located in Toronto, with a subordinate chairman for Montreal. More directly subordinate to Toronto are collectors, usually prominent persons chosen by the chairman, in Ottawa, Hamilton and London. As in the Liberal Party, the Conservative leaders try to maintain as much ignorance of the sources of the funds as is possible; inevitably, however, they may become aware of the key donors due to social associations.

The Party attempted in this period to separate fund raising from expenditures, and fund raisers usually did not take part in the allocation of funds after they were collected. Sometimes contributors might ear-mark part or all of their donations to a particular area or candidate. Expenditure was supervised by the national director and the finance committee. Below them were the provincial finance committees. The national director or organizer decided for the most part how to allocate the money. Evidence indicates that the national director has a great deal of freedom in making expenditures.[50]

Under Mr. Bell's direction, attempts were made to make all the provinces self-sufficient financially, but with the exception of British Columbia and Alberta the provinces required continued transfer payments from Ontario and Quebec. Manitoba was subsidized to only a limited degree. Saskatchewan received more than Manitoba; the most subsidized area was the Maritimes.

John Williams estimates that in the 1949 election, the Conservatives spent over $3,000,000 on both the national and local levels.[51] With Mr. Drew as leader, funds became more readily available than they had been in the immediate past. The 1949 campaign confirmed that Toronto had superseded Montreal as the most important source of funds for the Conservatives. It is estimated[52] that the cost of the 1953 campaign at the national level was about $2½ million. The British Columbia and Alberta organizations were fairly independent financially. About $4,000 was sent, on an average, to each constituency, for a total of about $1 million. The specific allocation was determined by the national headquarters, except for the Province of Quebec where the money was sent to Montreal to be redistributed. In some seats the grant covered little more than the candidate's deposit, but some important candidates, including the leader, received large sums covering their entire campaign expenditures.

When Mr. Diefenbaker became national leader in 1956 some important changes were made in the Party's method of party finance. Allister Grosart, on becoming national director, decided to pool all the available funds and to allocate to the provincial committees an amount equal to $3,000 multiplied by the number of constituencies in a province. This amount (e.g. Ontario 85 x $3,000=$255,000) was an unconditional grant, to be distributed among the constituencies in the province as the committee saw fit; Quebec was thus given money only in proportion to its parliamentary representation. Cries of over-centralization of party expenditures thus were stilled. The result was a more effective use of money because of a better on-the-spot assessment of local conditions.[53]

About $1 million[54] was available to the national headquarters in 1957, a low figure which may illustrate certain apprehensions among the Party's contributors concerning the Party's chances under a

---

[50]Confidential source.
[51]John R. Williams, *The Conservative Party of Canada, 1920-1949* (Durham, North Carolina: Duke University Press, 1956), p. 143.
[52]Confidential source.
[53]Confidential source.
[54]*Ibid.*

new leader.[55] Apparently, the decision was taken to allocate almost all
the money available to the provinces for use in the constituencies. The
remainder went into the leader's tour (estimated at $70,000), operation
of national headquarters, the printing of pamphlets (which were distributed by the candidates) and a minimal amount of national advertising,
(only one newspaper advertisement was purchased in 1957 by the national Party). Meisel maintains that contributions of "considerable magnitude" came into Conservative headquarters in the last three or four days
before the election, reflecting last-minute doubts in the business community as to the probable outcome.[56]

     In 1958, considerably more money was available to the
Conservatives, who now formed the government. About $6,000 per con-
stituency was sent to each provincial committee. The leader's tour cost
about $100,000. The national campaign cost close to $3,000,000, one
estimate being from $2,700,000, to $2,800,000.[57]

     The 1962 campaign was managed in much the same way
as the 1957 and 1958 campaigns. It is estimated that even more money
was now available, $3,000,000 or more being spent by central headquar-
ters, with between $6,000 and $9,000 being allocated per constituency.
Little information is available on the 1963 election, but it is apparent that
financial support for the national leadership was considerably diminished.
It has been alleged, without proof, that fund raisers did collect money, but
much of it was ear-marked for local or provincial Party use rather than
the national Party.

*   *   *   *   *

CONCLUSION

Party finance in Canada has undergone a steady evolution from Confederation to the present day. From the situation a century ago, when fund
raising and campaign expenditures were considered to be among the
regular duties of the party leaders, to the present situation in which fund
raising and campaign expenditures are the duties of party officials, separate and distinct from the party leadership as such, the years have
witnessed a steady trend toward the specialization and professionalization
of the various functions of political finance. Today the fund raisers and
those responsible for allocating campaign expenditures are usually separate, both from each and from the party leaders. The precise degree of
this separation, and the nature of the interdependence of these various
functions of party organizations, remain matters of dispute and conjecture.

     The purposes for which money is expended during the
election period have also changed with time. Around the Confederation
period, money was concentrated on organization, i.e., the mechanics of
bringing voters to the polls, and on maintaining newspapers as the major
means of communication with the voter. As the franchise widened, simple
organization became more difficult and the emphasis began to shift to
communications through the print media. Concomitant with this was an

increasing concentration of expenditure on the actual election period, rather than the more generalized pattern of expenditure whic had prevailed when the electorate was smaller. In the thirties, the print media were partially displaced by radio, which was in turn displaced by television in the late fifties.

Despite the changing patterns of expenditure there is no evidence to support the notion, often expressed, that elections were once inexpensive, but have become increasingly expensive in recent years. Elections in Canada have always been costly to the principals involved. If anything, the growth of specialized fund raising may have lessened the financial burden on the individual candidate; in the Confederation era, individuals could be financially ruined by political participation.

The experience of both the two older parties and the third parties which have arisen in the twentieth century demonstrate that mass fund raising as attempted so far, is an impractical method of party finance, and that widespread popular support can rarely be translated into widespread financial support.

Both the Liberal and Conservative Parties have, at various times, attempted to widen the base of financial support by mass fund raising. Such attempts have failed completely. The older parties have thus been forced by necessity to rely on a relatively small number of business sources. The CCF Party made a sustained effort to subsist on "grass-roots" financing, but this was very difficult and the Party in its last years went into a prolonged financial decline. Its successor, the New Democratic Party, has been much more successful, but its financial resources rest primarily on the trade unions. The experience of the Ralliement des Créditistes in the Province of Quebec shows that mass fund raising may be successful for brief periods in exceptional circumstances, but that it is not practicable on a sustained basis.

Successful fund raising has so far rested on a stable group base: such as business corporations or trade unions. Any attempts to reform political finance must take this fact into consideration.

RECOMMENDATIONS OF THE COMMITTEE ON ELECTION EXPENSES

I. Political parties should be legally recognized and, through the doctrine of agency, made legally responsible for their actions in raising and spending funds.

II. A degree of financial equality should be established among candidates and among political parties, by the extension of certain services and subsidies to all who qualify.

---

[55]*Ibid.* Meisel, on the other hand, estimates national expenditure at $1,700,000. See Meisel, p. 173.

[56]Meisel, p. 173.

[57]Confidential source.

III. An effort should be made to increase public participation in politics, by broadening the base of political contributions through tax concessions to donors.

IV. Cost of election campaigns should be reduced, by shortening the campaign period, by placing limitations on expenditures on mass media by candidates and parties, and by prohibiting the payment of poll workers on election day.

V. Public confidence in political financing should be strengthened, by requiring candidates and parties to disclose their incomes and expenditures.

VI. A Registry under the supervision of a Registrar should be established to audit and publish the financial reports required, and to enforce the provisions of the proposed "Election and Political Finances Act".

VII. Miscellaneous amendments to broadcasting legislation should be enacted to improve the political communications field.

10

Ad-Men and Scientists Run This Election

RICHARD GWYN

*

The twentieth century and Canadian politics come to terms this year: the nation will have its first scientific election. (1962)

For the first time the skills of sociologists, statisticians, advertising experts, pollsters, and mass-communications experts may be as decisive as the age-old talents of politicians.

Two completely new weapons are being brought into the fray: intensive, privately hired, public opinion surveys and sophisticated, probing, statistical analysis. To these are added the latest techniques of advertising and mass communications.

Here are some examples of what's happening:

Five major advertising firms will handle the Conservative party account. The Liberals are making an intensive statistical study of every marginal riding in the country. The Conservatives run a month-by-month private "Gallup poll" far more refined than the public survey. The Liberals have established "campaign colleges" in Ontario, the Maritimes, and British Columbia to teach party workers the latest techniques. The nearest Conservative equivalent is the day-long workshops for women organizers held regularly in Ottawa.

Voting results in every riding for the past three elections have been assessed by both major parties. Ridings are listed 1 to 265, working from "safe," through "marginal," to "irretrievably lost." This list is then altered to take account of local conditions such as changed population and strengths of competing candidates. The major campaign emphasis will be placed in ridings in the middle of the table, dubbed "marginal."

There are two basic types of surveys: polls, which assess party support in the country as a whole or in particular localities; and depth surveys, which gauge public thinking and thus produce material to fashion the real issues of the campaign. The cost of these runs ranges from $500 for a quickie poll in a single riding to $50,000 for a nation-

---

*Reprinted from *The Financial Post*, LVI, No. 17, April 28, 1962.

wide depth study. A report by a company making a survey can run to more than one hundred pages of close-typed statistics. One recently completed contained one hundred and fifty-one main and alternate questions.

Surveys are being used in individual constituencies. A week-by-week poll in the 1961 Esquimault-Saanich by-election showed the New Democratic Party in the lead till the day Tommy Douglas made a speech critical of the United States—which went down poorly in an area heavily dependent on American tourists. Surveys taken for this year's five Ontario by-elections forecast the result and pinned down the sales tax as the breaking point for Premier Robarts. The 1960 setback for the Diefenbaker government in the Peterborough by-election was accurately foreseen by the Conservatives weeks before the ballots were counted.

Some depth surveys do no more than confirm common-sense observations. But most change hunches into near-certainties or remove as serious issues many that have been played up by the newspapers (for example, nuclear weapons).

An election issue can be defined as something which enough people feel strongly enough about to switch their votes. Thus campaign experts think people who oppose nuclear weapons will vote anti-Conservative anyway.

The parties place great store in this hidden form of public pulse-taking. The sudden attack by the Conservatives, the less successful counterattack by the Liberals, on the issue of the government's record of keeping promises were both inspired by the findings of surveys. The Conservatives know from surveys that their description of the Liberals as a bunch of bureaucrats and autocrats finds an echo with some sections of the public. Emphasis by the Liberals on the slogan "the Pearson team" follows a mammoth survey in January on their leader's public image. . .

The Liberals have adopted the theory of winning on the margins, which recognizes the potential for winning a large number of ridings by a series of marginal gains in key areas and among certain population groups. They are making a detailed study of every marginal riding. Voting results at each polling station over the past three elections are calculated in terms of proportions won by each party. These are translated into areas marked "strong Conservative," "moderate Liberal," and so on. All unmarked areas are strictly marginal or contain a heavy preponderance of new voters—new subdivisions or apartment dwelling sites, for example.

It is in these latter areas that candidates will do their most intensive door-to-door canvassing. Areas marked moderate for one party or another are given secondary attention; those marked "strong," the least of all.

This emphasis on marginal areas within ridings is repeated at the national level in the allocation of campaign funds, advertising, and tours by big-name speakers to key constituencies.

The amount of extra effort that can be given to marginal

ridings is limited, and to ignore any constituency, however hopeless the contest, would be disastrous to party morale in the district. But within these limits, resources will be allocated where opportunities for gains are considered greatest.

Conservative organizers refuse to concede any seat as irretrievably won or lost. The bulk of Conservative effort is concentrated on determining national or regional voting trends and issues. Typical of these is the party's earlier-mentioned "Gallup poll." The sample taken is larger than that used in the public survey and is concentrated in no more than six selected ridings at a time. So, gradually, a picture is painted of party standings across the nation.

Another sampling technique used by the Conservatives is tape-recorded interviews with carefully chosen representatives of different population groups. These are played back endlessly by campaign planners to build up an impression of those issues about which the public feels strongly. Most highly regarded are those ad-lib comments that provide a clue to the way the person really feels.

Once the real issues—those which will influence votes—have been assessed, the parties construct a general line of approach based on these factors. "You tell people things you know they want to hear," explained one organizer.

Conservative campaign appeal, as now developing, will have two main elements: (1) Don't put back the same old gang you kicked out in 1957, and (2) Elect Diefenbaker, the man you can trust. Of key importance will be the Prime Minister's charismatic personality, his ability to project an image with which ordinary people can identify themselves. The approach of the Liberals draws heavily upon Kennedy's "New Frontier," and senior party workers evince great respect for his campaigning abilities. From the New Frontier are Liberal standbys such as: "The wasted years"; "We will get the economy moving again," and "We will restore Canada's lost international prestige."

"Until the campaign starts we're playing for fumbles as much as for field goals," said one organizer. This is an esoteric and difficult game. The purpose is to manoeuvre the opposition into a false position.

11

Mackenzie King as Leader

R. MacGREGOR DAWSON

*

. . . [The] attitude of Mackenzie King to political questions cannot be fully understood until one has grasped his conception of the role which the political party should perform in a democracy, and particularly in the Canadian democracy. He considered that the parties in Canada had two major functions: the propagation and carrying out of ideas and policies, and the bringing together of diverse and even conflicting groups and interests so as to secure a working agreement and a measure of common action. The second function was in his eyes even more important than the first; indeed its operation might necessitate party principles being temporarily shelved or substantially modified in order to secure the necessary consent among the rival forces within the party—the highest common factor on which all could unite. Such a conciliatory and mollifying influence was indispensable in a country like Canada where the bonds of national unity were weak and the centrifugal forces of race, religion, geography, economic interests, etc. were unusually strong; these, if not held in some restraint, might quite conceivably disrupt the state itself.

King's belief in the party system and his conviction that the party was the necessary means for achieving popular consent thus led him at times to make enormous concessions to preserve the unity of the Liberal party. It seemed to him short-sighted indeed to push a much needed reform through Parliament and into the statute books at the price of a divided support and the virtual paralysis of that party for years to come. Gladstone had tried it, and had not only disrupted his party and been driven from office, but also failed to achieve the immediate objective, Home Rule. The danger of pursuing King's policy is, of course, obvious, for the party leader may well confuse the retention of office with the necessity of maintaining party unity, and jettison all principles in a frantic effort to stay in power at any cost. . . .

Once King's ideas on the essential liberalism of the Farmer and Labour movements were accepted as valid, the attitude which the Liberal party should adopt in the existing political situation was virtually determined. Liberals, King said, should not rest content with welcoming

*Reprinted from *William Lyon Mackenzie King: A Political Biography*, University of Toronto Press, 1958.

only their erring brothers who had temporarily thrown in their lot with the Unionists, they should also regard the new radical movements with sympathy and make it easy for the parties of protest to make common cause with them. Expressed in concrete and realistic terms, the major problem was to find issues on which all could unite with the double purpose of strengthening the opposition to the Government and carrying out a common programme, although admittedly the need for compromise would severely restrict the area of effective action. Once the parties had developed confidence in each other through experience and association, they might well be prepared to make further advances which would lead ultimately to a permanent union. King's policy in dealing with the Farmers was to keep hammering away at the virtual identity of Liberal and Farmer policies, to persuade the Farmers, if possible, to work in immediate fellowship with the Liberals, and at all times to say and do nothing which would form a barrier to the union he was convinced would eventually prove to be inevitable.

Mackenzie King lost no time in applying this policy of reconciliation to all liberal-minded Canadians. The Liberal Unionists were the first in his mind, and following the lead of Laurier, he did his utmost to make it easy for them to rejoin the party. In a reply to J. E. Atkinson's warm letter of congratulation on the leadership, he wrote of this desire for reunion:

I am in most hearty accord with your suggestion that every effort should be made to emphasize the rapprochement which has already been effected in such large measures between Unionist and other Liberals. In this matter, there can be but one attitude from now on. The National Convention has laid down a platform of principles and policies. All who are in accord with views therein expressed, and who are willing to assist in making them prevail, must be recognized as members of a party whose past divisions and differences have faded from view in the larger single aim and purpose by which all true Liberals are now united. Only those are against us who are not for us; and this is a test which, in determining political allegiance, no man can apply to another, but each must apply to himself.

*   *   *   *   *

King did not believe that it was his job as the leader of the party to become the passionate advocate of new causes, however admirable, but to bring together, consolidate, and make operative a common will on all public questions when such a result was possible. Bold and imaginative ventures were invaluable aids in the creation of opinion, but they were luxuries which the reformers and pioneers could best afford. The political leader was bound in his endeavour by what was generally acceptable at any particular time. If King believed that he was unable on certain questions to obtain the consensus he sought, he could see no virtue in trying to force people's ideas into a mould which they resisted. So long as the majority of Canadians remained strongly isolationist and opposed to the League of Nations King would not try to convert them. Indeed, he would go further and capitalize on their common isolationism. It constituted one of the few issues on which he could find agreement—Ontario as well as Quebec, West as well as East—and he seized the opportunity to turn it to good account and use it as a binder to encourage co-operation not on this alone but on other questions as well. Whatever his own views on the functions of the League might be, King was ready to sink them, temporarily or permanently, if by doing so, he could accomplish what he considered to be the larger purpose. What King perceived in his early days as leader and what succeeding years confirmed, was that the Canadian people wanted no more commitments to and for the League of Nations than the minimum which was consistent with the maintenance of national self-respect. King gave them that minimum or even, at times, a little less.

*   *   *   *   *

The Chanak incident[1] provided an interesting contrast in Canadian political leadership, though the decisions were made under somewhat different circumstances, inasmuch as King had to furnish an immediate answer while Meighen could take his time—as he did—in announcing his position. King's cautious approach satisfied Liberals of all persuasions; Meighen's jingoistic appeal antagonized and probably alienated some of his Conservative following. Where King's policy tended to bring Progressives and Labour closer to the Liberals, Meighen's announcement tended to widen the existing gap between those groups and the Conservatives. King's prestige was greatly enhanced, and the country began to realize that while the Prime Minister might lack colour, he possessed both courage and common sense and was not to be hurried into mistaken policies on the impulse of the moment. The alleged necessity of consulting Parliament was his way of gaining time—to await events in Europe, to ascertain public opinion, and to give that opinion at the same time an opportunity to take shape and become stabilized—but it was also a policy, which Meighen's reproaches and Lloyd George's repeated requests for assurances made abundantly clear. If it turned out that Parliament had to be summoned (which was always possible) the Cabinet would have to bring down a policy for parliamentary approval and it might then have to be of a more positive nature. For the moment, however, the Cabinet considered that no case had yet been made to justify any overt action Some time later a Progressive member of Parliament put the matter succinctly when he suggested that the crisis demanded not so much a policy of "ready, aye, ready" as one of "steady, aye, steady"—certainly a fair epitome of King's policy at that time.

Mature consideration did not seem to improve Mr. Meighen's sensitivity. In 1925 he went a step further and antagonized also the right-wing Conservatives by giving a speech at Hamilton on what he felt should be done if war again threatened. The Government, he said, should decide on its policy, and not only should Parliament be called promptly, but the Government's decisions "should be submitted to the judgment of the people at a general election before troops should leave our shores." At the time he was getting ready to make this speech representative men in the Conservative party pleaded with him not to do so; but he persisted. It was followed by an immediate cry of protest, and all over the Dominion many Conservatives were incensed at his proposals. Two years later he rose in a Conservative national convention, and tried to justify what he had said; he was "as tenacious of his own opinions," wrote a commentator, "as he is indifferent to the protests of his party." The natural result was to revive the disagreement which his Hamilton speech had already caused among many Conservatives.

The difference between Meighen's approach to a political issue and that of Mackenzie King was drawn by Meighen himself over a decade later at a gathering of the Conservative party which was held to bid farewell to R. B. Bennett. In the course of his remarks Meighen touched on the subject of political leadership in terms which not only provided a clue to his own ideas but also quite clearly indicated Mackenzie King as the villain of the Canadian scene:

In our Dominion where sections abound, a Dominion of races, of classes and of creeds, of many languages and many origins, there are times when no Prime Minister can be true to his trust to the nation he has sworn to serve, save at the temporary sacrifice of the party he is appointed to lead. . . . If anyone tells me that fidelity to party and fidelity to country are always compatible, or that the wisdom of mere numbers is the wisdom of heaven, then I tell him that he loves applause far more than he loves truth. Loyalty to the ballot box is not necessarily loyalty to the nation; it is not even loyalty to the multitude. Democracy has failed and fallen in many lands, and political captains in Canada must have courage to lead rather than servility to follow, if our institutions are going to survive. There must be something better than an ambition to be reelected, or democracy will fall, even in this Dominion.

It is interesting that King and Meighen each advanced the heterogeneity of the Canadian people as a major justification of his special form of leadership. To Meighen the challenge had to be met by the formulation of some broad concept of the national interest which would transcend this diversity and in large measure obliterate it. Having formulated this concept, Meighen then invoked all the arts of rational persuasion to secure its popular acceptance. His confidence in the product of his own judgment was so profound and his advocacy so determined that the policy was open to little or no discussion, still less could it be recast or toned down in any way to meet the demands or soothe the feelings of dissenting groups or interests.

---

[1]When in 1922 Prime Minister Lloyd George asked Mr. King if Canada would be represented by a military force to help repulse Turkish advances into Greece, Mr. King replied that Parliament must decide, whereas Mr. Meighen said Canada's response should be "Ready, aye ready!"

Mackenzie King also perceived in this diversity of population a challenge but a different kind of opportunity. Opposing views, as he saw it, should not be expected to undergo any rapid conversion. Such a change would come through the slow influence of sympathetic association. The emphasis should always be placed on those things which people held in common and on which they could be induced to co-operate. Shared experiences would in time lead to increased tolerance, compromise, and understanding.

First across the gulf we cast
Kite-born threads, till lines are passed
And habit builds the bridge at last!

Nevertheless any fair appraisal would have to recognize a certain degree of truth in Meighen's criticism, and concede that King's leadership would have been improved had he been more venturesome and more willing to offer forthright guidance to the nation. King's tactics enabled him to secure and retain office—the indispensable first step. But King, too frequently, stopped right there; and because he was reluctant to press on and try to realize some independent conception of the national interest, his policies slipped into the mire of pure expediency. King was always reluctant to venture into the unknown. He avoided taking risks, and he would postpone action, if by so doing he could ensure a greater degree of safety. He dreaded unnecessary discussion which might lead to disagreement and even threaten the existing party solidarity on which the whole security of his position rested. He was not prepared to use his own power extensively in an effort to modify the character and scope of those common elements on which he sought to base his policy. He was too willing at times to yield his own judgment when confronted with opposing opinion. He was slow to admit that he had a duty as leader to exert a moderate pressure in the direction in which he believed the country should move. Franklin Roosevelt, for example, was able to follow King's general course, but with a significant difference. He found it possible to maintain this precarious balance, this unending compromise and adjustment between the leader and the led. Thus in the field of foreign policy Roosevelt was usually able to keep in touch with and even follow American opinion, while at the same time his confident personality was guiding that opinion in the general direction he desired.

Meighen's excessive self-confidence inclined him to be somewhat contemptuous of and superior to public opinion. King's excessive caution and search for common ground tended to make him too acquiescent and too sensitive to that opinion. Yet King was able to accomplish infinitely more. His method was the necessary approach to office, although admittedly a stronger realization of his duty to take the initiative would have added to his effectiveness. It was, of course, King's sensitivity to existing conflicts of belief and his search for existing areas of agreement which led to Meighen's taunts of loyalty to the ballot box and servility to public opinion. King might well reply that the best hockey player in the world is no use off the ice, that a party leader who cannot get elected and stay elected cannot govern and in due course will destroy the party he is supposed to lead. A condition precedent to the exercise of power in a democracy as elsewhere is to gain a place in the seats of the mighty.

Political leadership, in short, must always meet two tests: the ability to gain and stay in power, and the ability to use power once it has been gained. King's technique in bringing conflicting groups together make him a master in passing the first ordeal, though he allowed the same talent to undermine his effectiveness after he was in office. Meighen's technique never got him over the first barrier. He showed some ability to meet the second of the requirements of democratic leadership, but he was given little opportunity to demonstrate this capacity. There is, moreover, no escaping the fact that the same difficulties which prevented him from obtaining office would have been equally operative in preventing his staying there. In point of fact, they did exactly that, for on the two occasions when Meighen attained the Prime Ministership, he was unable to secure confirmation from the electorate.

12

Federal Strains Within
A Canadian Party

EDWIN R. BLACK

*

Unity is a rallying cry within the ranks of political parties everywhere: that it must be voiced so often and in so many different circumstances reveals some of the extent to which political parties are subject to internally divisive forces. To state, then, that Canada's major parties are peculiarly susceptible to quarrels over leadership is to direct attention to an unusual aspect of such disputes in this country—the dimension imparted to them by the federal system. Canadian parties do, of course, have difficulties analogous to those of parties in other countries, difficulties such as the disputes between Hugh Gaitskell and Aneurin Bevan or between Harold Macmillan and Peter Thorneycroft. But equally noteworthy in Canada are the frequent public squabbles between federal party chieftains and the provincial leaders, their theoretical subordinates. A simple pairing of names suggests some of them: Mackenzie King and Mitchell Hepburn of Ontario, George Drew and Deane Finlayson of British Columbia, Lester Pearson and Ross Thatcher of Saskatchewan. Whatever may be the causes of leadership feuds, in Canada they are always likely to be complicated by the federal system which, with its plurality of independent centres of political power, makes country-wide party discipline more difficult to maintain than it is in comparable unitary countries.

Two subjects have been raised, party leadership and the impact of federalism on the party system; as yet, neither has been investigated systematically. This paper is designed to explore the fringes of these subjects by examining a particular case—the dispute between the federal and provincial factions of the British Columbia Progressive Conservative Association—and by looking briefly at several other quarrels between federal and provincial leaders. Factors isolated from these disputes lead to a concluding statement of ten general propositions about the relationship of federalism to the party system. Special emphasis will be given to the peculiar problems of organization that a party faces in trying to operate at both the federal and provincial levels of the federal system.

*Reprinted from *The Dalhousie Review*, XLV, 3, 1965.

Quarrels within a political party can usually be traced to differences over policies and objectives, to conflicts of personalities and ambitions, or to differences in the perception of problems and their most appropriate solutions. It should be recognized, however, that these same differences impart vitality as well as discord to the system. The problem is to keep the expression of these differences within bounds, a task which becomes even more difficult if the party has an "open" tradition honouring healthy debate and the expression of diverse and even radically different viewpoints.

The course of debate and struggle within a party is analagous to an electrical system in which the leaders and clusterings of party opinion are represented by electrodes of varying capabilities. The party's *raison d'être*— its ultimate objective—is represented by the common field through which the electrodes interact. The system's activity depends upon maintenance of voltage differentials (i.e., opinion differences) between the electrodes, all or some of which are responsive to changes in the external environment. The organization's relative efficiency depends upon its ability to harmonize and integrate the different forces coursing through it. If the internal transmission and transforming facilities break down, the system's output of power is reduced. In most states the boundaries of the system are co-terminous with a single service area—the unitary state. But in a federation such as Canada there is a self-contained party organization within each province. This means that there are co-existing within the country whole series of similar parties which are frequently required to work together as national units. Attempts to combine these often disparate systems for the pursuit or maintenance of public office at the federal capital reveal the strengths and weaknesses of the overall integrating process.

Before considering a particular case, we should, perhaps, look briefly at the editorial-page model which rationalizes the two-fold concerns of a major Canadian party. According to the model, the Conservative party, for example, should be a unified, country-wide association of political activisits who work through provincial sub-divisions to achieve their goals. While the party's objectives—of ideological formulation, popular persuasion, and attainment of office—may be prosecuted at two independent levels of government, the party sub-division chiefs, the provincial leaders, are usually seen to be hierarchically inferior to the federal leader. The Progressive Conservative party in British Columbia does not always conform closely to the model.

*   *   *   *   *

"Federal-provincial schizophrenia" is what Aristotle would probably call a degenerate form of the "right state" of a political party. Our model suggests this "right" form obtains when the same political organism functions with equal efficiency in both the federal and provincial areas of its responsibility. The schizophrenic forms of organization are probably more common in the Canadian provinces than is the efficiently operating, dual function type. To its great cost, the Conservative party in British Columbia manifested its schizophrenic tendencies in a violent public quarrel; the resulting public attention made the situation especially difficult to repair.

The quarrel turned, essentially, on two issues: how federal activity in the province should be organized and who should direct it. Following the provincial association's collapse in the early 1930's, federal work in the province was handled by a committee appointed by members of Parliament and other candidates. On coming to the federal leadership in 1942, John Bracken undertook to revitalize Conservative organization throughout Canada. Where a province had an effective Conservative party association full responsibility was vested in the provincial leader. Where the party was notably weak, as in Quebec, a special organizer was named. British Columbia presented an unusual problem. An active provincial association existed, but its leaders were in coalition with the Liberals. An effective C.C.F. opposition was keeping the government on the defensive, and leading British Columbia Conservatives were frequently required to support or promote Liberal-inspired policies. To compound the problem, from Bracken's point of view, the provincial Tories tended to see the local picture in the same terms as did the Liberals and did not agree that there was any necessity for a thorough-going reorganization.

Deciding that a strong personal hand was needed, Bracken named Howard Green as his personal representative and gave him particular responsibility for all federal organization work in British Columbia. In practice, Bracken made the policy and tactical decisions and Green communicated them to the faithful in British Columbia. The then provincial leader (R. L. Maitland) accepted this arrangement, although his chief lieutenant, Herbert Anscomb, was angry at having to defer to Green or to anybody else in organizational concerns. Anscomb won the provincial leadership in 1946 but did little to improve the state of the party.

The coalition arrangement generated much internal party friction after the war. Anscomb and his close associates enjoyed many of the prerequisites of office and insisted on continuing with the coalition; they hoped thereby to gain both time and resources for rebuilding the party. But many other Conservatives thought that the coalition should have been terminated at the war's end. This group included the many who were out of favour with the gruff and sometimes arrogant provincial leader. More importantly, however, the dissidents also comprised returning veterans, older party workers who saw the organization degenerating, young party members eager for a change, and many party adherents who were concerned that the alliance with the Liberals was impairing the party's chances in the federal field. Liberal and Conservative party labels were not used during the 1945 and 1949 provincial elections, and the Conservative associations were ordered to work for the election of Coalition candidates no matter what their previous political stripe might have been. A sizable number of those discontented with Anscomb refused to participate, especially in the 1949 campaign; most prominent of all the abstainers were the members of Parliament and their close associates and supporters.

The provincial leader was openly challenged at the 1950 annual meeting. The federal wing of the party, the Young Conservatives, and others discontented with Anscomb, supported W. A. C. Bennett in what proved to be that M. L. A.'s second futile bid for the leadershsip. After beating off Bennett's threat fairly easily, Anscomb went on to elect nearly all his own people to the association executive, and again sought to control all campaign funds and the selection of federal candidates. Drew, taking the advice of his M.P.'s, refused to accede either to Anscomb's insistence on full organizational control or to his demand that the organizer be dismissed. The organizer, Frank Barker, was accused by the Anscomb faction of having directed Bennett's unsuccessful drive for the leadership. Soon after the convention, Barker was summarily locked out of the provincial Conservative office and his files were thrust into the hall. With the approval of the federal group, Barker opened another office despite the provincial leader's strong objections.

The 1952 provincial election was a disaster for the Conservatives, and Anscomb resigned; a protégé, Deane Finlayson, came out of the ensuing leadership contest with a comfortable lead over the candidate of the federal wing A. L. Bewley. Finlayson also sought to control federal organization work but was told that he would first have to demonstrate some competence both in the field and at the polls. He continued to insist on his "rights" as provincial leader. Finally, in 1954, to report the occasion from Finlayson's viewpoint,

After years of frustration, after failing in every means including the changing of leadership in the province and the changing of presidents; after promises of cooperation that were never kept, after dismemberment of the party and what appeared to be a deliberate effort to emasculate the party so it could no longer be a factor in provincial politics, the Executive decided upon drastic action. It moved a motion of non confidence in the National Leader on July 17th (1954).[1]

The provincial leader urged the necessity of approving his executive's motion. He charged that Drew had had secret dealings with various party opponents, that Drew was arrogant and dictatorial, and that Drew and his organizers had made a "saw-off" deal with Social Credit to the effect that Drew's group would keep out of Social Credit's way in British Columbia in return for Social Credit agreement not to oppose federal Conservative candidates. The federal party leaders in the province were "agents of malice and misery", Finlayson said, and he went on to predict that within two years Drew would be supplanted as national leader by John Diefenbaker. Angry debate filled the air for several hours, charges were hurled freely, and individuals were slandered on all sides. Eventually, a ballot was taken. The federal leader stood condemned by an

---

[1]Allan J. McDonell, ed., *A Factual Documented Statement of the Conservative Party's Position in British Columbia and Some of the Reasons for the Motion of No Confidence in the National Leader* (Vancouver, 1955), p. 20.

announced vote of 40 to 24. The party's three M.P.'s jumped to their feet and stalked from the room followed by twenty-one supporters, several of them in tears and all of them enraged.

During the weeks that followed, Conservatives ranged themselves defiantly into two antagonistic camps. The party's bitter internal strife was fully reported and exposed for all the voters to see. On the one side were Provincial Leader Finlayson, most of the executive of the provincial association, and some constituency association officers. On the other side were the members of Parliament, the Young Conservatives, and the other riding-association executives. Newspapers reported the dispute as a simple personality clash between Drew and Finlayson. The provincial leader's charge that the federal leader was denying him his rights as provincial leader and acting like a dictator seemed to accord with Drew's public image and was generally accepted outside the party. Many of those supporting the federal leader justified doing so on grounds that the provincial executive had acted unconstitutionally and had thereby gravely injured the party. Chiefly, however, it would seem that they supported Drew because they refused to relinquish to an untried provincial leader and his friends the full control of the party's federal organization, an organization built largely through the efforts of such men as Leon Ladner and the three M.P.'s, Green, Fulton and Pearkes. Formation of a separate organization to deal with all federal affairs was announced soon after the Vernon meeting.

The fight was a public one and many bitter words were exchanged as first one Conservative and then another held press conferences. During the month of July, 1954, newspapers reported almost daily incidents evidencing the split. An editorial in *The Vancouver Province,* headed "Suicide at Vernon", expressed a commonly held view of the affair:

>   *So far as the public knows, the vote at Vernon was based on nothing but the charge that George Drew and his federal party supporters were interfering with the provincial politicians. There was no major issue of policy. It was strictly a domestic row over the kitchen sink.*
>   *By resolution, George Drew stands condemned, not because he failed in matters of national policy, but because he butted in on Mr. Finlayson, the seatless leader of a seatless party.*[2]

Throughout the constituency associations, an ever-widening gulf became evident as supporters of both sides sought to put their group on record in support of either Finlayson or Drew. Those members of the constituency associations who found themselves in a local minority on the leadership loyalty queston sometimes sought help from the headquarters of either faction to set up a new association, but more often they simply quit active party work. Premier Bennett claimed that large numbers of disaffected Tories were joining his Social Credit "movement". In August, the federal group began reorganizing in earnest; the three M.P.'s divided responsibility for the province between themselves, established the Federal Council, and sought to ensure the loyalty of all the federal constituency associations. The executive of the Canadian association recognized the Federal Council as having sole responsibility for federal work in British Columbia.

Sporadic attempts at reconciliation were made, but without much apparent effect. The provincial association did not match the activity of the Federal Council in organizing, and although the Finlayson group claimed large numbers of supporters and carried on a vigorous press campaign, little that was tangible appeared to result. In March, 1955, the provincial wing published what it called *A Factual Documented Statement of the Conservative Party's Position in British Columbia and Some of the Reasons for the Motion of No Confidence in the National Leader.* This publication, which was widely distributed, presented a series of statements, letters and parts of letters, tracing the difficulties back to 1942 and Green's appointment by Bracken. The statement purported to demonstrate that Green had sought undue power for himself in opposition to the only legally constituted association, and that the two federal leaders had systematically supported Green's attempts to divide the party. The publication reiterated the association's claim to be the sole legitimate embodiment of the party in British Columbia and attacked the federal wing for setting up the Federal Council. The charge of "a saw-off with Social Credit" was repeated and was made a formal resolution of the provincial officers. In the provincial election held a year later, 1956, the Conservative share of the popular vote stood at an all-time low. Virtually every newspaper's interpretation of the vote attributed the Tories' dismal showing to the internal party split.

Much debate in British Columbia swirled about the institutional manifestations of the central party within the province, that is to say, the post of personal representative of the federal leader and the Federal Council. Both institutions require examination.

The designation of a personal representative began with John Bracken, was continued by George Drew, and with some modification by John Diefenbaker. Considering the controversy about the post, it was somewhat surprising to discover that so slight was the importance attached to the post by its holders that they were unable to recall with certainty exactly who had held the appointment during what years. The representative's duties were always vaguely defined and his powers were even less definite. All four of the people who held the post have agreed, however, that the primary function was that of funneling reliable information to and from the federal leader and the local organizations. From the time of the coalition government, the federal leaders were never convinced that much credence could be placed in situation assessments made by persons working closely with the Liberal party or by an association long accustomed to co-operating with the Liberals and essentially

---

[2]*The* Vancouver *Province* (July 20, 1954).

unchanged since the coalition. It was primarily to fill this gap in information that personal representatives were appointed.

Formation of the Federal Council did not at first supersede the personal representative's work, for the Council was more concerned with associational work and less with the divination of popular feeling. But as the Federal Council largely completed its task of building loyal party groups in every constituency, the Council's president assumed the additional task of obtaining information as well. Diefenbaker utilized the system he inherited in British Columbia but began to supplement information supplied by the Council with that of other advisers.

The Federal Council of British Columbia was not unique in the country-wide scheme of Conservative party organization, a consideration that received acknowledgement neither from the Council's opponents in the province nor from the press in its discussions of the party divisions. In 1959 the national organizer, Allister Grosart, gave the Federal Council an outline of party structures in other parts of the country. Quebec had a federal association overseeing three regional associations and "more than seventy-five riding associations, most of them fairly new". Manitoba had been organized on a strong federal-constituency basis after a coalition provincial government had resulted in the atrophy of many Conservative groups in the provincial ridings. Grosart said that the separate federal association was to be maintained in Manitoba until the provincial organization had been rebuilt and the two fields of work could be divided under one jurisdiction. A federal council was to be organized in Newfoundland in 1960. Grosart emphasized that no problems resulted wherever there was a strong provincial association and that separate federal organization was usually unnecessary. This situation was believed to obtain in Ontario, Nova Scotia, and New Brunswick. The federal organizer did not report on Prince Edward Island and noted that there were provincial but no federal associations in Saskatchewan and Alberta.

In other parties and in other situations, federal cabinet ministers have often been the party's effective chieftains within a province ruled by an opposition party. Where the party forms the provincial government, it seems safe to assert that the premier has had full control over all organizational work within the province—unless he has specifically declined interest in the federal work, as, for example, Ontario's Leslie Frost was thought to have done.

Today (1965), ten years after the Vernon resolution condemning the federal leader, reconciliation has been affected between the two factions. The Federal Council has been disbanded, the two offices merged, and the provincial leader made responsible for all federal organization in the province; during the federal and provincial election campaigns of 1963 the most thoroughgoing co-operation of the two wings was evident to press observers. Without detailing the transformation, it may be well to suggest a few of its significant aspects.

*   *   *   *   *

Selection of a new federal leader was significant for the

provincial situation. Diefenbaker was generally thought to have given aid and comfort to Finlayson in the quarrel with Drew, and it was Diefenbaker rather than Fulton, the British Columbia member of Parliament, who received the votes of provincial association delegates to the leadership convention. But while the new federal leader was on good terms with Finlayson, he did not disturb the organization of responsibility for federal work in the province. For their part, the Fulton-Green group constituted for the 1957 and 1958 general elections a campaign committee that included prominent members of the provincial faction. Members of the federal wing won election to the provincial executive while three of the M.P.'s succeeded to cabinet posts at Ottawa. Finlayson, after another provincial election shutout in 1960, resigned his post in despair. After a period in which the provincial leadership was deliberately left vacant, the Federal Council disappeared into a reconstructed provincial associaton. Within it were constituted two parallel committees, one charged with provincial responsibility and the other with federal duties. After helping to effect these changes, Federal Public Works Minister Fulton answered an almost unanimous draft to become provincial leader. One respected newspaperman reported from the 1963 leadership convention that "even the most cynical delegate agreed that due to the Fulton touch a bitter split between federal and provincial wings of the party was dead, buried and soon to be forgotten". Later, he commented that "in the long run, final healing of the . . . split may prove to be a more significant development politically than Fulton's tumultuous election as leader of the provincial Conservatives".[3] Head-table guests at the final luncheon included both Deane Finlayson and Herbert Anscomb. The new executive elected at the convention was composed of members who had not been associated with either of the two former factions.

As a summary of political difficulties in British Columbia, a few salient points should be noted:

1. During the 1940's the Conservative party as a whole was embarrassed by the anomaly of being in active alliance with the Liberals at the provincial seat of government and being in active opposition to them at Ottawa. 2. In the immediate postwar period, an organizational resurgence in the federal sphere was in marked contrast to the antebellum attitudes of the provincial leaders. 3. The established provincial faction was challenged unsuccessfully four times by leadership candidates enjoying the support of the federal wing. 4. While the dispute appeared to involve nothing more than the status of the provincial leader, the question embraced both the shape and control of all party organization in the province as well as the selection and final approval of candidates for both federal and provincial contests. 5. Even in the depths of electoral despair, the provincial faction maintained a firm grip on the only legal Conservative association and with it was able to censure the federal leader. 6. During the 1950's, the federal faction was always better able to raise

---

[3]Tom Hazlitt, "Fulton's Political Miracle," *The* Vancouver *Province* (January 28, 1963).

election funds than was the provincial faction; this situation further embittered the provincial partisans, but it does not seem to have been a significant factor contributing to the party division. 7. No aspect of the quarrel seemed to derive from differences over policy. (Can we attribute this to the lack of office-holding by the party, or does it simply confirm our impressions about the group's rather slight ideological commitment?) 8. Not until one of the two factions was able to attain public office were its representatives able to assimilate the other group.

*   *   *   *   *

Whenever leaders of the same party are caught quarreling in public, both supporters and commentators are wont to reduce the matter to a problem of differences in personality and to assert that the dispute lacks substantive content. This, for the leaders' party, may well be the most acceptable public face to put on the dispute if they are unable to deny its existence. The personality explanation has the attraction of simplicity and credibility, and it helps to reinforce Canadian reluctance to see important differences of principle as significant factors in the country's political life. Expressed as a general thesis, this explanation holds that federalism as such does not make an important difference to the leadership of the major parties, and that quarrels within them arise chiefly from natural jealousies and personality incompatibilities, just as they do in the parties of unitary states.

This thesis is, however, inadequate. While some of the internal disputes in Canada's federal parties do result from clashes of personality, something more than one man's inability to get along with another is required to split a party and range its members into factions. The divided organizational arrangements which manifested the Conservative split in British Columbia persisted for more than a decade and through three different pairs of federal and provincial leaders. It is, of course, reasonable to suggest that personality differences may trigger a dispute which rends a party in two. But if that division endures within a two-party or multi-party system, then we must look beyond the personalities for deeper conditions which themselves might have split the party eventually. Here we will probably find clues to the fissiparous forces which federalism attempts to contain.

Standing as something of an antithesis to the "personality" theory is the "party brokerage" theory. According to this idea, the successful party in a federal state serves as a broker or middleman between the provinces, which have diverse and often contradictory policy claims. Inter-factional quarrels are said to be reflections of these internal policy contradictions as the national party seeks to work out programme compromises which are acceptable both to those primarily oriented toward the provinces and to those oriented toward the country as a whole. The validity of this theory is dependent upon finding substantive policy content behind the internal party disputations. While we do not have to disagree with the assertion that Canada's major parties very seldom display coherent and consistent philosophies or policy orientations, there is enough truth in the statement, and so little evidence of policy differences in the British Columbia conflict, that the brokerage explanation is also unsatisfactory.

A synthesis of these ideas may be more serviceable. It may be put this way: The Canadian outlook favours, and, indeed, sometimes requires, politics of pragmatism rather than of policies or ideology; internal party disputes represent, from time to time, conflicts of personalities, attempts to reconcile divergent provincial policy demands, and problems resulting from the often disparate organizational needs of two groups within the party, the one group seeking federal victory and the other seeking victory at the provincial capital.

Some of the general propositions suggested by this study are outlined below . . .

1. Canada's major parties do not fit the model of unified country-wide parties with hierarchically inferior provincial sub-divisions; major party supporters do not exhibit the necessary degree of commitment. 2. Both the structure and the internal operation of a major party resemble that of the Canadian system of government. The sovereignty of provincial party units is as real and extensive as that of the provinces with respect to Ottawa. 3. Just as the virtual independence of a provincial government's policy-making depends to a considerable extent on its provincial resources, so the effective control of provincial organization by the local officers depends upon the local unit's political resources in comparison with those of the central party; such resources are considered to be size and commitment of membership, financial capabilities, quality and appeal of leadership, and, of course, electoral success. 4. Party organizers must deal with three types of active members: those whose political interests are primarily oriented in provincial terms, those whose interests find primary expression in central-government goals, and those whose interests are multi-faceted or else are concentrated on some aspect of political life comprehending both spheres of government—such as the attainment of ideological objectives or general governmental power for the party. 5. A party's policy objectives and organizational requirements in the federal and provincial arenas are often quite different, but both sets of leaders must rely in large measure on the same relatively small group of people and on the same resources for their field work. 6. The interests and energies of the party machinery within one province cannot be converted readily and with equal efficiency to both federal and provincial objectives. Attempts to treat the party as if it were readily convertible impose almost intolerable stresses on the organization, stresses which may be expected to become manifest in difficulties between the party leaders. 7. The public or private character of the expression and resolution of internal party differences is a reflection of the leadership skills and institutional machinary with which the groups are endowed, and of the party's electoral morale. 8. Even where a provincial party organization is controlled by relatively ineffectual persons, if they are determined in their leadership, representatives of the central party can undertake "corrective"

action only at considerable risk. 9. The provincial party is a highly-charged organism, with many internal stresses and tensions, which must be capable of frequent integration with as many as nine others of similar nature to produce a country-wide mechanism focussing its power on system-wide problems. 10. The pattern of authoritative relationships between central and provincial party groups will depend upon whether public office is held by one, neither, or both of the two party groups. These relationships will also be affected by the nature of any "rehabilitative" process through which an out-of-office party faction may be going and by the degree of ideological and policy solidarity between the central and the provincial units.

The Minor Parties

*

Canadian parties, although vague in their policies, are disciplined parliamentary groups requiring of their members a high degree of conformity. The leader has great authority, and there is little room for dissidence. Protest, then, must occur outside the old parties, and if it is to be effective, must itself assume the form of a political party. There have been many such parties in Canadian history, but here we refer only to three: the Progressive movement, which has now disappeared, and the Social Credit and New Democratic parties. Each achieved its greatest success in the West, where it was built upon the structure of voluntary organizations already existing among the farmers. Also, each appeared in a time of crisis.

The Progressive movement arose after World War I as a farmers' party to protest against capitalist domination in Canadian economic and political life. It attracted wide support from the frontier provinces of Alberta and Saskatchewan, as well as from the farmers of Manitoba and Ontario. Its eastern support weakened its militant sectionalism and prompted some of its leaders to move into the Liberal party. Others formed alliances with labour, leading to the formation of the C.C.F. party (now the New Democratic Party). The failure of the Progressive (U.F.A.) government of Alberta to cope with the depression opened the door to the Social Credit party under the fervent, messianic leadership of William Aberhart.

13

The Progressive Tradition in Canadian Politics

W. L. MORTON

*

. . . The Progressive movement was a revolt against a concept of the nature of Canadian economic policy and of Canadian political practice. The concept of Canadian economic policy which the Progressives had formed and on which they acted was that of a metropolitan economy designed, by the control of tariffs, railways, and credit, to draw wealth from the hinterlands and the countryside into the commercial and industrial centres of central Canada. The concept of Canadian political practice which the Progressives had formed and on which they acted was that the classic national parties were the instruments used by the commercial, industrial, and financial interests of metropolitan Canada to implement the National Policy of tariff protection and railway construction by dividing the vote of the electorate on "political" issues and by the compromises and majority decisions of the legislative caucus.

To what extent did these concepts correspond to actuality, what success had the Progressive revolt against them, and what are the consequences of its success or failure in Canadian history?

That the national economic policy of the period was mercantilist in its inspiration and metropolitan in its operation may be affirmed without subscribing to the heated conviction that deliberate greed or malice entered into its formulation, or even that it rested on the blind and selfish inertia of its beneficiaries. Arch Dale's cartoons in the *Grain Grower's Guide* of bloated capitalists siphoning off the hard-earned dollars of the western farmer were effective for their purpose and are amusing comments on an epoch in Canadian history, but they belong to the realm of folk-lore rather than to that of historical interpretation. The National Policy was designed to make central Canada into a commercial and industrial empire, based on the development of the hinterlands of the West and North by the construction of railways to serve both East and West. During the Laurier boom, conditions were favourable, and great success was enjoyed in exploiting the virgin lands of the continental West.

*Reprinted from *The Progressive Party in Canada*, University of Toronto Press, 1950.

When those conditions passed, an adjustment of the policy was necessary. The metropolitan East was challenged by the frontier West it had called into being; the old National Policy was confronted by the New. The adjustment could be either a modification of the policy towards freer international trade, as by an agreement for reciprocity with the United States, or by the metropolitan area assuming, as part of the whole country, the costs of increased benefits to the hinterland areas.

It was to force such an adjustment that the farmers took political action in 1919. Unfortunately, as the controversy over the Wheat Board revealed, they at once fell into confusion about which alternative they would pursue. They strove for results as far apart as a tariff for revenue, and a system of open and organized lobbying in group government, which would have been in practice a scramble for economic benefits distributed by the state. The farmers in the movement represented conflicting interests themselves, and were also responsive to the forces impelling the swift transition from the free economy of pre-war years to the economic nationalism of the 1930's. The seeming unity of purpose of 1919 to 1921 was soon dissolved. In federal politics, the agrarian voters of the West for the most part returned to the Liberal party. In economic matters, the great body of farmers found hope in the new co-operative movement which gave rise to the Wheat Pools. But resentment of the long Liberal domination, and the vision of a stable farm income ensured by government action through a wheat board, remained to drive Conservative voters to support new, anti-Liberal parties, to maintain the U.F.A. in power in Alberta, and to erode the old economic individualism of the farmer with the hope of state action, which would counter the discrimination of the tariff by underpinning the farm economy.

The Progressives, nevertheless, gained certain material benefits for their constituents, especially in the matter of railway rates and communications. The restoration of the Crow's Nest Pass rates, the completion of the Hudson Bay Railway and the proliferation of branch lines in the nineteen-twenties, were their work or owed much to their effort. "With a split representation from the West," wrote the *Free Press* in 1930, "the Crow's Nest Pass rates would never have been restored. The 'National Policy' on this question, favoured along St. James Street, would have been imposed upon both parties had there not been a parliamentary contingent from the West free from control in caucus by an eastern majority."[1] This was spoken in the authentic accents of Progressivism, and it expressed, no doubt, a partial and limited view. If national politics were a struggle for sectional benefits, however, the Progressives had won a measure of success.

At the same time, the Progressives influenced Liberal fiscal policy to the extent of forcing abstention from increases in the tariff and ultimately of actual reduction. Their electoral success of 1921 checked a swing towards economic nationalism evident in most countries after the

---

[1]"The Fruits of the Progressive Movement," *Manitoba Free Press*, (August 6, 1930), 13.

war, even in free-trade Britain, and notably in the United States. After the disappointments of the Liberal budgets from 1922 to 1929, they seemed at long last to be on the threshold of success in the Dunning budget of 1930. Indeed, the Conservatives were able to use the cry of western domination with effect in Quebec in 1930.[2] Otherwise their successes, as in the re-imposition of the Crow's Nest Pass rates on east-bound wheat and flour and in the construction of the Hudson Bay Railway, were in the nature of sectional concessions won from the dominant metropolitan area. On the whole, the Progressive movement left the metropolitan economy of central Canada unaltered in substance or spirit.

Against the concept they held of Canadian political practice the Progressives revolted with notable results. Again, of course, they were divided. There were those who revolted against the composite party because in caucus a sectional group might be consistently outvoted. These, the Manitoban or Liberal Progressives, sought to force a realignment of parties along the lines of the liberal and conservative elements in the electorate. They wished, not to abolish the practices and conventions of party government, but to use them in the interests of the primary producers, as a party of liberal principle. The others were the doctrinaire or Albertan Progressives, who rejected party government as such, and proposed to replace it and its accompanying conventions by group government.

Both, however, were in revolt against the traditional parties as the instruments of the beneficiaries of the metropolitan economy. Did this concept correspond with actuality? While the Progressive view, undoubtedly, was a caricature of the relations of the national parties and the beneficiaries of the metropolitan economy, the caricature has that grasp of salient features which makes a caricature recognizable. Both parties from 1896 on were the practically indistinguishable proponents of the National Policy, and they acted through the caucus, the party-managed nominating convention, and the distribution of campaign funds.

It was these three focal points of party government at which the Progressives struck. That sovereignty had passed from the legislature to the majority in caucus they recognized, and also that that meant the subordination of the weaker to the more populous sections of the country. Henry Spencer said before the United Farmers of Canada (Saskatchewan Section) in 1931: "Of 240 odd members in the Dominion, the great majority went from Eastern Canada, and so it didn't matter which group was in the majority. The Western vote was so absolutely submerged in the caucuses, that however good a man might be, his vote was lost. That was the reason we took independent action."[3] To restore sovereignty to the legislature, and to make sectional views known, the Progressives refused to be bound by decisions taken in caucus. Nominating conventions they proposed to take away from the parties, and restore to the electorate. Campaign funds filled by private donations, they wished to replace by public subscriptions and a levy on party members.

The revolt against caucus, however, could only have succeeded by reversing the development of parliamenary government. No modern cabinet in the parliamentary system could undertake the vast work of the annual financial and legislative programme without reasonable assurance of the consistent support of its followers. The independence of the legislatures of an earlier day was no longer possible; parliament had become the critic, not the master, of cabinets. The popular control of nomination and provision of campaign expenses depended, moreover, upon a zeal for public affairs the electorate failed to display for any length of time. The Progressives put a challenge to democracy which only the U.F.A. met successfully.

Did the restoration of the old parties in 1930, then, and the rise of the C.C.F. and Social Credit parties, essentially composite parties like the old, mark a complete defeat of the Progressive revolt against the party system? To a great extent it did. Yet the old order of Macdonald and Laurier, when party affiliation was hereditary and party chieftains were almost deified, was not restored. The two-party system did not return in its former strength. The rules and conventions of parliament made provision for more than two parties. The electorate became more independent, indeed, to the point of political indifference. The authority of the whip became lighter, the bonds of caucus weaker, than in the old days. These were effects of the Progressive movement, and constituted its mark on Canadian political life.

The mere modification of political conventions and modes was perhaps a slight result of so much effort. Yet where could the sectional and agrarian revolt have led except to secession or class war, or to an acceptance of the composite party once more chastened, no doubt, but essentially unchanged? A free society is an endless compromise between anarchy and authority, union and secession. To compromise, no doubt, is to corrupt—to corrupt the simplicity of principle, the clarity of policy— but if so, then all politics corrupt and federal politics, the politics of the vast sectional and communal aggregations, especially. To this conclusion all purists, all doctrinaires, and all Progressives, must ultimately come or abstain from power. The logical alternative is Robespierre guillotining the guillotiner.

Yet the Progressive insurgence was not merely a sectional protest against a metropolitan economy, it was also an agrarian protest against the growing urban domination of the Canadian economy and of national politics. As such, it was closely allied to the sectional protest. As an agrarian protest, the Progressive movement was a response to the industrialization of the economy, and the commercialization and mechanization of agriculture. In the years of the Progressive movement Canada was undergoing an industrial and urban revolution. To meet the challenge of the coming order, the old, hard-working farmer with his faith in long hours and sweat was ill-equipped. He had to be made over into a manager, a business man, and a skilled technician. The work was largely done

²*Ibid.*
³*Minutes of Annual Convention of United Farmers of Canada* (Saskatchewan Section) (1931), p. 317.

in the farm organizations from which the Progressive party sprang. The professional men, and especially the lawyers, whom the old parties put before the voters to elect were inadequate, not so much to make the legislative adjustments required by the transition from manual to mechanized agriculture, but to express the resentment and discontent the farmer experienced in the throes of the transition, and to speed the work of adjustment. This task the Progressive movement performed, particularly in the two agricultural provinces it captured and held, Manitoba and Alberta. Its very success caused its passing, for the farmer came into business in the co-operatives, into politics in the parties, old or new, to stay. He stayed, not to protest further, but to get on with the job of looking afer the interests of the new commercialized and mechanized agriculture. In this aspect the Progressive movement was the expression of the last phase of the transformation of the old semi-subsistence agriculture into the business of farming. With the Progressive revolt, farming ceased to be a way of life and became simply another occupation. Countryman and city dweller no longer inhabited separate social orders; the city had prevailed over the country, but in prevailing had learned, not a little because of the Progressive movement, to respect the countryman. No one after 1921 would have thought of writing Gadsby's "Sons of the Soil," in which the farmers of the great anti-conscription delegation of 1918 had been ridiculed by a slick and too clever journalist.[4]

In a larger view, also, the Progressive movement marked a profound transformation. Behind the sectional protest lay not only resentment of the National Policy and of its agents, the political parties. Behind it lay also resentment of the inequality of the provinces of the continental West in Confederation. They had been created with limitations, imposed "for the purposes of the Dominion." They entered Confederation, not as full partners, as sister provinces, but as subordinate communities, subject to the land, fiscal and railway policies of the metropolitan provinces and the special interests of the French Canadian in the French dispersion in the West. They were, in short, colonies under the form of provinces "in a federation denoting equality."[5] The Progressive party was a full-blown expression of the West's resentment of its colonial status. As such, it was one phase of the development of the Canadian nation.

As such, also, it had a great measure of success. Not since the days of the revolt has the West been subjected to the indifference, the neglect, and the fumbling administration which provoked the troubles of 1869, the Rebellion of 1885, and the movement itself. The swaggering hopes of the boom days, that the West would dominate confederation by holding a balance of power in Ottawa, were happily not realized. But the increase in cabinet representation from the one lone minister of Laurier's day to the minimal three of the present, was not merely an exercise in abstract justice, but a response to the political weight of the West in the Union Government and to the force of the Progressive movement. The choice of western leaders by political parties from 1920 on was a similar response to the political power and electoral independence of the West. At the same time, it is to be observed that just as the Dunning budget denoted the beginning of Progressive success in fiscal matters so the transfer of the natural resources in 1930, the purposes of the Dominion having been fulfilled, marked the end of the colonial subordination and the achievement of equality of status by the West in Confederation. This, too, was a response to western pressure embodied in the federal Progressive party and the provincial governments the movement threw up. The progressive movement, in short, marked the achievement of political maturity by the West, and the symbols of equality could no longer be withheld.

Yet the resolution of the sectional animosities, of the narrow complacency of the East, and the equally narrow assertiveness of the West, was to be accomplished, not by the bitter exchanges of the 1920's or by enforced concessions. The work of reconciliation, a work of time, of patience, of manoeuvre, the Progressive party advanced by proving that the West, too much tried, would and could resort to independent political action. The work might have been completed in that way. It was, however, completed by tragedy. No sooner had the West, through the progressive movement, begun to win a modification of the National Policy and no sooner had it achieved equality of status in Confederation, than depression drove the country into a defensive economic nationalism. Drought ruined the agrarian economy of the West, and threatened the great co-operatives and the provincial governments with general bankruptcy. The West was saved by federal action, and from the disaster of the thirties came, in East and West, a deeper sense of interdependence than the past had known. The Rowell-Sirois Commission, the great inquest provoked by the disaster, accepted and elaborated the basic thesis of the Progressive movement, that in a federal union of free citizens and equal communities, there must be such equality of economic opportunity and such equality of political status as human ingenuity may contrive and goodwill advance.[6]

[4]H. F. Gadsby, "The Sons of the Soil," *Toronto Saturday Night* (June 1, 1918), 4.

[5]C. C. Lingard, *Territorial Government in Canada: The Autonomy Question in the Old North-West Territories* (Toronto: University of Toronto Press, 1946), p. 251.

[6]See R. McQueen, "Economic Aspects of Federalism," *Canadian Journal of Economics and Political Science*, I (August, 1935), 352-367 for a sober analysis of the points involved.

14

Interpretations of the
Social Credit Movement

JOHN A. IRVING

*

The Social Credit upsurge in Alberta was essentially a people's movement which sought to reform, but not to revolutionize, the existing social order by changing the pattern of certain institutions. . . . During the years it rose to political power, this movement passed through the stages of social unrest, popular excitement, formalization, and institutionalization; and it exhibited, in the course of its evolution, the mechanisms of agitation, *esprit de corps*, morale, ideology, and operating tactics. Considered as a phenomenon of mass psychology, the Social Credit movement may best be interpreted in terms of a tripartite pattern which involves its philosophy, its leadership, and its strategy and tactics. . . . The philosophy of Social Credit includes both a severe criticism of certain phases of the present capitalistic system and a number of constructive proposals for its reform. The psychological functions of this philosophy in the development of the Social Credit movement in Alberta will be discussed here in terms of four principal factors—the social context, the desire for meaning, the satisfaction of needs and the conditions of suggestibility.

On its negative or critical side, Social Credit appealed to Albertans for two reasons: it exploited the preferred group tendencies connected with economics and politics that had been developing in the province for over a generation; and in "explaining" the causes of the depression it did not run counter to, but rather accentuated, the extremely hostile attitudes towards the existing economic system that had arisen in a period characerized by "poverty in the midst of plenty."

Of these preferred group tendencies, the most significant was the criticism of the capitalistic banking and financial system that had long been encouraged by the United Farmers of Alberta. . . . At its annual conventions, especially during the decade preceding 1935, there were bitter debates on resolutions attacking the system and calling loudly for its reform, and indicating that there was scarcely a U.F.A. local that did not have a member or members dedicated to the task of keeping up an

---

*Reprinted from *The Social Credit Movement in Alberta*, University of Toronto Press, Toronto, 1959.

incessant criticism of the monetary system. When Major Douglas himself appeared before the Agricultural Committee of the Alberta legislature in the spring of 1934, the U.F.A. members applauded his devastating criticisms of the system, while at the same time they were highly dubious of his constructive proposals. On its critical side, the philosophy of Social Credit definitely fitted into old social norms; in this respect, Albertans were perhaps more suggestible to the appeal of Social Credit than the people of any other Canadian province.

During the depression, which, for a variety of reasons, was probably felt with greater severity in Alberta than in any other part of Canada, social unrest and widespread discontent developed on a hitherto unparalleled scale, but the provincial government, grown conservative through long years in office, offered no solution of the people's economic problems. Further . . . the representatives of the Eastern financial interests who visited Alberta to discuss the payment of loans and mortgages were insistent that the obligations of the hard-pressed farmers must be met in full: the lowering of interest rates was unthinkable; there could certainly be no adjustment whatever of principal indebtedness. Confronted with the depression on these terms, it is not surprising that thousands of people had developed embittered and hostile attitudes towards both the government and the monetary and financial system. Social Credit was a philosophy made to order for distribution among people with such political and economic attitudes.

In recent years social psychologists have emphasized the importance of the "desire for meaning" in the individual's organization of his experience. The desire for meaning arises when primary, or even derived, needs are frustrated of realization, that is, in critical situations. These situations arise when an individual finds himself involved in a chaotic social environment which he cannot interpret and which he wants to interpret. In such circumstances people who have become accustomed to the established order of society are susceptible to social change. Under the impact of an appropriate philosophy, old values may be overthrown and new social norms may arise.

The feature of the depression which puzzled Albertans most was the discrepancy between the abundance of goods produced and offered for sale on the one hand and the shortage of purchasing power in the hands of the consumer on the other. According to the Social Credit analysis, this discrepancy was simply due to the fact that under the monetary and financial system the rate of flow of purchasing power to the masses was always less than the rate of flow of prices, that is, the purchasing power of consumers was always less than the cost of production. It was also argued that in Alberta the depression, although an inevitable and recurrent feature of an unreformed monetary system, had been accentuated by the machinations of bankers and financiers (the "Fifty Big Shots") who controlled financial credit. To thousands of people this "explanation" of the depression seemed to make meaningful the grievous shortage of purchasing power from which they were suffering, the paradox of "poverty in the midst of plenty." Social Credit interpreted the chaotic external environment in a form simple enough to be "understood," and during the rise of the movement the A plus B Theorem became part of the everyday vocabulary of nearly all adult Albertans.

As the depression increased in severity, Alberta passed into a phase approaching social disorganization: phychologically considered, conditions could scarcely have been more ideal for the setting up of new social norms. Social Credit thus satisfied the desire for meaning and intelligibility amidst a chaotic social environment. On its positive or constructive side, Social Credit advocated new norms, and the upsurge of the movement represented an active attempt to realize a new social order through a specific programme of monetary and financial reform. It was maintained that if the Social Credit proposals could only secure legislative approval, the horrors of the depression would automatically end and a new world would surely come into being. There are also indications that to many of Aberhart's personal religious following the philosophy took on the character of an eschatology, a prohpetic vision of a divinely ordained future for the world.

The major factor in the psychological appeal of the philosophy oi Social Credit was unquestonably the promise it held out for the satisfaction of the primary needs of food, clothing, and shelter. In a depressed and debt-ridden province where thousands of people were unemployed and living on relief, and where farmers were forced to sell their products at such incredibly low levels that they were often on the verge of starvation, the prospect of a basic dividend and a just price had an almost irresistible attraction.

In its offer of a basic dividend, generally understood to be $25 a month for each adult citizen, the Social Credit plan resembled to a certain extent the Townsend Plan which was attracting millions of adherents in the United States, especially in California, at the same time. This "fountain pen money" (as it was called in derision by the opponents of Social Credit) would provide every family with economic security and would banish forever the fear of poverty. Further, the basic dividend was to be presented without any eleemosynary taint, for was it not the people's right, their cultural heritage? Like many another panacea in the long procession of schemes for the salvation of society, the promise of a basic dividend gave the leader of the social credit movement the chance to take his followers along a Glory Road.

The social context, the desire for meaning, and the prospect of satisfying their needs combined to produce in Albertans a psychological condition in which they were extremely open to the appeal of Social Credit. At the same time, most of them lacked sufficient knowledge of philosophy and the social sciences to enable them to assess its claim to be *the* authentic interpretation of their world. Unable to deal with Social Credit in any critical way, thousands of people accepted it because it brought order into their confused world. They were at once bewildered and had the will to believe. They were in a condition of readiness to respond, and the philosophy of Social Credit lent itself admirably to short-cut rationalizations in the form of slogans and symbols. For those who could not understand the philosophy as a whole, slogans like "Control of Credit," "Monetization of Natural Resources," "Basic Dividend," "Just Price," and "Cultural Heritage" became crowded with meaning. No small part of the appeal of Social Credit was simply due to the fact that it met so well the conditions of suggestibility which existed in Alberta at the time that Aberhart began his crusade in 1932.

An emphasis on the profound and multivalent appeal of the philosophy of Social Credit to the people of Alberta must not obscure the importance of the leadership of William Aberhart as a major factor in the rise of the Social Credit movement. . . . Aberhart brought to the movement his great prestige as an educationist and religious leader: it is doubtful if the movement would have won political power in Alberta without his leadership. This does not imply that we should think of him as a sort of genius with a mystic power of prestige that compelled assent and loyalty for Aberhart, like the leader in any field of social life, was both cause and effect. He was the product of the life of his people, and his power lay in his offer to lead in a direction in which those people wished to go, to resolve a difficulty for which no other man had so good a solution.

In his leadership of a mass movement, Aberhart combined the functions of the prophet with the executive capacities of the great planner and organizer. As a prophetic leader, Aberhart may be interpreted in terms of his unification of Christianity and the philosophy of Social Credit, his resolution of his followers' problems of ego involvement, and his charismatic appeal.

Aberhart's leadership gave the Social Credit movement a threefold religious context: he used the excellent facilities of the Calgary Prophetic Bible Institute as the headquarters of the movement; he attracted into the movement most of his large personal religious following which had been built up over a period of some twenty years; and he identified unmistakably the philosphy of Social Credit with the variety of Bible prophecy and Christian fundamentalism he had long been advocating. Aberhart had no hesitation in presenting Social Credit to Albertans as a Divine Plan for the salvation of society, the parallel in the economic sphere of the Divine Plan for the salvation of the individual. While such an approach infuriated many institutional religious and political leaders, it had a powerful attraction for thousands of people who were undoubtedly led in this way to join the movement.

Aberhart's presentation of Social Credit as a Divine Plan enabled him to insist that ultimate victory was inevitable: the cosmic forces were all on his side. In building up this feeling of inevitability in his following, he swept into the movement many persons who might otherwise have hesitated, but who wished to be on the winning side. He was shrewd enough, however, not to rely entirely upon the Divine Plan for the cosmos: he also used extensively the secular appeal. The names of the noblemen, dignitaries of the Church and state, and "experts," mostly in *England,* who accepted the proposals of Social Credit were constantly invoked as an answer to the criticisms of orthodox economists in *Canada.* No name, apart from that of Major Douglas himself, was more useful in this connection than that of Dean Hewlett Johnson, of Canterbury Cathedral, who at the time was an ardent advocate of Social Credit. To Aberhart's earlier prestige as an educational and religious leader there was now added the halo that came from his advocacy of a philosophy which not only mirrored the Divine Design, but which had the support of many great and powerful authorities on earth as well.

As a result of the depression, such economic chaos had developed in Alberta that the majority of the people were experiencing at least the threat of economic insecurity, if they had not already become unemployed, been forced to the verge of starvation, or gone on relief. . . . There was a widespread disturbance of cultural norms and frames of reference, and thousands of people felt that they had lost their status in society. This impairment of status was naturally accompanied by problems of ego involvement. In a society that had emphasized so strongly that individual effort was the key to success and respectability, many people now appeared as hopeless failures: they were obsessed with feelings of guilt for their inability to cope with the system. To these people, Aberhart's explanation of the "real" causes of the depression—and of their plight—brought a new outlook on life. In making clear to them that they were not personally responsible for their desperate situation, in naming the bankers and financiers as the "devils" who had ruined them, he lifted (as in the religious confessional or the psychiatric clinic) the heavy burden of the guilt of failure from their lives and started them on the road back from ego displacement to ego enhancement.

In a society in which the individual is also motivated by the desire to maintain or increase his own feelings of self-regard, Aberhart helped his followers to achieve ego enhancement by insisting on their direct participation in the activities of the Social Credit movement. Through incessant *personal* effort, a new orientation was given to their lives and . . . many of them exhibited surprising qualities of local leadership. In addition, the movement appealed to their feelings of self-regard in that it promised a restored, a redefined, or a greatly improved status for all of them when victory should be achieved. Aberhart's success as a leader was partly due to his ability to persuade so many people to work so vigorously for the "cause": these people, on the other hand, were willing to work so hard because they experienced thereby so much psychological healing of their disorganized lives. They escaped from the horrors of the depression by developing new ego involvements in the Social Credit movement.

Although Aberhart always paraded his Queen's University degree and his titles as Principal of Crescent Heights High School and Dean of the Prophetic Bible Institute, he was careful also to preserve membership character with his followers. To maintain a "folksy" appeal, he had an act . . . in which he would come to the platform in a tatttered, patched up "coat of many colours" to illustrate the fallacious approaches of various well-known political leaders to the problems of the depression. His grammatical errors, although made unintentionally, served to increase this folksy appeal. He received rich and poor alike in his office at the Bible Institute, with the same unflagging interest in their problems. He appeared to his followers as a man who was absolutely devoted to their cause. It is not surprising that people identified themselves with a leader who possssed such characteristics. This identification included an acceptance of *his* objectives as *their* objectives, of *his* unusual mixture of religion and economics as *their* interpretation of the world. His followers were so convinced of his sincerity and conviction that they felt, in their turn, that he identified himself with them, and Aberhart naturally encouraged the development of this attitude.

Ego involvement in the movement became so acute for many people that they refused to discuss the validity of the Social Credit proposals with opponents or, finally, even to listen to the speeches of leaders of other political parties, whose meetings they boycotted. By the summer of 1935 a large number of Social Crediters had developed such intolerance that they viewed any attemtp to analyse Social Credit theories critically as a personal attack on William Aberhart. As we have seen, the incisive, scientific analyses of Social Credit presented by the vice-president of the U.F.A., Norman F. Priestley, in a brilliant series of radio broadcasts, lashed them to fury: they retaliated not by rational arguments but by writing abusive and even scurrilous letters to Priestley, questioning his right to criticise "that Man of God, William Aberhart." Nor would they listen to Professor Angus, spokesman for the Economic Safety League. Two weeks before the election, several of the U.F.A. leaders finally realized the nature of the social movement with which they were confronted. "A dead calm," one of the then Cabinet ministers has put it, "descended over our meetings. We moved like ghosts across Alberta, and everywhere the Social Crediters faced us in ice-cold silence. We carried out our assignments and kept up a bold front, but I knew we had hopelessly lost."

The social disintegration into which Alberta drifted as the depression wore on had produced a state of mind in which thousands of people were expressing a desire for a strong-willed, dauntless leader who would take them out of the wilderness: they realized, however dimly in many instances, that only collective action under a great leader could solve their problems. Aberhart's imposing physical presence, his performances as orator and organizer, his resolute and inflexible will, his infinite resourcefulness, his ability to hypnotize people by his voice, his contagious belief in himself—all these characteristics combined to produce in many people the attitude that "Here is the *Leader*." In the crises which occurred at various times it was always personal allegiance and absolute loyalty to William Aberhart that finally prevailed, and not any agreement on thought or action. Charismatic leadership gave singular unity and additional drive and momentum to a movement that already maintained, on the philosophical side, the inevitability of the realization of Social Credit in the world. To the assertion that Social Credit could not, under the B.N.A. Act, be applied in the province of Alberta, his followers had one simple, confident answer—"William Aberhart will find a way. If we all stand behind him we can build a new world under his leadership."

If Aberhart's character as the prophet of the Social Credit movement gave his leadership a Messianic quality, his ability as an organizer and planner was no less remarkable. Around his person the whole movement gravitated and, with the exception of the short period in the spring of 1934, he maintained undisputed control over its development. The strategy and tactics that gradually emerged in the course of this development may be considered in terms of six major factors: systematic instruction, a people's movement, the use of old norms, the media of propaganda, dramatization, and the groups.

Throughout its . . . rise the Social Credit movement . . . emphasized its continuity with a long-existing religious movement. But, as a movement in its own right, it was born in the basement of the Bible Institute the night its leader began systematic instruction in the literature of Social Credit. Those who received this instruction had an irresistible feeling that they had gone back to school to study the causes of the depression and its remedy under a master teacher. The experiment was so successful that its members enthusiastically invited others to take part. Systematic instruction was the dynamic [factor] underlying the organization of the groups. As the movement developed, hundreds of people had been so well trained in the philosophy of Social Credit that they could organize and conduct new study groups on their own initiative. Organization within the organization gathered momentum and enabled Aberhart to extend the movement indefinitely.

The response of the people was, indeed, so enthusiastic that Aberhart was able, after a few months, to maintain truly that it was a "people's movement." He invariably said to his audiences, "It's *your* movement; *you* must carry it to others; I can't solve the problems of the depression but *you* can. Study! Study! Study! And then *you* carry the truths of Social Credit to others." Sometimes the appeal was grimmer, especially after the decision to take the movement into politics, as in the radio refrain, "If *you* have not suffered enough, it is *your* God-given right to suffer more; but if *you* wish to elect *your own* representatives to implement the Social remedy, this is *your* only way out." A person whose interest in Social Credit had been aroused was immediately put to work for the movement, in his family circle, among his relatives, in his neighbourhood district. These tactics account for both the tremendous drawing-power of Social Credit meetings and the remarkable coverage of Alberta that the movement achieved in a short time. People were attracted to a movement which gave so many signs of being aggressive and dynamic.

The structure of the Social Credit organization was given added strength because it paralleled so closely that of the U.F.A. which had been functioning in Alberta for nearly twenty-five years. . . . Aberhart's study groups corresponded to the U.F.A. locals; his zones (usually containing ten or a dozen groups) were modelled on the U.F.A. districts; there was little difference in the constituency organizations of the two movements; and, finally, the Social Credit League was inspired by the U.F.A. provincial convention. For nearly two-and-a-half years, Aberhart, as well as other Social Credit leaders and speakers, had the use of both organizations: as we have seen, they engaged actively in functional penetration of the U.F.A. locals until the Social Credit movement was finally transformed into a political party in April, 1935, only five months before the election. The similarity in the organizational structure of the two movements and Aberhart's tactics of functional penetration made it easier for movements of the U.F.A. to transfer their allegiance to the Social Credit movement. . . . In some locals nearly the whole membership deserted their leaders and went over to Social Credit groups.

Apart from the remarkable personal activity of the people themselves, Social Credit ideas were promoted mainly through the use of the radio, the lengthy speaking tours of Aberhart and Manning in the summers of 1933 and 1934 (and later of numerous local and secondary leaders), the *Social Credit Chronicle*, and the large-scale distribution of literature. Paradoxically enough, newspapers hostile to the movement (and eventually there were scarcely any exceptions) helped to spread the philosophy. The very publicity they gave to the movement through the violence and bitterness of their personal attacks on Aberhart, and the ridicule they heaped on the Social Credit proposals boomeranged; they turned people to the movement who might otherwise merely have watched the great contest from the side-lines.

The most effective medium of propaganda was unquestionably Aberhart's use of the radio. As we have seen, he had already had nearly ten years of experience as a broadcaster; a representative of the British Broadcasting Corporation who visited Canada in the middle 1930's declared there was no device or technique of the radio speaker that Aberhart had not thoroughly mastered; a former Prime Minister of Canada concluded that "Aberhart had the greatest mass appeal of any leader in Canadian history." Whoever has observed in Alberta the far-flung loneliness of the country-side (as in the vista from the great hill east of Cochrane on the Banff road) can appreciate the psychological significance of the penetration of Aberhart's radio voice into thousands of isolated farm homes. He thundered his exposition of Social Credit in a voice which had many tones and ranged up and down the octaves, but perhaps his greatest attraction was his capacity to project his personality over the air. Through his radio addresses, Aberhart built up contacts in every region of Alberta except the Peace River and the far north, to which the Calgary radio station CFCN could scarcely penetrate at that time. Correspondence resulted from these contacts; radio instructions for the formation of groups were sent out and the movement was on its way even in the most isolated districts. It may be doubted if there could have been a Social Credit movement without Aberhart's use of the radio.

Aberhart brought to the promotion of Social Credit ideas all the techniques of dramatic appeal he had developed during twenty-five years as an expounder on Sunday afternoons of Bible prophecy and Christian fundamentalism: whether in religion or politics he could always be depended on to give the public a good show. . . . The response of the people was aroused and sustained through the wide publicity he was able to secure for the movement at each critical stage in its development: by the use of numerous devices such as petitions, appeals to the U.F.A. government, the straw vote, the radio calls for "One Hundred Honest Men," mass meetings, and great picnics and teas. He thus kept the movement rolling so effectively that people listened to the radio or read their papers eagerly for news of it and tried to anticipate what he would be up to next. Even the split in the movement which occurred in the spring of 1934 merely heightened the tension among the people and dramatized anew the movement.

Dramatic effects were perhaps nowhere so successful as in his radio plays in which a cast of characters representing various vested interests (the Banking system, the mortgage companies, industry, etc.) argued with Aberhart and Manning (always the heroes of the piece) the merits of Social Credit. The most spectacular of these was, of course, "the Man From Mars" series. . . . The opponents of Social Credit were never able to put their case before the public with anything approaching Aberhart's effectiveness, and his use of dramatization must be considered an important psychological factor in the appeal of the movement.

The study groups were the genuine organizational foundation of the movement. When public enthusiasm for Social Credit was approaching the stage of mass hysteria in the summer of 1935 there were 63 groups in Calgary alone, and some 1,800 in the whole province. Membership in the groups ranged from 10 to 800; many of them had between 100 and 200. The groups were privileged to send delegates directly to the Central Council or later to the Social Credit League in proportion to their numbers; they also functioned as the principal medium through which funds were raised for the movement. Groups usually held weekly or fortnightly meetings, and for years the main item on the agenda was the study of Social Credit literature.

Other social movements have used the group form of organization, but a close examination of the Social Credit groups suggests that they probably played a much more important role in Alberta than in movements elsewhere. Considered psychologically, the groups had three important functions: they sustained the microcosm; they developed a remarkable type of primitive comradeship; and, as the movement changed into a political party, they maintained in the minds of their members the hope of the ultimate realization of Social Credit in the world.

Why did Social Credit, rather than some other philosophy, for example socialism, become so widely accepted among the people of Alberta as the hope of salvation? Would Aberhart have been equally successful as the leader of a socialistic movement? Only speculative answers can be given to such questions, but various considerations may be adduced. Let us explore the possibilities in terms of philosophy, leadership, and methods.

. . . Social Credit fitted in with the norms of a province where monetary reform as a solution of economic problems had long been advocated. As such, it exhibited a remarkable congruence with preferred group tendencies. Socialism, as contrasted with Social Credit, had no real roots in the Alberta community. The weakness of the appeal of socialism may be attested by the fact that its devotees among the U.F.A. Members of Parliament were themselves strongly attracted to monetary reform in general, and to Social Credit in particular, both as an explanation and as a solution of the problems created by the depression. The indecision that existed in the minds of leading Alberta founders of the C.C.F. concerning the competing claims of socialism and Social Credit confirms our view that the existing social norms were heavily weighted in favour of the latter.

Given more favourable circumstances than actually existed for its reception in the Alberta of the 1930's, it is conceivable that the philosophy of socialism could have been presented in such a way as to satisfy "the desire for meaning" of the better educated classes of the community. Socialism offers at least as plausible an explanation of the cause and cure of depressions as Social Credit. But the former represents a much more penetrating, as well as a much more comprehensive, critique of the capitalistic system than the latter. Then, too, the objectives of socialism seem to be much more remote and difficult of realization than those of Social Credit. As such, the latter offered the more immediate and, therefore, under depression conditions, the more attractive lure of the satisfaction of needs than the former. Social Credit was undoubtedly presented in such a grossly over-simplified form that even the most economically and politically illiterate person thought he understood it. It may be doubted whether even Aberhart could have presented socialism in such a way that it would have met the conditions of suggestibility that existed in Alberta during the 1930's. Nor should it be forgotten that Social Credit lends itself admirably to the kind of exposition of which Aberhart was capable, whereas socialism does not.

Socialism is not, in fact, the type of philosophy that would have appealed, in any significant sense, to a man of Aberhart's capacities and temperament. Whether considered in terms of nature or nurture, Aberhart was an arch-conservative in education, religion, and politics. The Social Credit movement has always been at great pains to appear as a *reform* rather than a revolutionary movement. As such, it has differentiated itself sharply from socialism (whether Fabian or Marxian) in several important respects. It seeks a limited objective, the transformation of the monetary and financial system of capitalism (it will make capitalism "work"), never the revolutionary reconstruction of society at large. It is strongly steeped in the current *mores* of capitalistic society. It attempts to establish a claim on existing institutions by emphasizing its respectability and its essentially Christian character. Finally, as a merging of social reformist and religious interests, Social Credit has constantly reaffirmed

the ideal values of Christian capitalistic society. Aberhart would not, therefore, have been equally successful as the leader of a socialist movement
for the reason that the philosophy of socialism was utterly foreign to his
mind and personality. But it would probably be difficult to discover a leader
whose intellectual and emotional capacities were more ideally suited for
the acceptance and propagation of the philosophy of Social Credit.

In the light, then, of the conditions that existed in Alberta,
as well as of Aberhart's actual capacities and personality, it was inevitable
that a Social Credit rather than a socialist movement would prevail. This
conclusion is confirmed by the historical fact that socialism was, in reality, an alternative to Social Credit in 1935. While it is true that socialism
appeared as such an alternative only within the equivocal context of the
U.F.A. movement, it was still an alternative. Surely the inability of socialist ideas to revitalize the decaying U.F.A. movement may be adduced in
further support of our argument.

Indeed, for well over two decades following its disengage-
ment from the U.F.A. in 1938, the C.C.F. was unable to make headway
against the Social Credit movement. The perennial failure of the C.C.F. in
the province of its birth to defeat the Social Credit party may be taken as
a final justification of our view that not even Aberhart could have led a
socialist movement to victory in 1935. But such a final justification requires a consideration of the bitter struggle between the Social Credit and
socialist movements in Alberta in the year following the memorable election of 1935. . . .

15

The C.C.F. in Saskatchewan

S. M. LIPSET

*

The rapid acceptance of new ideas and movements in Saskatchewan can be attributed mainly to the high degree of organization. The small rural communities are forced to adjust to changing economic and social situations. Interest in political and economic matters is continually being stimulated. Farmers derive most of their ideas and knowledge of larger problems and policies from well-informed neighbours who hold community posts.

The Wheat Pool, the co-operatives, the agrarian Progressive Party of the 1920's, and the C.C.F. were all built rapidly through this structure of organized farmer opinion. The role of the social structure of the western wheat belt in facilitating the rise of new movements has never been sufficiently appreciated by historians and sociologists. To the economic and cultural factors usually associated with the development of these movements should be added the variable of social structure. Repeated challenges and crises forced the western farmers to create many more community institutions (especially co-operatives and economic pressure groups) than are necessary in a more stable area. These groups in turn provided a structural basis for immediate action in critical situations.

Though it was a new radical party, the C.C.F. did not have to build up an organization from scratch. It was organized from the start by the local "class" and community leaders of rural Saskatchewan. The fact that the province was so well organized on an occupational basis enabled the new party to obtain the support of the politically conscious community leaders. By the early 1940's, C.C.F. committees, composed in the main of the same people who were the officials of other rural organizations, were operating in almost every district in the province. It was this "machine" that brought the C.C.F. to power.

Today the C.C.F. had become the political voice of the organized agrarian community. The organized farmers are brought into direct contact with "their" government by active participation in a class political party that controls the state.

---

*Reprinted from *Agrarian Socialism*, University of California Press, Berkeley and Los Angeles, 1950.

The basic unit of political organization in rural Saskatchewan is the poll, the smallest voting district. Each provincial constituency is divided into from one hundred to two hundred polls. The C.C.F. has attempted to build up in each district a working committee of two or three people who will take charge of C.C.F. educational work among the one hundred to two hundred voters in the poll. Above the local organizations is the constituency. A C.C.F. constituency has a committee of twelve to twenty-five members and an executive committee of seven to twelve members. The committees are elected at annual conventions, which are attended by three delegates from each poll. The leading body of the entire party is the Provincial Council, which has representatives from each constituency and meets several times a year. The provincial party organization supervises the work of each constituency body. Between Council meetings, the party is governed by an executive body of nine. This provincial organization is controlled by the annual provincial convention. Each constituency convention elects ten delegates to the provincial convention. The convention elects top party officers and determines policy.[1]

If the formal pattern of the C.C.F. party organization were actually followed, about 24,000 people would be active party members, either as members of poll committees or as delegates to the party conventions and committees. Actually, this optimum figure is never reached, for many districts have no active poll committees. In recent years the average attendance at the fifty annual C.C.F. constituency conventions has been about 100 delegates, 5,000 people in all. Many more electors, however, are active in the local organizations than attend as convention delegates. One could safely estimate that between 10,000 and 15,000 people take part in the actual operation of the party.

Between elections, this activity does not include much formal party work. Poll committees usually meet once or twice a year to discuss the work of the local and larger party bodies. They arrange public meetings for party leaders and enroll new members. In some areas, committees meet regularly to discuss party policy and to analyze books and outlines suggested by the provincial office. The constituency committees, which have about 1,000 members, have much greater responsibilities and consequently meet from six to twelve times a year. These committees are the grass-roots bodies which influence the work of the C.C.F. members of the legislature and the provincial party.

The fact that the majority of C.C.F. members and officials are not continuously active in party work does not mean that they are not acting politically in other community roles. Most of the active C.C.F. members have administrative tasks in rural organizations. They are members of local co-operative store boards, Wheat Pool committees, and U.F.C. executive bodies, and do not differentiate between their activities in these organizations and in the C.C.F. One informant expressed this feeling clearly.

It's really all one movement that we have here. We are building socialism through the Wheat Pool, through our co-op store,

*through our U.F.C. local, as well as through the C.C.F. They are all part
of one movement, the "people's movement." Sometimes one organization
or fight is more important than the other, but we need them all. The fact
that our poll committee doesn't meet except before conventions doesn't
mean the C.C.F.'ers here don't care about the party. We feel that we are
building the C.C.F. when we build our co-op store, and we are building
co-operation and destroying the profit system when we built the C.C.F.*

At first glance the relationship between the C.C.F. and
other rural community organizations appears similar to the pattern of
party-society relations advocated by the Communist Party. Communists
want to be the vanguard of the working class, the class leaders. To
accomplish this, they attempt to permeate working-class organizations
and become their officials. In the Soviet Union, Communists are placed in
key positions in trade-unions, co-operatives, and local governments. In
democratic countries they use the tactics of "boring from within" to
achieve positions of leadership.[2]

In Saskatchewan, however, the "vanguard," the leaders of
the farming community, started the C.C.F. As a result, C.C.F. activity
and community activity are closely interrelated. This situation is not a
result of any planned action, but is, rather, a consequence of the tight
organization of the farming community on an occupational basis. The
C.C.F. is the class party, the farmers' party, and thus controls the farmers' organizations. Many leaders of the C.C.F. and of rural organizations
are not aware of this close interrelationship. The party makes no direct
efforts to influence other institutions and has no explicit policy for its
members to follow in them. There are no C.C.F. caucuses in the co-operatives or other rural groups. In practice, however, most of the secondary
leaders are C.C.F. members and therefore support the policy of the party
and the C.C.F. government. The leaders are, in fact, continually engaged
in political activity.

The relationship between the C.C.F. and rural community
organizations is a two-way affair. C.C.F. leaders in their capacity as local
government officials and co-operative leaders know the needs of the
community and the effect of government policies on the rural community.
They use the party organization as a direct channel of communication to
the legislature and the cabinet. A stream of resolutions moves constantly
from local and constituency committees to the Provincial Council and the
government.

Since the election of 1944, interest in C.C.F. conventions
and governing committees has grown greatly. Through participation in
this organization at least 10,000 people are led to feel that they are taking
a direct part in the establishment of government policy. The vitality of

---

[1]C.C.F. (Saskatchewan Section), *Handbook* (Regina, 1946).
[2]Commission of the Central Committee of the Communist Party
of the Soviet Union, *History of the Communist Party of the
Soviet Union* (New York: International Publishers, 1939), pp.
46-49.

grass-roots participation in rural Saskatchewan leads to vigorous criticism of the activities of the government and the party. The active members in the C.C.F. are mainly experienced local leaders, who represent the grass-roots, not the summits, of the rural community. The C.C.F. differs from many European socialist parties and the nonsocialist parties in the United States and Canada in that its secondary leaders are unpaid and receive little additional status from their party position. The party officials had status in the community before they became C.C.F. leaders, and therefore are relatively independent of top control. This pattern of grass-roots democracy runs through all the farmers' movements in Saskatchewan, and the C.C.F. is only continuing it. In order to perpetuate interest and loyalty to the party, C.C.F. leaders are almost forced to encourage criticism and suggestions from the rank and file. Many C.C.F. leaders, from Premier Douglas down, reiterate that they are only the servants of the majority of the party. Theoretically, the party leadership and the government must accept any policy adopted by the provincial convention.

Many members of the C.C.F. now conceive of government as a tool to be manipulated by the people. They come to constituency conventions fully prepared to let the government know their opinions. The resolutions adopted at conventions reveal the operation of this conception of direct democracy:

That the Government investigate and pass legislation which will stop completely the overloading and crowding of live stock in stock cars, trucks or any other vechicle.

That a stop be made to the shipping of live stock unfit for human consumption to packing houses or stock yards. The only exception being stock clearly designated for purposes other than human consumption.[3]

Whereas the Department of Health is prepared to go to considerable work and expense to have all citizens tested for T.B. to have the disease controlled and

Whereas after the test has been taken and even if your family shows no signs of the disease they may go home and drink milk from a diseased cow

Therefore be it resolved that the Government make an extensive test of all cattle as soon as possible regardless of whether the present veterinary profession have time to do it all or not.[4]

That we the delegates of Saltcoats Convention, especially the women members, desire the Government to investigate the possibility of the Woolen Mill handling woven materials, as blankets from this class of goods fulfill many useful purposes on the farm.[5]

The lack of inhibitions in criticizing government policy can be seen in a number of resolutions.

Be it resolved that we consider the five C.C.F. Cabinet Ministers who talked and voted against the resolution to exempt single men up to $1,200 and married men up to $2,500 on the Federal Income Tax, were badly out of line . . . especially Mr. Fines, who actually implied that he *would tax the lower paid classes exactly as the Capitalist King Government is doing.[6]*

Whereas the existence of natural gas and oil in commercial quantities in the Province of Saskatchewan has been proven conclusively;

And whereas the C.C.F. as a Socialist Party believes in and advocates the public ownership of the natural resources of this Province for the benefit of the people of Saskatchewan;

And whereas a resolution was passed at the 1945 Provincial Convention urging the Government of Saskatchewan to undertake the development and distribution of natural gas and oil in this Province;

And whereas natural gas and oil in the Province of Saskatchewan continues to be extensively exploited by private persons and concerns;

Therefore be it resolved that the Government of Saskatchewan be called upon to show cause why the exploitation of these resources has been allowed to fall into private hands.

And be it further resolved that the Government of Saskatchewan be immediately called upon to place these resources under social ownership, control and operation for the immense benefit of the people of Saskatchewan.[7]

Free forums, such as the constituency conventions provide, strengthen the C.C.F. in innumerable ways. The top leaders can never depart far from the thinking of the rank and file without being made aware of it. The conventions serve, also, to preserve the vitality and support of the party. In interviews many C.C.F. members stressed this existence of direct democracy through the party.

Well, what did you think of that speech? I really made B. [a Cabinet Minister] squirm. Don't misunderstand it though. I think B. is doing a good job, but like all men, he makes mistakes and he has to be told about them. That's the wonderful thing about this party. The members really run it. No one in this room would have the least hesitation about telling anyone from Coldwell or Douglas down that he is wrong if he thinks so. Can you see any Liberal supporter doing that to old Gardiner? Why, did you know the Liberals haven't had a convention since 1933.[8]

To what degree can the formal structure and appearance of grass-roots democracy in the C.C.F. be said to be real? Do the people really govern? One cabinet minister, in discussing the role of conventions, said:

---

[3]C.C.F. (Saskatchewan Section), *Provincial Convention Delegates Handbook* (Regina, 1945), p. 33.

[4]*Ibid.*, p. 35.

[5]*Ibid.*, 1946, p. 51.

[6]*Ibid.*, p. 45.

[7]*Ibid.*, p. 51. It should be noted that the last two resolutions were passed at constituency conventions at which cabinet ministers were present.

[8]The Saskatchewan Liberal party held a convention in 1947.

They are today the most important part of the C.C.F. organization. I think we are doing good work and that the majority of the people approve our policies. However this will not keep us in power. A lot of good governments have been defeated and lost power. Our people will not actively support and work for the C.C.F. once their feeling of "Get the Rascals out" is over. . . .

The one thing that maintains our active support is the feeling that the people run the government, that we are only their servants. The conventions reinforce that feeling every year. It is therefore important that we never refuse to carry out anything demanded at the Provincial Convention unless we have a darn good explanation. Our supporters will put up with mistakes or with inefficiency, but they won't stand for dictation. The one thing that can kill the C.C.F. is the idea that we are another party like the Liberals and Conservatives, that the government is composed of another group of politicians and "heelers" who come around every four years for votes.

Cabinet ministers and party leaders appear to act on these principles. *This does not mean that they do not make policy.* In fact, almost all important provincial policies are set by the cabinet and the members of the legislature. At provincial conventions the final form of resolutions, suggesting changes in policy, is usually determined by top leaders. This control, however, is exercised by men who combine superior oratorical ability, status, and information. When the leaders oppose a resolution they are able to control the overwhelming majority of delegates.

In the 1946 convention a resolution proposing government ownership of gas and oil appeared to be favoured by the majority of the delegates, for it had been a traditional demand of the farmers' movement and of the C.C.F. Two cabinet ministers armed with statistical data were able to convince the convention that the oil and gas fields were not yet proved commercial fields and that the cost of developing them as a risk investment was beyond the financial ability of the province.

On certain issues, however, government and party leaders have been voted down and accepted their defeat. The 1946 provincial convention adopted two resolutions recommending changes in government policy that had previously been rejected by the cabinet and the C.C.F. legislative caucus: one supported the right of married women to work for the government, and the other urged the forty-four-hour week for labour with no reduction in pay. At the following session of the legislature both proposals of the convention were adopted.

There has been, however, one major issue in which the government has not completely followed convention instructions. The 1945 and 1946 conventions urged the government to fill all policy-making positions in the civil service with persons who support C.C.F. ideals. The cabinet at first refused, but gradually has been making concessions to the pressure from the conventions.

Direct democracy in the C.C.F. and other Saskatchewan

farm organizations is limited by the extent of the knowledge, experience, and interests of the secondary leaders. C.C.F. conventions fail to pass resolutions on a multitude of important problems because the delegates lack opinions about, or knowledge of, these problems. The conventions rarely bother with the details of a government health scheme, the methods of operation of government industry, the problems of debt refunding or repayment, priorities in economic planning, or provincial proposals to Dominion-provincial conferences, though these administrative details may be more important than the broad over-all policies with which the resolutions deal. Other important issues neglected by the conventions are foreign policy and other aspects of national affairs that do not affect agriculture. The overwhelming majority of resolutions reflect the day-to-day economic and social concerns of farmers and workers: farm regulations, provincial tax legislation, roads, liquor laws, and social services.[9]

The extensive grass-roots discussion of governmental problems is not new in the history of the province. Long before the C.C.F. was formed, the Saskatchewan Grain Growers' Association met in annual district and provincial conventions to adopt policies to be urged on governments. The annual meeting of the S.G.G.A. was known as the "Farmers' Parliament" and was well attended. The Liberal Party, which then controlled the province, paid close attention to the actions of these conventions and wherever possible implemented the recommendations of the S.G.G.A. In order to maintain the support of the organized farmers, it offered cabinet posts to Grain Growers' officials.[10] The provincial Liberals lost their hold on the farmers' movement when the Progressives were formed in 1920, because the federal Liberal Party would not meet many of the agrarian demands.

The fact that extensive participation in the Saskatchewan C.C.F. is not a result of the growth of a new political movement or of some characteristic inherent in the C.C.F. becomes clear if the organization is compared with the party elsewhere in Canada where it has been successful. Of those voting for the C.C.F. in Saskatchewan, 15 per cent were party members. The British Columbia C.C.F., which is largely an urban working-class movement, won 39 per cent of the total vote in the 1946 provincial election, but less than 5 per cent of its supporters are members of the party. In one Vancouver constituency that has elected socialist or C.C.F. candidates since 1930, party leaders do not know who their supporters are, and only a handful of them are in the party.[11] In Toronto the C.C.F. received 133,443 votes in 1945, but has never enlisted more than 3.8 per cent of this figure in the movement. Actually, the Toronto C.C.F. has considerably less than 1,000 active members. The growth of the C.C.F. movement in Toronto and Vancouver has not been the result of, nor has it resulted in, an increase in direct political

---

[9]C.C.F. Convention, *Handbooks*, 1945, 1946, 1947.
[10]Hopkins Moorehouse, *Deep Furrows* (Toronto: George J. McLeod, Ltd., 1918), pp. 230-233, 265.
[11]From interviews with C.C.F. leaders.

participation by the masses. The party in these cities resembles the traditional North American parties, with little direct contact between the organization and the major part of the electorate.

If one notes the differences between the community structure of Saskatchewan and that of cities such as Toronto and Vancouver (1950), the relationship between structure and the extent of political activity becomes clear. The 600,000 rural residents of Saskatchewan elect 2,100 members of municipal councils and 15,000 members of school boards. Large cities, however, have an insignificant number of community positions compared to their total population. The 800,000 citizens of Toronto elect only 24 members of a council and 18 members of the school board.

In most North American cities the majority of political and community posts are held by members of the middle and upper classes.[12] The city councils are filled with lawyers and other business or professional people. Many community organizations such as hospital boards, Y.M. C.A. boards, and community chests are dominated by members of the upper classes. This again is in striking contrast to rural Saskatchewan, where farmers must fill these posts themselves.

Trade-unionism is the major institutional exception in urban life in which workers are given an opportunity to hold office and take responsiblity. The ratio of officials to total union membership, however, is often very low. There are many union locals with thousands of members and two to twenty officials. In Saskatchewan the ratio of members to officials in the co-operatives and educational organizations ranges from five to one to twenty to one. The Saskatchewan Wheat Pool, the largest farm organization, has a total membership of 60,000 to 70,000. About 11,000 farmers are elected members of Wheat Pool committees in their localities. One out of every six members of this organization, which most closely approximates a trade-union in rural Saskatchewan, is a local official who meets regularly with others from six to twelve times a year to discuss and act on local, provincial, and national matters. Local members usually attend meetings twice a year. The average local Pool organization has about sixty members.

The co-operative movement is extremely weak in the urban areas of Canada and the United States. In contrast with Europe, co-operatives in America have not succeeded in interesting many workers. The co-operatives, therefore, do not serve as a basis for training leaders and creating channels of communication between workers and larger institutions. The few urban co-operatives that do exist tend to be led by members of the middle class. The breakdown or absence of real neighborhoods in urban centres has also served to prevent the formation of a local corps of leaders. The political machine has provided the only effective urban leadership group, and it could hardly be expected to be a vehicle for new ideas and for social change. Outside the factory, the urban working class is dispersed. There are few channels for genuine intraclass communication.

The building of a new mass political organization is, therefore, much more difficult in a city than in a rural community or small town. It is almost impossible to locate the informal leaders of the lower classes. The people are not accustomed to making political decisions. In the anonymity of city living, organized person-to-person political contact is difficult.

* * * * *

Widespread community participation and political interest have developed in Saskatchewan in response to the environmental and economic problems involved in creating a stable community. No one factor—the small units of government, the vulnerable one-crop economy, the "one-class" society, the sparse settlement of the area, the continual economic and climatic hazards—developed because of an interest in maintaining an active grass-roots democracy or a concern for politics. The combination of all these factors, however, has made for a healthy and active democracy. Unplanned structural conditions have facilitated rapid popular response to economic and social challenges and the acceptance of new methods and ideas.

The Saskatchewan pattern, while offering confirmation of the "small democracy" theories, provides no panacea for those who would plan society so as to create the basis for popular community activity. Early in the nineteenth century Thomas Jefferson advocated "general political organization on the basis of small units, small enough so that all its members could have direct communication with one another and take care of all small community affairs."[13] This and similar proposals have been ignored, for small communities were not functional in the development of a great industrial nation. In the nineteenth century, anyone who objected to the growth of large cities was called a "reactionary" or a "utopian" trying to block the march of civilization.

The small agrarian community in Saskatchewan has been preserved only because this pattern was functional in the wheat economy. The grain companies, the co-operatives, the political parties, and the farmers, all would have preferred larger communities and more centralization. They would laugh at the rational democrat's argument for their type of living and their type of economy. To the people of the West, decentralization has meant poor community services and little access to many material and cultural values. They welcomed the automobile and better roads, which are resulting in the breakdown of the smaller communities and the growth of large towns and cities. It remains true, however, that the smaller the community and organizational unit, and the less economically and socially stratified the society, the better are the possibilities for grass-roots political activity. Saskatchewan demonstrates that widespread and continuous political interest is not incompatible with efficient, large-scale organization.

---

[12]Gunnar Myrdal, *An American Dilemma* (New York: Harper & Row, Publishers, 1944), p. 714.

[13]John Dewey, *Freedom and Culture* (New York: G. P. Putnam's Sons, 1939), p. 159.

16

The New Democratic Party And Canadian Politics

W. BAKER and T. PRICE

*

Canada has long had two major national parties, built around a considerable diversity of interests. The Borden coalition of 1917 and the Progressive Party of the early 1920's were temporary departures from a developing two-party system; and even with minor parties contesting every election since 1921, until recently the main question following national elections has been: which of the major parties has won enough seats to form a majority in the House of Commons? It is only in the 1960's that a permanent multiple party system has been considered possible.

One reason for the apparent break-up of the two-party system, was the emergence in 1932 of the CCF, and in 1961 of its successor, the New Democratic Party. The persistence and evident increasing strength of the New Democratic Party, moreover, could be the single most significant factor in sustaining minority government. Since 1961 the New Democratic Party has continued a philosophy and style of politics that originated with the CCF. Many of the early CCF'ers were outspoken and aggressive democratic socialists. The *Regina Manifesto* of 1933 contained the declaration, "We aim to replace the present capitalistic system, with its inherent injustice and inhumanity, by a social order from which the domination and exploitation of one class by another will be eliminated, in which economic planning will supersede unregulated private enterprise and competition, and in which genuine democratic self-government based upon economic equality will be possible"; and the programme subsequently outlined covered the socialization of all financial machinery, the socialization of transportation, communications, electric power, and a variety of other essential industries, a national plan of external trade, socialized health services, a national labour code, and a national progressive taxation policy.[1] It was a happy circumstance for the CCF that the capitalistic system was based in central Canada, so that agrarian radicals could combine with labour and a scattering of intellectuals under the democratic socialist banner. The growth of the CCF as a political party was aided by the great depression which demonstrated the failure of capitalism.

Organized to wrest political, economic, and social advantage from entrenched elites, the CCF was competing with the major political parties that had shown an ability to work with these elites. Therefore, it was necessary to develop a political style incorporating grass-roots financing, the use of volunteer campaigners, and the involvement of the party rank and file in party decisions. That the CCF continued to exist at all, in contrast to the early demise of the Progressives as a political party, and in the face of determined efforts by the Liberals to reduce its impact, was itself an accomplishment.[2] During its thirty years as a national party the CCF demonstrated that democratic socialism, albeit flexibly defined, could form the basis of organized political activity outside the framework of the major parties.

Post-war prosperity and Liberal success in attracting the left-wing voter robbed the CCF of some of its elan. By the mid 1950's some of its leaders pressed for a more pragmatic approach and for greater attention to political organization. The party's Winnipeg Declaration of 1956 embodied a revised democratic socialism, in which an emphasis on the mixed economy and on public-private co-operation in social planning was substituted for widespread public ownership.[3] The aims of 1956 were essentially the same as those of 1933. Reviewing the position of the socialist in 1956, David Lewis, as one of the leading spokesmen of the CCF, stressed that the socialist ends were a classless or egalitarian society, both within the confines of a single nation and worldwide; human freedom, "a society in which the worth and dignity of every human being is recognized; economic and social security; and a lasting peace based on freedom and equality among nations." The party's means to achieve these ends, however, were to be different from those of the founders, particularly concerning the extent of public ownership. Lewis stated the change in the following way: "Socialists . . . can no longer regard nationalization as an automatic panacea for all ills . . . [D]evelopments . . . have . . . shown that there are available in the modern economy, tools of control and of planning which can be effectively applied without actually replacing private with public ownership in all spheres. . . . Public ownership in a democratic society and under a democratic socialist government will never cover more than a part of the economy."[4]

The changed attitude towards nationalization was significant and reaction to the new position was varied. On the one hand, this

---

[1]See Kenneth McNaught, *A Prophet in Politics* (Toronto: University of Toronto Press, 1959), and particularly Chapter 18, for a discussion of the origins and programme of the early CCF.

[2]J. W. Pickersgill, *The Mackenzie King Record* (Toronto: University of Toronto Press, 1960) includes extracts from King's diary to indicate how carefully King attempted to "cut the ground . . . from under the CCF," p. 601.

[3]*The Winnipeg Declaration of Principles*, adopted at the CCF National Convention in July of 1956, is cited and discussed in Leo Zakuta, *A Protestant Movement Becalmed: A Study of Change in the CCF* (Toronto: University of Toronto Press, 1964). See particularly pp. 169-73.

[4]David Lewis, *A Socialist Takes Stock* (Toronto: Ontario Woodsworth Memorial Foundation, 1956).

was hailed as evidence of the healthy flexibility of democratic socialism; traditional doctrine was modified because of a new awareness of the threat to the individual from big bureaucracy and mass society generally, coupled with an awareness that other means existed for reducing the power of the corporate elite and creating a more egalitarian society. On the other hand, the CCF was criticized by Zakuta for temporizing like the major parties, "the move from idealistic sect to pragmatic church".[5]

The CCF was attempting to come to grips with its political environment without losing its identity as the party of the democratic left. It had demonstrated its ability as policy innovator and as a goad to the major parties. It had been a useful funnel for public pressure for a more egalitarian society, but even at its zenith in the early 1940's, its success was moderate. This was no longer considered sufficient by a party that sought to further its social objectives by forming the government as it had done in Saskatchewan.

In 1956, the Trades and Labour Congress and the Canadian Congress of Labour had united to form the Canadian Labour Congress (CLC). The 1958 Winnipeg convention of the CLC virtually decided the future of the CCF. While elements from the Canadian labour movement had been strongly invoved in the CCF, it had never really become the political arm of labour. The TLC in particular had tended to believe, with Samuel Gompers, that the labour vote must remain uncommitted, to be used judiciously to gain favours from the government. Increasing labour struggles in the 1950's, coupled with concern over government attitudes to organized labour, led labour leaders to come out strongly for increased involvement in party politics.

At its second convention, in April of 1958, the CLC overwhelmingly supported a resolution calling for the formation of a new party as "an effective alternative force to the old parties." The executive of the CLC was instructed to join with the CCF, interested farm organizations, and others to form a new political party. The CLC supported CCF ideals and practices, but believed a new party would both emphasize labour's commitment and create a broader base on which to build needed electoral strength.

There had always been a strong pro-CCF group within the CCL, and a smaller one within the TLC; at first such CCF groups worked hard to get the CLC to endorse the CCF. Recognizing the possibility of an initial convention rebuff by rank and file union members, and fearing that this would lead to a reversion by the CLC to an uncommitted position, they became convinced that it was the better strategy to work for a new party.

The founding convention of the New Democratic Party was held in Ottawa, between July 31st and August 4th, 1961. The programme did not differ significantly from that of the 1956 Winnipeg Declaration.[6] The major emphasis was on a planned economy, the regulation of the abuses of the capitalist system, improved social welfare, and the general enrichment of life through cultural and recreational measures. A neutralist foreign policy was rejected, and a more internationalist role for Canada with less dependence on the United States was suggested. A non-nuclear defence policy was advocated, with Canada to support the United Nations and maintain a mobile peace-keeping force. Finally, firmer measures to reduce foreign control of Canadian industry were advocated. These policies have remained and around them specific proposals have been built.

The New Democratic Party differed from the CCF in two important respects: resolute attempts were made to involve French Canada in the party, and a closer link was established with organized labour. The New Democratic Party was formed with the expectation that it would become a major, national party. If the CCF ever hoped realistically for national power, it sought it as the reform party of the economically and socially disadvantaged. While accepting this, the New Democratic Party sought to broaden its electoral base considerably, by seeking French-Canadian support as a first step.

The programme adopted by the founding convention included a statement attributing to the federal system the role of insuring "the united development of the two nations which originally associated to form the Canadian partnership . . ." A second paragraph entitled "Canada as a Nation", read:

> Our pride in Canada as a nation is enhanced by our consciousness of the two national cultures which form the basis of Canadian life. We are indeed aware that those who have their roots in the French-speaking community frequently and legitimately use the word "nation" to describe French Canada itself. The New Democratic Party believes that true Canadian unity depends upon equal recognition and respect for both the main cultures of our country.[7]

French-Canadian involvement was also encouraged by the constitutional provision for "a President and an Associate President, one of whom shall be English-speaking and one French-speaking," and for "a Secretary and Associate Secretary, one of whom shall be English-speaking and one French-speaking." There was provision, finally, in a 1963 amendment, for

---

[5]See Leo Zakuta, "Membership in a Becalmed Protest Movement," *Canadian Journal of Economics and Political Science,* XXIV, 2 (1958), 190.

[6]W. D. G. Hunter suggests that pragmatism is the keynote of the programme adopted in 1961: "Instead of boldly proclaiming its faith in socialism . . . the party offers a collection of *ad hoc* Keynesian remedies which it believes will promote progress and stability, lessen inequality and insecurity, advance health and welfare, and preserve human rights and liberties." W. D. G. Hunter, "The New Democratic Party: Antecedents, Policies, Prospects," *Queen's Quarterly,* Autumn (1962), 367.

[7]*Federal Programme of the New Democratic Party,* adopted by its Founding Convention (Ottawa, July 31 - August 4, 1961). pp. 20-21.

a Bi-cultural Council, "to ensure the continuing co-operation of English and French-speaking elements."[8]

The second major change in 1961 was the closer link with the trade unions. The constitution provided for this through affiliated memberships open to "trade unions, farm groups, co-operatives, women's organizations, and other groups and organizations."[9] Affiliated groups were given the right to submit resolutions and to be represented at the governing Convention in the proportion, roughly, of one delegate per thousand members, thus preventing the trade unions achieving the voting dominance in the Convention which they have gained in the British Labour Party. Much more important than this formal provision, however, was the close working relationship between CLC and former CCF leaders, first established during the formative days of transition, and continued after the party was successfully launched. Both the CCF and the CLC agreed from the outset that while ties would be strong they should be somewhat informal, to allay fears of labour dominance. The refusal of Stanley Knowles, then Executive Vice-President of the CLC, to become a vice-president of the party when it was first formed, despite his important role, indicates how scrupulously some of the founders worked to establish the desired relationship. In 1962, prior to announcing his candidacy for a Commons' seat, he severed all formal connections with the CLC and resigned his post.[10]

Organized labour in Canada has remained committed to political action in support of the New Democrats since 1958. Moreover, its tangible support of the party has grown over the years. In December, 1961, 278 locals with a total of 71,010 members were affiliated with the party. By September, 1962, this had risen to 612 locals with 186,295 members; and on August 31st, 1966, there were 679 affiliated locals with a total affiliated membership of 242,000.[11]" This is not a particularly striking growth, especially since membership in the CLC exceeds 1,200,000 members. However, during 1966 a new drive began within the CLC to increase its affiliated membership in the NDP to 300,000 members for 1967. If the drive is successful, the financial base of the NDP will be $180,000 annually from affiliation dues alone.

The gains from increased union interest are broader than merely the increase in affiliation fees. If the interests of the party and organized labour continue to coincide, some of the organizational skill and union finances will go towards strengthening the NDP as a political force. Moreover, in many urban constituencies union members are the party's most reliable workers.

The New Democrats also looked for support from farmers. The early CCFers professed to see a labour-farmer affinity that never did, for them, become a strong alliance. The agrarian west appeared to be pitted against the industrial east, rather than the struggling farmer and worker standing together against the industrial and commercial elites. The western farmer simply did not identify himself with the urban worker. Even in 1966 the National Farmers Union would not become affiliated with the NDP, despite strong approaches by the party, because it wished to remain free to negotiate with all governments, as needs dictated. However, this has not prevented NFU leaders from being active within the party. Moreover, during the past two years, the farmers appear to have adopted some of the techniques of organized labour in seeking political advantage, and the party has been able to take their side in battles with government. There is no evidence, however, that farm support for the NDP approaches that of labour, although the party still hopes to recapture the prairie farmer's vote.

Although the CCF received its initial impetus from western agrarian protest, and the New Democratic Party was strongly promoted by the Canadian Labour Congress and its affiliated unions, the NDP's electoral support does not betray overwhelming reliance on these groups. For a left wing political party, it shows surprisingly little class or occupational bias in its composition or electoral support. This is consistent with the findings of Alford and Regenstreif, that over a period of time there is no clear class-party affinity, whether judged by income, education, or occupation. The most important variations in party support seem to be regional and religious.[12]

The NDP, like the other parties, has clear bases of regional strength. The rural support developed by the CCF in Saskatchewan has dwindled in the last ten years, although it remains fairly powerful at the provincial level, in the absence of any other strong opposition contender. The bases of strength today are areas in which there is a degree of working class consciousness and strong trade unions. These are in parts of British Columbia, in Winnipeg, in certain mining constituencies in Northern Ontario, and in downtown constituencies in Toronto and Hamilton.[13]

---

[8]*The Federal Constitution of the New Democratic Party*, adopted by its Founding Convention (Ottawa, July 31 - August 4, 1961), pp. 9-10, and as amended August, 1963.

[9]While the NDP still hopes to affiliate all kinds of groups (farmer, ethnic, co-operative, etc.), only labour has taken advantage of this provision. That farm groups did not participate was a particular disappointment.

[10]William E. Lyons, *The New Democratic Party in the Canadian Political System* (Unpublished Ph.D. thesis, Pennsylvania State University, 1965), p. 458.

[11]The figures for this paragraph were provided from the Central Records of the New Democratic Party (Ottawa).

[12]Robert Alford, "The Social Bases of Political Cleavage in 1962," John Meisel (ed.), *Papers on the 1962 Election* (Toronto: University of Toronto Press, 1964), pp. 202-3. Peter Regenstreif, *Parties and Voting in Canada: The Diefenbaker Interlude* (Toronto: Longmans, 1965), p. 98.

[13]In a CIPO survey during the 1962 election it was found that the approximate farm and trade union support in the NDP's four best provinces were:

	T.U.	Farm
Ont.	25	8
Sask.	57	18
Man.	39	
B.C.	35	14

R. Alford, *ibid.*, pp. 218, 222.

Both the CCF and the NDP have enjoyed a considerable degree of middle and upper class support, though understandably for a left wing party, proportionately less than the Conservatives and the Liberals have received.[14] The NDP, being unable to attract solid class or occupational support from all regions, is forced to battle for support on the same terms as the other parties. That is, it must canvass for the support of professional, white-collar and unskilled workers, small business men, voters from all classes and all regions. This appeal is reflected in the slate of candidates presented in federal elections, and in the membership and top leadership of the party.

Participation in political activity has been found to be higher among those on the upper levels of the social scale.[15] It is not surprising that the bulk of NDP leadership has been middle class.[16] The party has preferred to select middle class candidates with a fairly high level of education, particularly in urban constituencies of varied social composition where the chances of success seem good. In the 1965 federal election over 50 per cent of the party's candidates could be termed middle class; only 20 per cent were employed as skilled or unskilled workers.[17]

The NDP's support and its most active organizations and membership are now found in the larger urban areas. Even in the 1962 election, the party's first, its strength was over 20 percent in ridings which were urban by 60 per cent or over.[18]

This has increased in the subsequent two elections; the NDP's fate seems tied to urbanization. The mobile individual in the urban environment is likely to break his traditional ties and change his voting pattern. This might explain why the NDP does relatively well in the urban areas and poorly in long-settled, traditional areas such as rural Quebec and the Atlantic Provinces.

The New Democratic Party differs from the CCF in its emphasis on techniques of organization. While the CCF in its earliest years exhibited a certain disdain for organization, the New Democrats have shown the reverse. To a grass-roots structure similar to that of the CCF has been added a central group of organizers. The move towards more effective organization is explained in part by a realization of the difficulties of stimulating, maintaining, and co-ordinating the activities of rank and file members and supporters. Many leading New Democrats believe that the party depends on far greater grass-roots support and involvement than the Liberals and Conservatives command.

From the beginning it was agreed that the New Democratic Party would remain a "grass-roots" party in financing and organization. New Democrats, like the CCF, saw the power base of the Liberals and Conservatives firmly embedded within the community of large industrial and commercial interests, and saw this further reflected in sources of finance, leadership, and in legislative activities.

The organizational structure of the party is, in general, similar to that of the CCF. There is a single hierarchy from the poll committee within the constituency organization, through the respective provincial conventions with their governing councils and executives, to the Federal Convention with its governing Council and Executive. This is not a federalized organization, however, although membership in the party is granted at the provincial level. It is one party, decentralized in form, seeking viable organizations in every constituency. The individual party member is given a role in policy-making through his active control of the delegates attending the all-important provincial and national conventions, and through his part in framing policy resolutions at the constituency level for consideration at the conventions. The federal constitution states that "the Convention shall be the supreme governing body of the Party, and shall have final authority in all matters of federal policy, programme and constitution"; and the power of the Federal Council to govern between the biennial conventions is derived from the Convention. Similar provisions exist in the provincial constitutions, concerning the provincial conventions and councils.

Between conventions the chief policy-making bodies are the Federal Council and the respective provincial councils. Within a province, each riding has the right to send a representative to the council, although in practice inactive ridings will probably not do so, and even some of the more active ridings will miss council meetings if they are held some distance from the riding. Policy questions are discussed at council meetings, and new topics that have arisen since the last convention are taken up. Where the provincial caucus is small, as in Ontario, and where influential party figures are outside the caucus, the council can exert decisive influence on the caucus.

The permanent staff of the party, while small, is influential. The Federal Secretary and the various provincial secretaries are particularly important. In the Federal Office there is a permanent Director of

---

[14]Party support by Socio-Economic Status, 1962.

	A (high)	B	C	D (low)	Total
NDP	8%	7%	14%	10%	12
Liberal	37%	37%	38%	40%	38
P.C.	39%	45%	33%	33%	36

Ibid., p. 210.

[15]S. M. Lipset, *Political Man* (New York: Doubleday, 1959), Chapter VII.

[16]In a survey of five Ottawa ridings in 1965, Howat Noble found that 76.5 per cent of party members (Blishen scale) were upper and lower middle class. This is exceptional, due probably to the non-industrial nature of the city, but even in industrial areas such as Windsor 50 per cent is not uncommon. Howat P. Noble, *Membership Participation and Political Organization: A Study of the New Democratic Party in Five Provincial Ridings in the Inter-Election Period 1963-65* (Unpublished M.A. thesis, Carleton University, April, 1966).

[17]Middle class candidates such as Tom Berger, Vancouver-Burrard, Charles Gifford, Notre Dame de Grace, and Charles Taylor, Mount Royal, have done well in middle class areas and have raised the hope of the NDP in constituencies where working class support alone would be insufficient to ensure victory.

[18]J. Meisel (ed.), *op. cit.*, p. 281.

Organization, a Director of Research, and a Director of Publicity. In Ontario a Director of Organization was appointed in 1966, and the latter supervises the activities of ten Ontario organizers in addition to supervising fund-raising activities.

The New Democratic Party has developed its own style of contesting elections. The essence of this approach is set down in the party's manual, *With Your Help*. Briefly, a New Democratic campaign is intended to capitalize on the party's greatest strength, its volunteer workers, and to overcome its greatest weakness, a lack of sufficient funds for mailings, heavy advertising, and television exposure. The New Democrats have had considerable success in concentrating on particular ridings in by-election campaigns. For these campaigns additional funds and workers were brought in from neighbouring areas. It is clear therefore that the New Democrats can apply their approach successfully in isolated by-elections. It is less clear that it will work in general elections, where relatively small resources must be more broadly allocated.

One asset the New Democrats have at present is solidarity between provincial and federal levels. Provincial politicians help in federal campaigns and vice versa, and money and organizers are transferred as needed. There also appears to be a great degree of solidarity across provincial boundaries, with few rivalries and differences among the provincial groups. This extends further, to voters; New Democratic support is roughly similar in both provincial and federal elections.

The grass-roots pattern of organization has some strong parallels in the area of financing, as much of the financial support for the New Democratic Party still comes from the membership and individual supporters, in small amounts. There is a basic membership fee collected in the local constituency (consisting in Ontario of five dollars a year), the amount being set by the individual provincial conventions. If there is more than one member from the same family, the additional fee is one dollar per member. Members who are unemployed also pay only one dollar a year, while pensioners receive a life membership for one dollar. The youth membership is $2.50 yearly. Finally, there is provision for "sustaining members", who pay twelve dollars yearly. From the five dollar regular membership, forwarded by the local constituency, the provincial office retains $3.50, sending one dollar to the Federal Office and returning fifty cents to the constituency.

In addition to the membership, an important source of funds is the affiliated unions. The party receives an income based on five cents per month for each member of an affiliated union, (the only members exempted by the union being those who specifically request exemption.) Income from affiliated unions is paid directly to the federal office, and from the five cents per affiliated member received each month, two cents are sent to the appropriate provincial party. Should an affiliated union member become an individual member, and request that this be done, sixty cents is deducted from his annual fee and the appropriate adjustment is made between the federal and provincial offices. In practice, most party members who are trade unionists pay the full membership fee.

The major remaining source of funds is the special fund-raising campaign, normally conducted just before elections. Such campaigns include direct (and often successful) appeals to the unions; raffles, picnics, passing the hat at meetings, fund-raising dinners, and special twenty-five cent weekly clubs in the factories also help. Each riding is asked to submit a budget to the provincial office, well in advance of election day, giving an estimate of anticipated receipts and expenditures. Those ridings with an organization capable of sustaining a strong campaign are expected to make a contribution to the provincial office of twenty per cent of election fund revenues. Some of this revenue is then used in weak constituencies, for deposits and a minimum of publicity, and some for central campaign expenditures. For by-elections special appeals go out from the provincial office to all constituency executives. For the 1966 by-election in Kenora, for example, the provincial office appealed to each constituency for a contribution based on five to ten cents per member.

The unions have made important contributions at election times, either to the provincial NDP office or to the constituency associations, over and above the regular affiliation fees. In a number of urban constituencies in Ontario a considerable part of the election fund comes from direct union contributions, in an amount usually decided at special union meetings to which few rank and file union members actually go. Many unions have a special Political Action Committee fund, from which such special contributions can be drawn. and even some non-affiliated unions contribute in this way.

Judging by the perennial shortage of funds at all levels of the party, fund-raising has been difficult. Even in 1966, when income from union affiliations was higher than it has ever been, individual and sustaining memberships were expected to account for half of the total income of the federal office ($91,000 out of an anticipated $181,000). The financial base depends, therefore, upon the enthusiasm and dedication of a large, militant corps of local leaders.

Despite its problems, the NDP fares much better financially than did the CCF, even in its peak years. There are more members, giving more, and there is greatly increased union support. In the election of 1962 the NDP spent $500,000 and in 1963 it spent from $400,000 to $500,000. Most of this was collected in Saskatchewan, British Columbia, and Ontario, and transfers were made to the remaining provinces. In the 1965 election, the NDP estimated that it had raised and spent, at all levels, $1,000,000. Despite this impressive increase in available funds, the NDP still operates on a budget far below that of the Liberals or the Conservatives.[19]

It is rather curious, in view of the growth in financial

---

[19]Further information on the financing of the New Democratic Party is available in the *Report of the Committee on Election Expenses, 1966*, Queen's Printer (1966).

strength of the party, that except in Ontario and Saskatchewan its paid membership appears to have remained relatively constant. No accurate figures are available on membership growth, but the summary of income from memberships in the national office is one rough indicator; from 1962 to 1965 the income from individual memberships was as follows: 1962—$39,633; 1963—$31,194; 1964—$40,843; 1965—$45,386. This suggests that a slight growth trend has been evident since 1963, but it in no way parallels the growth in electoral support. One reason may be that the constituency organizations do not put their best efforts into membership drives, because most of the money raised from memberships goes out of the constituency.

The membership picture may be changing, however, if Ontario is typical. From a membership of 12,600 in July of 1964, a special membership drive in 1966 had resulted by July in a membership of 21,000. This reflects in part the efforts of the central organizers. The party is seeking to build a large grass-roots base and, in Ontario particularly, much effort is being applied to extending and diversifying the membership base. Yet in general, only a small corps of militants take an active, continuing interest between elections.

A changing financial and membership picture may be indicative of a party's growth trends. It is results at the polls, however, even though they reflect to some extent discontent with the major parties, which are most important. In its first general election in 1962, the New Democratic Party received 13.5 per cent of the popular vote, gaining nineteen seats in the House of Commons (ten in British Columbia, six in Ontario, two in Manitoba, and one in Nova Scotia). In 1963, with 13.2 per cent of the popular vote, its representation went down to seventeen (nine in British Columbia, six in Ontario, and two in Manitoba). In 1965 its support rose to 17.9 per cent of the popular vote; and it won 21 seats in the House (nine in British Columbia. nine in Ontario, and three in Manitoba).

The popular vote in each province for recent elections shows that the NDP has increased its vote in six provinces, roughly held its own in two, and lost ground only in Prince Edward Island and Newfoundland, where it is at present an insignificant political force.[20]

In provincial elections since 1965, and in the results of various Gallup polls, the party has also shown gains. In the Alberta election of September, 1966, it won its first seat. At about the same time, in the British Columbia election, its share of the popular vote rose from 28 per cent to 34 per cent and the party won two extra seats, for a total of sixteen. In the Manitoba election of June, 1966, it won four additional seats, with a popular vote of 23 per cent, in contrast to the 13 per cent received in 1962. While its strength in Manitoba is greatest in urban Winnipeg (9 seats), it won two rural seats and ran a close second in two more. Finally, and most striking of all, in the nation-wide Gallup poll of November, 1966, the NDP and Conservatives were each put at 26 per cent.

While their ultimate goal is to govern nationally, the New Democrats appear to be placing their greatest emphasis at present on increasing their strength at the provincial level. In this they are following the traditional path of Canadian national parties where the immediate hopes of governing nationally are slim. The prospects for provincial power are brightest in Saskatchewan, where the Liberals took office with an extremely narrow margin in several constituencies. In British Columbia the party has a solid base of support and, as in Saskatchewan, forms the official opposition. In Manitoba, it has 20 to 25 per cent of the provincial vote. In Quebec, while the party is organized to contest federal elections only, it has come close to winning several Montreal federal constituencies, and is currently organizing in rural areas. A number of the party's leading national figures are from the Province of Quebec: Frank Scott, Charles Taylor, Michael Oliver, Robert Cliche and Thérèse Casgrain. In the Maritimes, the New Democrats are very weak, strength being evident only in Cape Breton.

It is in Ontario that the most strenuous efforts of the New Democrats are being made. With only eight members in the Ontario legislature they have nevertheless behaved during recent sessions as if they, and not the Liberals, were the official opposition party. They see the provincial Liberals in the greatest disarray; the October, 1966 Gallup poll gave the New Democrats 31 per cent in Ontario, behind the Conservatives but well ahead of the Liberals. A 1966 provincial convention slogan, "67 seats in '67", is a rallying cry rather than a serious prediction, but the New Democrats do anticipate gains sufficient to place them as the official opposition, in serious contention for the right to govern. By 1971 they expect to have become accepted by the electorate as a serious alternative to the Conservatives.

New Democrats appeared more optimistic in 1966 than in the founding years 1959 to 1961. The basis for this optimism was the performance of their elected representatives at both federal and provincial levels; the growth in percentage of popular vote as reflected in elections and in various public opinion polls; the existence of the nucleus of a strong permanent organization in Ottawa and certain provinces; a more favourably inclined, or at least accepting press than that existing for the CCF; a sense of permanency stemming from the revenue base provided by the affiliated unions—and knowledge of the CLC's strong drive to increase this support; and, finally, a belief that the public is growing increasingly disenchanted with the performance of the Liberals and Conservatives in the Federal Parliament.

In the last resort, however, whether the New Democratic Party succeeds will depend neither on the current strength of its financial base, nor on its new corps of organizers, but on whether its political style and basic philosophy are more attuned to the political temper of the next decade then those of the old parties.

---

[20]See appendix for the relevant election statistics.

Regional Politics

---

*

Canadian politics has, since Confederation, been dominated by central Canada—especially the commercial and manufacturing interests of the Toronto and Montreal regions. Concessions have been granted to the outlying areas in the form of subsidies for provincial governments, improvements in communications, or support for particular industries. The attitude of the Maritimes to this situation has been cautiously conservative. They have gone on supporting the old parties, hoping for "better terms" from Ottawa. They have preferred to be on the winning side in national elections and to express their protest within the old party structure.

The same cannot be said of French Canada or the West. They have expressed their dissatisfaction in ways that require special examination. Mr. Guindon analyses the social changes in French Canada underlying the changed outlook of Quebec.

Mr. Smith takes issue with other writers on the nature of the party system in western Canada and supplies an interpretation of the radical, yet conservative politics of that region.

Mr. Robin explains the distinctive nature of politics in British Columbia.

17

Social Unrest, Social Class and Quebec's Bureaucratic Revolution

HUBERT GUINDON

*

I. POLITICAL STRUCTURES AND THEIR LEGITIMATIONS

* * * * * *

Political structures need legitimations . . . Formal political empires collapsed because of a bankruptcy in legitimations which are created by intellectuals and become sacred values for the other social groups.

Withdrawal of the support from political structures by wide segments of the intelligentsia therefore becomes a crucial clue of imminent political instability. When this disenchantment of intellectuals is widely publicized and finds massive support in the lower social strata, the political regime, short of tyranny, is doomed. For a political structure is, in the final analysis, a moral order requiring for its existence consensus.

Confederation is a political structure. For growing numbers of French Canadian intellectuals its legitimations are unconvincing. . . . Where does Confederation as a political structure stand within French Canada? Intellectual disenchantment with Confederation is widespread within the French Canadian intelligentsia, including the social scientists. This disenchantment of intellectuals, artists, writers, newspapermen, film directors, etc., has been widely publicized in all forms of mass media. Furthermore, wide segments of French Canada's new middle class are either openly committed to, or sympathetic with, this heightened nationalist feeling if not with separatism itself. This disenchantment, measured by belief in separatism, has not yet found massive support in the rural and lower urban social strata, but has met rather with indifference, apathy, and skepticism, seldom however with outright hostility. Had massive support from these social strata been forthcoming, the separatist idea would have been acted upon. Paradoxical as it may seem, it is the uneducated, unskilled and semi-skilled French Canadian farmer and worker, the "ignorant," "joual"-speaking French Canadian, oft-maligned and spoofed at by his ethnic middle class and the perfect fit of the anti-French Canadian stereotype, who is at present quite unconsciously holding Confederation, unsettled as it is, on its shaky legs.

*Reprinted from *Queen's Quarterly*, LXXI, No. 2, 1964.

This leads me to raise specifically, the questions I shall attempt to answer in this essay. Why has the lower-class French Canadian been relatively immune to separatist agitation? Why has the new French Canadian middle class become virulently nationalist and, to an important extent, separatist? Why has the emergence of this new middle class heightened ethnic tensions in Confederation? What is the nature of social unrest in the lower social strata?

II. SOCIAL UNREST AND THE NEW MIDDLE CLASS

The emergence of what is commonly called the new middle class is not something specific to French Canada; quite on the contrary, the growth of such a class was rather belated, in fact, essentially a post-war phenomenon. With the growth and the increased size of large-scale formal organizations of business and government, the middle class was overwhelmingly transformed into a bureaucratically employed white collar group with professional and semi-professional status, displacing the dominant "entrepreneurial," self-employed character of the middle class in the last century. The new middle class is a product of the bureaucratic expansion of organizations.

1. The Growth and Characteristics of the New Middle Class in French Canada.

Structurally, the French Canadian new middle class is the same as its counterparts in industrially developed societies. But the circumstances of its emergence and some of its characteristics are somewhat at variance with most.

The bureaucratic revolution is, demographically speaking, the result of mass exodus from country to city. The demographic pressure created a need for expansion of the urban institutions serving this influx. In the process of expansion the urban institutions changed character, becoming large-scale organizations, marked by increased specialization. This bureaucratic revolution opened new channels of upward mobility. It required diversified staffs, trained in new skills. The growth of bureaucratic urban institutions became the structural basis of a new social class called the new middle class.

The French Canadian new middle class, I have said, is somewhat different in some of its social-psychological characteristics from other new middle classes. First of all, its emergence was more dramatic and sudden than in many cases. Secondly, the ethnic cultural traditions from which it came provided no models for the broad spectrum of the new occupational roles. Thirdly, French Canadian bureaucracies are to be found overwhelming in the public and semi-public sectors as against the area of private enterprise. Finally, the bureaucratic revolution, in French Canada, has not changed the power elite of French Canadian society; it has not displaced, but rather rejuvenated traditional elites. Much of the unrest, in my opinion, in the French Canadian new middle class can be related to these special characteristics.

2. The Duplessis Era and the New Middle Class

New middle class unrest dates back to the mid and late fifties. The post-war period saw a massive migration of French Canadians to the cities. . . . This massive urbanization altered the existing nature of urban institutions. Urban institutions of welfare, health, and education had to increase their size, their staffs, and their budgets rapidly to meet the new demographic needs. This bureaucratic growth was being stifled by Duplessis' discretionary habit in distributing public funds. In the process, the economic and status interests of this new middle class were not being met. Salaries could not be increased. Why? Because of Duplessis. Staff could not be hired. Why? Because of Duplessis.

Duplessis became a symbol of oppression, of reactionary government. He was depicted as a tyrant corrupting political mores. A persistent theme of Duplessis' political oratory was his opposition to "bureaucracy." Even though ideologically neutral, the theme was becoming increasingly impertinent structurally. The celebrated attack on the political mores of the Union Nationale Party by Fathers Dion and O'Neil paved the way for a new bureaucratic type of political morality. The growth of semi-public bureaucratic institutions required greatly increased and predictable amounts of money from the provincial treasury. Because he refused to meet these class demands, Duplessis was emotionally and unanimously resented by the new middle class. Where Duplessis failed, Sauvé succeeded. By a single declaration of policy, namely, increased grants to universities, hospital insurance and increased salaries to civil servants, he immediately got the emotional endorsement of the new middle class for the very same party. His untimely death was perceived by members of this social class as a tragic personal loss. Duplessis stifled the class interests and the status aspiration of the new middle class; he was resented. Sauvé decided to meet them; he was acclaimed.

3. The New Middle Class and the Lesage Regime

With the death of Duplessis, the critical importance of the new middle class on politics became unchallenged. Following in Sauvé's footsteps, the Liberal Party under Jean Lesage proceeded to base its political strength on the enthusiastic support of the new middle class, recently become politically aroused and vocal.

The link between the Liberal Party and the new middle class can easily be established. Its existence can be shown in terms of (a) the "nucleus" of its political support, (b) the choice of "competent" administrative personnel in the civil service, and (c) the nature of its legislative reforms. The "volunteer" workers of the Liberal Party in the past elections were urban, more highly educated, younger, new middle class people. The concern for qualified personnel in the expanding provincial civil service spells the end of the "self-made" man or politically appointed party supporter. The party man must also be professionally qualified.

The Liberal legislative reform is a bureaucratic reform. It

has sought to expand and strengthen the bureaucratic services of education, health and welfare. The Quebec renaissance or silent revolution, or whatever it is called, is a bureaucratic revolution. The tremendous expenditures in educaion and health are coupled with a constant concern with increasing the salaries of white collar occupations in these institutions. Current concern for portable pensions equally reflects the interests of the new middle class.

4. From Anti-Duplessism to Separatism

It is not, in my opinion, by sheer coincidence that separatism became a social force only after the death of Duplessis. By stifling the status aspirations of the new middle class, Duplessis became a scapegoat upon which its frustrations could be vented. Middle class unrest did not die with Duplessis. The middle classes, however, did lose a scapegoat.

The Liberal Party, champion of bureaucratic reform, endeavouring to meet the aspirations of this social class could not easily be indicted. Unrest in new middle class circles took on the form of separatist agitation. The class origins of separatism can be ascertained both in terms of the social location of its supporters and the class nature of its grievances.

Separatist leaders as well as their rank and file are to be found among the better-educated, younger, professional and semi-professional, salaried, white collar ranks. This class constitutes the core of its support. The nature of separatist grievances also underlines its class bias. Separatist discontent, in the final analysis, boils down to protest against real or imagined restricted occupational mobility. The objects of separatist indictment are the promotion practices of the federally operated bureaucracies, of crown and private corporations. This class bias is also the reason why the separatist appeal has gone by largely unheeded by the rural classes and the lower social strata of the cities.

5. Nationalist Unrest, the Liberal Regime and Confederation

Sheer coincidence cannot alone account for the fact that separatism and disenchantment with Confederation appeared on the political scene, in its massive form, after the Liberal regime came into power and not during the Duplessis era.

Meeting the status aspirations of the new middle class in French Canada, as the Liberals surely know by now, is an expensive proposition. . . . The income squeeze that resulted from trying to meet new middle class demands created a political crisis in dominion-provincial relations.

Ethnic tensions, unheard of during the Duplessis era, were brought back once again to the forefront of public discussion. *Maîtres chez nous,* the Liberal Party's slogan in the last election, is actually the official endorsement of a forty-year old slogan first put forward by Lionel Groulx[1] . . .

His was a voice in the desert until the new middle class made it theirs. . . . Many of the current themes of political concern are to be explicitly found in his writings. Ambivalence towards foreign capitalists and foreign labour unions, indignation at the handing over of natural resources to foreign investors, the lack of an entrepreneurial bourgeoisie, the positive role of the state in economic affairs, the lack of proper academic institutions and training for the world of business, the "bi-national" theory of Confederation, all of these themes are clearly and eloquently pleaded in his writings.

The financial strain of the French Canadian bureaucratic revolution and the nationalist ideology of the French Canadian new middle class, have brought about a reinterpretation of Confederation specifically and of ethnic co-habitation generally. The reinterpretation is not new; its widespread acceptance in the new middle class is.

Confederation is on probation. The French Canadian new middle class does not view it as something valuable in itself. It is to be judged on its merits as a means to achieving national aspirations. It has, for a long time, been viewed as an instrument of British Canadian nationalism. With the rise of ethnic tensions this view is becoming widespread in many circles and a postulate of the political analysis of separatist groups of every tendency.

What, in effect, needs clarification is the history of ethnic co-habitation in Canada. Ethnic accommodation, it seems to me, has been historically constructed, successfully in Quebec, on a basis of mutually desired self-segregated institutions. In the fields of education, religion, welfare, leisure and residence, institutional self-segregation has been total. The only two areas of societal living where inter-ethnic contact has been institutionalized are those of work and politics.

The pattern of ethnic contact in the area of work was established with the introduction of industrialization. Anglo-Saxon industry moved into a society faced with an acute population surplus, a distinctive political and religious elite, a developing set of institutions anchored in the rural parish. This society, politically stable, economically conservative, and technically unskilled, provided ideal conditions for investing Anglo-Saxon capitalists; they could invest their capital, open industries, and be supplied with an abundant source of unskilled labour seeking employment. The managerial and technical levels were filled, with no protest, by the incoming group, who also brought along their own set of institutions, servicing their own nationals.

This social setting provided an easy introduction to industry. The French Canadian elite was ideologically co-operative, sensitive only about its continued control over its demographic substructures. This fitted in quite well with the aims of the incoming groups, who could develop their economic pursuits and enterprises with minimum involvement in the local society. There was a minimum of involvement in local politics. The local elite of politicians and the clergy welcomed the transaction of business and the development of business institutions. All this took place with no unrest whatsoever. Industry was relieving the economic burden of the demographic surplus of French Canadian rural society. The local elites' leadership was not being challenged.

This pattern of mutually satisfying, self-segregated institutions worked with no dissent up to and including the Second World War. This historical pattern is now being challenged . . . by the recently emerged French Canadian new middle class. Making room for this new social class in the managerial levels of industry and government is the crucial test of Canadian unity. This cannot be achieved without the shedding of old habits that surrounded the traditional ethnic division of labour.

III. SOCIAL UNREST IN THE RURAL AND LOWER URBAN SOCIAL CLASSES

1. The Créditiste Episode

New middle class unrest, vocal and well publicized, overshadowed another social unrest, that of the lower social class of country and city, until the unforeseen sweep of rural Quebec by Réal Caouette's Créditiste movement.

Indeed, for the first time in Quebec's political history, the rural lower classes, . . . instead of sending to the federal parliament traditional middle class professionals, elected class peers to represent them. . . .

The Creditiste appeal successfully tapped the unrest of farmer and unskilled worker where the middle class separatist protest failed. The Créditiste criticism of the traditional parties found fertile soil in the economically deprived regions of rural Quebec. "You have nothing to lose" went the slogan. Another major theme was the right to economic security. Economic security to middle class people means decent pension plans. To a sizeable part of the French Canadian population it means something quite different. It means stable employment, a year-round job, the right not to live in the constant fear of unemployment. Caouette, who is no new middle class symbol by any means, but a small entrepreneur, the product of the barren Abitibi region, spoke their language. His charge that the old parties really do not care or cannot change their socio-economic plight, comes dangerously close to regional historic truth, for this state of economic insecurity has been a pattern that dates back almost a century.

. . . Duplessis, whatever his short-comings, based his political machine on the rural and lower-urban social strata. After the ousting of the Union Nationale from power, these classes felt unrepresented, uncared for, with no significant voice in the political arena. Duplessis had never been viewed as a dictator or tyrant in these strata. The Lesage

---

[1]Lionel Groulx, *Directives*, les editions du Zodiaque, 1937, p. 20.

resolve to dissolve patronage increased the number of Créditiste supporters because of disenchanted rural Liberals who had expected the continued exercise of patronage by their own group.

The possibly unanticipated effect of the crackdown on
patronage, in actual fact, was to halt or substantially reduce the flow of
provincial funds to the lower social strata. Holding up the new "bureaucratic" political morality was a hidden net reorienting public expenditures
to other social classes. In the light of this interpretation, the Créditiste
slogan "you have nothing to lose" takes on added meaning. Whatever the
dubious ethics of the political organizers of Duplessis may have been, and
whatever the size of the cake they kept as their part, they managed, in
their own devious ways to let the rest funnel down in numerous bits into
kinship systems. With the Liberal regime, the cake is properly and cere-
moniously cut, but the slices are fewer and the number of guests greatly
reduced.

Uprootedness is more characteristic of French Canada's
new middle class than of its urban proletariat. The traditional pattern of
land inheritance, of keeping the farm intact and handing it over to only
one heir, coupled with the high rural birth rate has meant that moving,
looking for work, settling elsewhere, is not a dramatic event in the life-
cycle of the rural surplus population and it has been provided for in the
cultural script.

What have not been provided for by the cultural traditions
are the role models for the new middle class occupations. For this reason,
the traditional culture is something far from sacred and useful, very often
the object of contempt and ridicule within new middle class circles. Part
of the anxiety and anguish of the new middle class psyche may be traced
to this lack of cultural continuity.

*   *   *   *   *

IV. SUMMARY

The emergence of a new middle class in French Canada is
a structural change that cannot be wished away. Its status aspirations are
challenging the historical pattern of the ethnic division of labour.
Whether its heightened national mood will lead to the separatist experiment is dependent upon two things: (a) on how successful the present
political and economic structure of the Canadian society will be in coping
with its bureaucratic aspirations, and (b) on the future direction of lower
class unrest.

The bureaucratic revolution of the last few years in Quebec
has brought to the surface latent resentment in French Canadian society.
The traditionally conservative substructure of French Canadian society
has expressed discontent of its own. Its course has not, until now, been in
the same direction. But who can say with absolute confidence that it will
never be?

Bold, imaginative and responsible decisions are in order
from the power elites of this country, whoever they may be. It is doubtful
that the current concept of "co-operative federalism" in its present confused and blurred state will tide us over.

18

Prairie Revolt, Federalism and the Party System

DENIS SMITH

*

The leaders of the three western movements of political protest, the Progressives, the C.C.F., and Social Credit, insisted in their national campaigns from 1921 to 1958 that their purpose was not to complicate the Canadian party system by creating permanent minor groups, but to simplify it by forcing a realignment of political loyalty throughout the country. The professed national aim of each party was to create a national two-party system divided on lines of principle, through which the reforms desired by each group might be adopted. The three parties of prairie origin argued either that the Liberal and Conservative parties were alike, offering the voter no choice, or that one of the two older parties was not fulfilling its proper function. Frequently they argued both.

The hope of political realignment first expressed on the prairies by the grain growers' organizations and John W. Dafoe after 1917 is echoed today by the leaders of the New Democratic Party, whose object is to create "a broadly based people's political movement, which embraces the C.C.F., the labour movement, farm organizations, professional people and other liberally-minded persons interested in basic social reform and reconstruction through our parliamentary system of government."[1] The political history of the prairies since 1917 cannot encourage those who still seek such a change. In forty years the three parties originating in the prairies have all failed to bring about a political transformation at Ottawa, and each has eventually been rejected by its own prairie followers in federal general elections. The recurrent wish in western Canada for a new national party may be partly discounted as the rationalization of ambitious politicians; but its persistence cannot be so easily explained. Pursuit of the aim reflects, in one sense, a failure to see the reality of the Canadian political system, and in another, a grasp of the

---

*Based on *Politics and the Party System in the Three Prairie Provinces, 1917-1958*, B. Litt. thesis, Oxford University, 1959.

[1]Resolution of the Canadian Labour Congress, 1958 convention, quoted in Stanley Knowles, *The New Party* (Toronto: McClelland & Stewart, Ltd., 1961), p. 127.

necessities of political action in a parliamentary system of responsible government.

The model which prairie political reformers hoped to reproduce was their simplified image of the British party system. Liberal Unionists and Progressives after 1917 desired new Liberal and Conservative parties on the late nineteenth-century British pattern; the C.C.F. after 1935 hoped for a division of loyalties on Conservative-Labour lines; Social Credit after 1953 pictured itself as the conservative opponent of an increasingly socialist Liberal party. None of the advocates of realignment saw clearly in their enthusiasm; their half-conscious equation of Canadian politics with an ill-formed image of British politics ignored the organization and attitudes of Canadian political parties.

*   *   *   *   *

The federal composition of the Liberal and Conservative parties, and of the new prairie parties after 1920, was a clear sign to prairie reformers of the nature of Canadian parties. Neither of the old parties was a monolithic whole. Within the national parties, the prairie units of both Liberals and Conservatives were relatively progressive, especially in the inter-war years. In their empirical way, prairie Liberals and Conservatives have often been more enterprising in proposing reform that would benefit the rural prairie economy than have been the Progressives in Manitoba or the U.F.A. and Social Credit in Alberta. The basic measures of crop insurance and credit reform desired by prairie farmers were adopted by Liberal governments in all three provinces before 1921. To make their appeal in the West, Liberals and Conservatives have frequently played down their relationship with their more conservative eastern branches. Even in the apparently homogeneous political region within the prairies, separate provincial traditions, tactical needs, and provincial jealousies have made co-operation between the three prairie units of the old parties difficult.

In the Progressive party, the C.C.F., and Social Credit, for similar reasons, provincial autonomy from the beginning vitiated attempts to unify policy and organization. The single-minded provincialism of Henry Wise Wood in Alberta prevented the establishment of a national Progressive organization; the U.F.A.'s parochialism was an equal hindrance to the C.C.F. in its early years; the Social Credit party escaped serious inter-provincial conflict before 1962 only because it was an insignificant force in federal politics outside Alberta. In spite of the common economic interest of the three grain-growing provinces, the provinces have three distinct political systems to which any party must adapt. The new parties have never had to face the more serious problem, constantly confronting the two old parties, of adjusting themselves within national parties having influential blocs of supporters and members of Parliament in the Maritimes, Quebec, and Ontario. The national unity of the Social Credit party was severely challenged for the first time in 1962 by the federal success of M. Caouette and his followers in Quebec.

Prairie reformers were too inclined to impose a European pattern when they claimed that nothing distinguishes the national Liberal and Conservative parties. The familiar distinction between Right and Left does not apply in Canada. Like the Republican and Democratic parties, Canadian parties are, first, alternate groups of officeholders. They are distinguished not by precise differences of policy when in office, but by continuing and deep differences of sentiment and approach which reflect the special ambivalence of Canada's history and position in the world. A new national party, to be successful, must either capture old citadels of sentiment from the existing parties or lay claim to new sentiments and attitudes that, unrecognized by the old parties, reflect new challenges faced by the country. The failure of the new prairie parties resulted from the country's failure to see any but the traditional problems and to consider any but the traditional responses.

The Conservative party represents and contains the latent anti-Americanism which has been the precondition of the country's existence since 1867. Without always exposing this feeling in its crudity, the party has come to power in 1911, 1930, and 1957 on surges of anti-American emotion and when in office has been prepared to contemplate legislative restrictions on American economic and cultural influence in Canada, if such restrictions promise political advantage. When the anti-American devil slumbers in Canadian breasts, the Conservative party loses some of its sense of purpose. The national Liberal party, in contrast, has represented the opposite desire of Canadians: to conciliate the United States, to avoid antagonizing the giant, to enter into a North American partnership.

The Conservative party's weakness in western Canada during the period from 1917 to 1958 can be partly explained by this difference of sentiment. The prairie provinces contained a large proportion of former American citizens; the closest neighbours of isolated westerners were not central Canadians but fellow farmers in Montana, North Dakota, and Minnesota; the ideas of American farm radicals were congenial on the Canadian prairies; the most obvious market for prairie wheat and source of cheap commodities was the United States. Anti-Americanism was irrelevant to prairie needs; prairie interests and associations called instead for anti-eastern feeling. In 1930, when the country was caught by the anti-American mood, Alberta and Saskatchewan were the provinces least affected.[2] The relative absence of this sentiment in the West before 1957 gave an advantage to the Liberal party, or to any other party which did not share the Conservative tradition.

The other side of this coin is the difference in emphasis given to the British relation; and again the Conservatives were at a disadvantage on the prairies in this period because the Anglophilia of Arthur Meighen, R. B. Bennett, and George Drew met indifference or positive

---

[2]The Conservative party received 34 per cent of the popular vote in Alberta, 38 per cent in Saskatchewan, 46 per cent in Manitoba and 49 per cent in the whole country.

distaste from the large numbers of Americans and continental Europeans on the prairies, and from all whose concern in the inter-war years was, with John W. Dafoe, to make Canada independent of Great Britain. It was only when the issue had long been settled that a faintly pro-British reaction to the Liberal party's reiteration of its prejudice set in on the prairies and elsewhere, to the benefit of the Conservative party in 1957 and 1958.

In domestic policy, too, the differences between the parties have been native ones. In this century, the Liberal party has been the public guardian or, more accurately, the propagandist of racial unity between French and English, while the Conservative party has repeatedly antagonized or ignored French Canada. These contrary tendencies had their effect on the prairies, particularly in the defeat of the provincial Liberal government of Saskatchewan by the Conservatives in 1929. The national Liberal party, by the inclination of its leaders and the necessity of accommodating its Quebec followers, has been pragmatic in its encouragement of national development and backward in social policy. The Conservative party has the bolder radical legislative tradition (although it is piecemeal), typified by Macdonald's assistance to the C.P.R., Borden's nationalization of the C.N.R. and civil service reforms, Bennett's abortive social legislation, and Diefenbaker's welfare legislation, assistance to farmers, and commitment to northern development. In the inter-war era of retrenchment, Mackenzie King's quietism was more in tune with the western Canadian spirit than with a policy of national expansion and legislative activity. The reforming surge of 1917 had died on the prairies by 1921, and the provincial governments, too, of whatever political flavour, were unimaginative and cautious for a decade afterwards.

Conservative devotion to the British connection has included a notably stronger reverence for British parliamentary institutions than that of the Liberal party. The Conservative party is quicker to detect and deplore departures from traditional parliamentary practice (or to show guilt for them, if the party itself is responsible) than the Liberal party; the Liberal party is more inclined to accept American partisan practices, especially in its relationship with the senior civil service. (There are exceptions. Some prominent Liberals since 1921 have been parliamentary traditionalists, but they have not been influential in the party's leadership. The Conservative party and the C.C.F. have had many more articulate defenders of the parliamentary system.) The Liberal party, by intent and long habit in office, has established with the federal civil service ties of sentiment which the Conservative party cannot match when it is in office.

All these differences are in feeling, experience, and approach rather than in clear-cut policy. The western advocates of the new parties after 1917, looking for more logical and cerebral distinctions between the old parties, did not see that the existing national parties already had a prescriptive hold on the deepest sentiments dividing the Canadian electorate.

The Progressives left the Liberal party because they saw that it was a loose federation of provincial groups, dominated by members from the populous, industrial provinces. The party's belief in a low tariff seemed nothing but an empty gesture to the West; in the party caucus the western members could rarely gain acceptance for their views. T. A. Crerar of Manitoba drew the same lesson from his experience in the Unionist cabinet from 1917 to 1919.[3] The sentiment for a low tariff seemed after the First World War to be the only dominant political feeling that had not been appropriated by either of the old parties. Yet it soon turned out to be old hat; the West was not seriously interested in major tariff reform after 1925. The Progressives had no other permanent objective of national policy.

One element in the Progressive revolt was, of course, the belief that the expanding West lacked the power to which it was entitled in the Liberal caucus. Equity required that each region should have power in the party commensurate with its economic and social position in the country. No politician would deny this right, and Mackenzie King, whose political life was typified by his efforts to balance delicately the power and interests of all parts of the country and to remain in power by doing so, would scarcely ignore it. The Progressives could expect that, gradually, the old parties would out of prudence and a sense of justice, grant the West a balanced place in party councils. King did this in the Liberal party by increasing prairie representation in the House of Commons in 1924 and offering cabinet posts to influential westerners like Crerar, C.A. Dunning, A. B. Hudson, J. S. Woodsworth and J. G. Gardiner. The display of western power within the Liberal caucus, and outside it, made it expedient for King to make concessions of policy to the prairies: the restored Crow's Nest Pass Agreement, the 1924 budget, the Hudson Bay Railway, the Old Age Pension Act of 1926, the budget of 1930, and the social welfare measures and financial agreements of 1940 and afterwards. The prairie political revolt, by achieving such concessions of position and policy at Ottawa, may be considered successful. But it was not, and could not be successful in its wider purpose of transforming the Canadian party system. The concessions did *not* mean that the Liberal party had been captured by western Liberals: they were the limited rewards of compromise.

Because they failed to accept the inevitable heterogeneity of national political parties or to recognize the differences between the two old parties, the prophets of a reformed party system on the prairie set out to achieve the impossible. But if Canadian parties are loose federations like American parties, why did not the West find satisfaction through them, as American regional protest groups usually do? In Canada, western politicians realized that the parliamentary system imposes on

---

[3]*See A. B. Hudson Papers*, No. 55, T. A. Crerar to A. B. Hudson (March 12, 1919); *Dafoe Papers*, John W. Dafoe to Sir Clifford Sifton (July 21, 1919); *Borden Papers*, O.C. Series, File 571, T. A. Crerar to R. L. Borden (June 4, 1919).

regional groups restraints which cannot be overcome within the major parties. In the congressional system, regional interest groups have better opportunities for enforcing their wills in primaries, and in Congress by log-rolling that avoids party lines, by filibustering, or by seeking a presidential veto. If they do not always succeed, American regional groups can at least talk freely within the existing party framework. But the need for party discipline in a parliamentary system limits regional interests to only two opportunities to put their cases: in the privacy of the cabinet and the party caucus. Prairie members of the old parties found it impossible to persuade their supporters that they were acting in their interest, when the dominant eastern sections of the parties were able to force their policies through in private.[4]

Prairie political rebels made further use of the available instruments of power in a federal system by capturing the provincial governments in the prairies. The parliamentary system forced western politicians out of the old parties; the federal constitution gave the new parties footholds of prestige and patronage in the provinces and made possible their survival, in a lingering half-life, even though the federal parliamentary groups of Progressives, C.C.F., and Social Credit were virtually impotent. The achievement of power in provincial elections was easier for the new parties than gaining power at Ottawa, because they could turn the profound prairie sentiments of insecurity, xenophobia, pioneering righteousness, and resentment of exploitation against the Liberals and Conservatives, who appeared with some justification to be the local agents of a colonial power—eastern Canada. Once the Progressives, the U.F.A., the Social Credit, and the C.C..F had come to power in the West, they sought to retain power for the same reasons any party does: habit, the enjoyment of power, the rewards of patronage, belief in their mission, the defence of their self-respect.

For ten years after 1917, the *Manitoba Free Press* advocated a complete separation between the federal and provincial units of all political parties.[5] It did so partly because it considered the problems facing a provincial legislature to be closer to those of a municipal council than of a sovereign parliament; partly because it assumed that the federal system, by its nature, involved continuous conflict over national policy between the provinces and the federal government; and partly because it wished the West to take the lead in creating a new two-party system at Ottawa by forming the core of a new national Liberal party. After ten years of testing, the *Free Press* abandoned its theory in the face of federal and provincial party systems was that by the very existence of two intransigent fact. The germ of truth in this prescription for separating the levels of government, two separate systems of policy-making and competition for power were created. There was illogic and injustice in a party system which made a provincial branch of a party suffer for the unpopularity of its federal associate, or vice versa.

But to expect that politicians would make two insulated realms was as unrealistic as to expect a simplified national two-party system. National party leaders will encourage the growth of provincial party units, as Mackenzie King and James Gardiner did, to make shows of strength and to provide organizations that they can use in federal elections. Men who enter provincial politics early in their careers will be drawn to Ottawa and the greater opportunities for responsibility and renown that it offers; they will find it useful, while in provincial politics, to conciliate the national party leaders who may later help them. Even a Progressive like John Bracken, who claimed in the 1920's to keep Manitoba politics free of federal complications, accepted national Liberal help after 1928 and at last agreed to take the leadership of a national party.[6] A provincial party leader will deny his federal loyalties when the federal party is unpopular and parade them when it is popular. The relationship is one of prudence, resting on a basis of common sentiment, and not of principle. The first objective of a party is to seek or maintain power, and Canadian parties will pursue this objective by denying their associations if this seems desirable. The temptation to do so would have been the same for the new parties if they too, had become major parties.

There is slight evidence that a provincial government controlled by a separate provincial party can gain more concessions from Ottawa, as the *Manitiba Free Press* implied by arguing for two levels of

---

[4]Regional tension within the parties seems also to have contributed to the erosion in Canada of the parliamentary practice of collective cabinet responsibility. It appears that one of the responses of the Liberal and Conservative parties to the centrifugal forces of Canadian regionalism has been tacitly to abandon strict cabinet unanimity in public statements of policy. See, for example, the conflicting statements on the South Saskatchewan dam made by Hon. James G. Gardiner, the Minister of Agriculture, and Rt. Hon. Louis St. Laurent, the Prime Minister, as reported in the Toronto *Globe and Mail*, June 4, 1954, July 18, 1956, May 8, 1957, and commented upon by Arthur Blakely in the *Montreal Gazette*, February 14, 1957.

[5]See, inter alia, *Manitoba Free Press* (April 7, 1922) editorial, 11; (April 27, 1922), 13; (April 28, 1922), editorial, 15; (June 2, 1921), editorial, 13; (June 22, 1927), editorial, 15; (July 8, 1922), editorial, 11; *Dafoe Papers*, John W. Dafoe to Sir Clifford Sifton (July 7, 1922).

[6]The federal power to make judicial and other patronage appointments has been one effective means by which the party in power at Ottawa has sustained weak provincial branches in the prairies, and incidentally made it difficult for the new parties to attract lawyers. Politicians who are lawyers, and who have hopes of being appointed to the bench, will be reluctant to lose the chance by breaking with the two major federal parties. Four prairie Liberal leaders received appointments to the bench from 1920 to 1930: J. R. Boyle (1924) and C. R. Mitchell (1926) of Alberta, W. M. Martin (1922) of Saskatchewan, and H. A. Robson (1929) of Manitoba. A. B. Hudson, the Manitoba Liberal who turned Progressive with John W. Dafoe and T. A. Crerar after 1919, was soon enticed back into the Liberal party by Mackenzie King, and was eventually appointed (1936) to the Supreme Court of Canada. Premier T. C. Norris of Manitoba (1915-1922), who flirted with the provincial farmers' party from 1920 to 1922, but never clearly repudiated his federal Liberal associations, was rewarded in 1928 by appointment to the Federal Board of Railway Commissioners. There is a certain predisposition to expect such appointments in the old parties.

party system. The prairie provinces took nine years after 1921 to obtain the natural resources that the federal government had retained, although during this time two of the governments were opposed to the federal Liberal administration. The decision to transfer control of resources came when the Dominion's immigration and settlement programme had been completed and control was no longer necessary for its purposes, not when opposition parties came to power in the prairies.[7] Prime Minister King decided to build the Hudson Bay Railway in order to bring Premier C. A. Dunning of Saskatchewan (a Liberal) into his cabinet and to gain the Saskatchewan Liberal Party's aid in the federal campaign of 1925, not to appease an unrelated provincial government.[8] Prime Minister Bennett gave financial assistance to prairie governments during the depression irrespective of party, and Prime Minister King, despite his "five-cent" speech of 1930, did so after he returned to power in 1935. In all these cases, the federal attitude to the provinces depended upon dictates of equity, national interest, and national party advantage, not upon the complexions of the provincial regimes.

Prairie politics since 1917 shows that Frank H. Underhill's hypothesis that the real centres of political opposition in Canada are in the provincial governments requires more careful definition.[9] He sees "a peculiar and uniquely Canadian phenomenon" developing: a party system in which a powerful majority party at Ottawa, faced by a divided and ineffective opposition, is meeting its real opposition in the governments of the provinces. The theory was stimulated by knowledge of the long period of Liberal dominance at Ottawa before June 1957, and of the existence then of a growing number of provincial governments under the control of other parties.[10] It is defended by reference to voting statistics, showing that at times a significant proportion of the electorate votes for one party in provincial elections and for another party in federal elections. The implication of this cross-voting apparently is that the public acts more or less consciously to create a balance between the party in power at Ottawa and opposition governments in the provinces.

Local politicians at times do find it convenient to criticize federal policy. But this is not to say that the real opposition comes from the provinces. Provincial governments are not designed to oppose the party in power at Ottawa, for they are usually preoccupied with duties of a different nature than those performed by the federal government. If Professor Underhill's theory is interpreted to mean that opposition parties use provincial stepping stones to achieve national power, it also requires qualification. Provincial elections in 1921, 1929, 1934, and 1935 did reveal prairie dissatisfaction with the incumbent governments at Ottawa and added to the tides that later brought their defeat. An opposition party may gain by provincial election victories if the timing of elections permits. But provincial victories are not prerequisites of national victory, as the Conservative party showed in the West in 1957 and 1958. Voters sometimes support one party in provincial elections and another in federal elections, but this may be as much the result of a desire to cast a vote for a candidate with a chance of election as of a desire to oppose the federal government in local elections. In the voters' minds, at least, if not in the politicians', the fields of federal and provincial politics are frequently unrelated. Professor Underhill's theory reduces to the simple fact that the attitudes of provincial governments and the results of provincial elections are two signs, among others, of the public mood in a federal system.

A theory of the prairie party system of greater ideological complexity has been proposed by C. B. Macpherson in his *Democracy in Alberta*.[11] From a position of economic determinism, he concludes that there has emerged in Alberta, and the other two prairie provinces, and "less definitely but perceptibly, in Canada as a whole,"[12] a new kind of party system that is neither plebiscitary democracy, nor the familiar two-party system of democratic theory, nor a one-party system. He calls it a "quasi-party system." He notices that in 1921 and 1935 radical parties came to power in Alberta virtually unopposed, and opposition to them in the legislatures remained weak. He notices, too, that both the U.F.A. and Social Credit gave up their radicalism under the pressures of office. He is not satisfied that this retreat into conservatism can be explained by Michels' theory of the need to create a bureaucracy to carry out reforms, and by the desire of the leaders to increase their power. He believes that "they were . . . compelled to take a relatively conservative position when they saw where they really stood in relation to the established economy. . . . It was not that the exigencies of government, as such, caused the leaders on attaining office to become orthodox both in their economic policies and in their practice of democracy. Rather, the exigencies of governing a society of independent producers, in revolt against outside domination but not against property, brought out the conservatism inherent in *petit-bourgeois* agrarian radicalism."[13]

He explains the long dominance in Alberta of a single party, faced by a weak legislative opposition, as essentially the result of the homogeneous *petit-bourgeois* illusions held by Alberta farmers, who

---

[7]V. C. Fowke, *Canadian Agricultural Policy* (Toronto: University of Toronto Press, 1947), pp. 240, 270.

[8]See *A. B. Hudson Papers*, Memorandum (1925), No. 71; *Dafoe Papers*, John W. Dafoe to Sir Clicord Sifton (November 20, 1925); *Canadian Annual Review* (1925-1926), pp. 30, 31; *Manitoba Free Press* (October 10, 1925), 1.

[9]See his *Canadian Political Parties* (Ottawa: The Canadian Historical Association, Historical Booklets No. 8, 1957), p. 19.

[10]Before the federal election of June 1957, seven of the ten provinces were governed by the Conservative, Social Credit, C.C.F. or Union Nationale parties; three provinces of small population, Manitoba, Prince Edward Island, and Newfoundland, were Liberal.

[11]C. B. Macpherson, *Democracy in Alberta* (Toronto: University of Toronto Press, 1953), pp. 3-27, 215-250.

[12]*Ibid.*, p. 215.

[13]*Ibid.*, p. 220.

believe themselves to have more independence than they actually have, and who have revolted in politics in an effort to realize the independence they crave. The farmers and their political representatives fluctuate between radical discontent with the external forces that control their economic security, and conservatism when they find that they cannot fundamentally alter their insecurity without destroying the economic system. They give their support, in outbursts of dissatisfaction, to one dominant party that talks of reform but is really conservative.

Macpherson introduces the phrase "quasi-party system" because he believes that the political system of Alberta is peculiar and permanent. It is not equivalent to the common Anglo-American two- or three-party system, in which the alternating parties act as brokers among sectional and interest groups, hindrances to oligarchy, and moderators of class conflict. He regards a party system primarily as a means of moderating class conflict; but referring to Alberta, he suggests, "... the absence of any serious opposition of classes within the province meant that alternate parties were not needed either to express or to moderate a perennial conflict of interests."[14] The Alberta "quasi-party system," in Professor Macpherson's view, maintains democracy and moderates a class conflict that is not an internal one in the province, but one between the province and outside centres of capital. The system either controls class conflict by giving an outlet to the class feeling of the province or conceals the conflict by demagogic appeals for unity in the pursuit of impossible objects.

Macpherson's criteria for recognizing a "quasi-party system" seem to be long tenure of power by one party, a week opposition, and a tendency of the party in power to become Jacobin, irresponsible to the people and renewing its authority by periodic plebiscites. He considers this to be the only possible system in Alberta, and perhaps in Canada, because, he maintains, the foundations for a two-party system do not exist.

The long dominance of single parties in Alberta, Saskatchewan, and Manitoba has not primarily been the result of the behaviour of a *petit bourgeois* community in revolt against semicolonial domination from the East. Reaction against the East has been a recurrent factor in prairie politics, but not an exclusive one. The charismatic power and political intuition of a few men has been as important, especially in Alberta. Henry Wise Wood, William Aberhart, Ernest Manning, Tommy Douglas, and John Diefenbaker were successful because they possessed unique talents of persuasiveness, timing, and awareness of the western mentality and were also blessed with good fortune; not because the prairies were occupied by independent producers.

Prairie governments have not been consistently opposed to the East and the old parties, as Macpherson implies: the Liberal party which ruled Saskatchewan from 1905 to 1944 (with one interruption) was for most of the time in open, even defiant, union with the federal Liberal party. The Progressive government of Manitoba gradually, though unobtrusively, moved into the federal Liberal camp after 1928, and from 1931 described itself as a Liberal-Progressive coalition.

Opposition in the prairie legislatures has, as Professor Macpherson notes, been weak in numbers and effectiveness. The numerical weakness of opposition groups in the legislatures, however, does not reflect the absence of opposition voters. Popular support for prairie governments has never been unusually high by the standards of other democratic countries. No prairie party has received more than fifty-eight per cent of the popular vote in a provincial election since 1917. In the elections in which single parties swept over four-fifths of the constituencies, they were able to do so because the opposition votes were divided among a large number of candidates and distributed fairly uniformly among the constituencies.[15] Opponents of the dominant prairie parties have frequently been unable to combine in opposition for reasons of federal party interest. (This was especially the case in Alberta from 1937 to 1940 when there was wide dissatisfaction with Premier Aberhart, yet provincial Liberals and Conservatives were pulled apart by the demands of the Federal party organizations.)

Insipid legislative opposition has been partly the product of a non-partisan approach to politics on the prairies. But this does not mean that westerners, because they share a common economic position, are incapable of supporting competitive political parties. There are more strictly political reasons for the failure of opposition on the prairies. The nonpartisan movement after 1917 was created by the frontier farmer's distaste for privilege that was much more than a simple economic impulse, by moral reaction against the excesses of the provincial Liberal and Conservative parties, and by a sense of common grievance against the political and economic power of central Canada. The political calm in the provincial legislatures lasted for several years after 1921; but it signified a return to moderation in politics rather than the triumph of a fundamental nonpartisan tradition.

Professor Macpherson's suggestion that the alternate party system never took firm root in western Canada must, in the light of prairie voting statistics, be modified. What have not taken root are the conventions of parliamentary debate and opposition within the provincial legislatures. The centre of the political battle has rarely been in the legislatures. Prairie legislatures had no independent traditions, self-respect, or position in society before universal suffrage, as did the British House of Commons. They have never acquired them; politicians and the public still regard the legislatures as slightly strange, imported contrivances to be treated with awe but ordinarily to be ignored. Political leaders seek sustenance through public acclaim on the hustings, not through legislative

---

[14]*Ibid.*, p. 21.

[15]The leading party won over four-fifths of the seats in Saskatchewan in 1917, 1925, 1934, 1944, and 1952; in Alberta in 1935, 1944, 1948, 1952, and 1959.

debate.[16] Successful politicians on the prairies (being practical men) have developed the talents—and parties, the forms of organization—required for their purposes. Political groups in the legislature have no coherence or permanence but depend for their life on the mood of a public with few inherited loyalties. The achievement of power comes not from the accumulation of cases against the governments in the legislatures (the public is unaware of any continuity that there may be in legislative debate), but more directly from management of the vote by an efficient machine, from long-term public attachment to a leader, or from demagogic appeals that turn sudden changes of public feeling to partisan advantage. Party competition exists, but it is manifested in tidal changes in voting habits rather than in day-to-day debate in the legislatures. A restrained plebiscitary system of democracy exists on the prairies; it does not merit Professor Macpherson's description as a "quasi-party system."

The final safeguard of democracy, the opportunity to replace a government by popular vote, is preserved by the fluid party system of western Canada. But the more immediate advantage of a free party system, a conscientious legislative opposition, does not exist. Cabinets tend to justify their acts by appeals to the electorate over the heads of legislators; they are not in the habit of submitting policies to critical scrutiny by the legislative opposition. The public does not demand it, and members do not train themselves for the work. The farmer's conventions in all three provinces before and after the First World War, and the C.C.F. conventions in Saskatchewan after 1944, for a few years substituted their criticism for that of the legislatures. But they had neither the skills nor the machinery of criticism that an alert legislature may develop, and their influence was ephemeral. Tolerance for persistent critical opposition, and the security and institutional aids such opposition requires are still absent in prairie politics; prairie society is neither self-confident enough nor distant enough from its days of romantic innocence and isolation to recognize their values.

---

[16]The level of legislative debate has been mediocre, and there has been little incentive to raise it. For most of the period, no reports of debates were kept for the information of the public. Saskatchewan, however, has broadcast the first seventy-five minutes of each day's debates since 1946, and transcripts of debates have been available to members since 1947. Manitoba introduced a provincial Hansard for the first time in October 1958. It is significant that in the heat of the 1962 Saskatchewan medical care controversy, there was no discussion of the value of a legislative session until the doctors' strike was in progress. The entire controversy occurred outside the legislature, through press conferences, radio and television statements, and newspaper advertisements. When the legislature did meet in August, it accomplished its work of amendment in a single day with virtually no debate.

19

The Social Basis of Party Politics in British Columbia

MARTIN ROBIN

*

It seems that the farther west one goes, the greater is the proclivity for radical politics. Saskatchewan was governed for twenty years by North America's only socialist government and today the New Democratic party is the major opposition party in the provincial legislature. Alberta has re-elected since 1935 a Social Credit government which presently shows little sign of senility or decay. British Columbia is twice blessed. The Social Credit government first elected in 1952 has been returned in every succeeding election. Premier W. A. C. Bennett has enjoyed the fruits of office longer than any other premier in British Columbia's history. Facing him in the legislature is the New Democratic Party, the major opposition in the provincial house since 1942. The moribund Conservative Party holds no provincial seats while Liberal representation is limited to five. The British Columbia situation is plainly unique both in the West and in the entire country. In no other province are the two federal minor parties—Social Credit and New Democratic—major parties in the legislature.

The British Columbia anomaly derives in part from the peculiar nature of the coast social structure. Extreme social cleavages, based primarily on class differences, have prevented the emergence of the non-ideological omnibus politics widely advertised by North American political scientists. High social tension and a weakly developed consensus are enduring elements of the British Columbia political culture.

The British Columbia labour movement, which provides the principal electoral, financial, and organizational base of the New Democratic Party, is the most militant and politically conscious in the country. Both British. and American influences have contributed to the radical predispositions of coast workers. British unionists, who comprised the great majority of the organized workers in English-speaking Canada in the first decades of the present century, brought with them both trade union and political organizational skills. Many had taken part in independent labour and socialist politics in Britain and launched into similar

*Reprinted from *Queen's Quarterly*, LXXII, No. 4, 1966.

activities in British Columbia soon after their arrival. They were particularly active in the building trades and coal mining unions which drew heavily from radical areas in the north and midlands of Britain.

The influence of American unionism on the Canadian working class has generally been conservative, but the American immigrant in the mining areas of the interior of British Columbia was an entirely different worker than the craft unionists who dominated the American Federation of Labor. The Pacific Northwest labour unions were always a thorn in the side of the labour aristocrats who dominated the American labour movement before the advent of the CIO, and British Columbia was not immune to the radical western American influence. The United Mine Workers became a powerful force on the Island and in the Eastern Kootenays, while the American Labor Union, Industrial Workers of the World, and Western Federation of Miners all had a substantial following among the many American immigrant labourers in the southern interior, coastal, and lower mainland regions. The metal miners in particular, fresh from the legendary labour wars fought in Colorado, Idaho, and Utah at the turn of the century and later, transplanted onto Canadian soil the fierce independence so characteristic of the frontier metaliferrous mining areas in the Northwest.

The radical background of the Unionists was but one element of a complex of factors which contributed to the militant stance of the British Columbia labour movement. Employers in the coast province have vehemently opposed the pressures of trade unions on property rights. Their public image, and pattern of behaviour, have historically conformed more to the Robber Baron stereotype than to that of the Industrial Statesman. Bitter labour wars, fought for union recognition, attended the growth of unionism in all parts of the province and oriental labourers were imported and used to lower wage rates and break strikes. The structure of industry has further contributed to class opposition. Highly capitalized extractive industries like lumbering, mining, and fishing, assured that industrial unionism, with its ideological orientation, has always been well-represented in the provincial labour movement. The ratio of ideological industrial unionism to craft business unionism is higher in British Columbia than in any other province in the country. Construction and lumber workers have been vulnerable to seasonal and cyclical unemployment and high job turnover. The provincial economy, with its specialized resource based industries and restricted internal markets, has been unstable and dependent upon shifting and uncertain export markets. Northwest American wage structures and living standards have served as significant reference standards and their demonstration effect on union demands has been considerable. The closed nature of many homogeneous, single-industry mining and lumbering communities with no middle class to mediate industrial conflict, in which class lines are clearly drawn, has contributed to the development of an intense working class consciousness. The force of traditional conservative institutions like the church, family, and an "enlightened" middle class, have been notably reduced in geographically isolated communities populated by mobile and radical working men. The

British Columbia labour movement is today the most highly organized and strike prone in the Dominion; 42.7 per cent of the paid labour force in the province are in trade unions compared to less than 33 per cent for Canada as a whole. From 1949 to 1959 the nonagricultural labour force in British Columbia, comprising 10 per cent of the total force of the country, contributed 15 per cent of all strikes and lockouts. Industrial disputes in British Columbia have been longer and more difficult to settle than in other areas of the country.

The political consequences of labour militancy are many but the most important result has been the alignment of the organized labour movement with the New Democratic Party. The socialist movement in British Columbia originally took root in communities populated by radical unionists and socialist organization expanded coscomitantly with the rise of industrial unionism at the turn of the century. Unlike all other provinces in Canada, socialism settled on the ground floor of industrial development in the coast province and socialist politicians claimed the affiliations of large blocs of unionists at the very beginning of the growth of the organized labour movement. In Ontario, the only other province where the NDP has a moderately strong urban and working class base, socialist organization appeared after the working class and trade unions had been disciplined electorally and ideologically by the elite dominated Liberal and Conservative parties. The socialists had to break down an established structure of political loyalties. Their task was considerably less onerous in British Columbia where a weakly developed party system, structurally generated class conflict, and a traditionally radical working class population concentrated in key industrial constituencies, combined to facilitate early radical political representation. In Ontario, it was not until 1943 that the CCF was able to gain the status of official opposition, a position it was subsequently unable to maintain. As early as 1912 the Socialist Party of Canada, a doctrinaire-Marxist predecessor of the CCF, constituted itself His Majesty's Loyal Opposition in the British Columbia provincial legislature. The socialist and independent labour share of the popular vote between 1903 and 1933 wavered between 10 and 20 per cent. But since the provincial election of 1933 the CCF-NDP vote had consistently remained around 30 per cent. In the 1945 and 1949 provincial elections the CCF-NDP gained 37.6 per cent and 35.1 per cent of the popular vote.

The status of the NDP as the perennial official opposition is facilitated by the close and enduring ties between party and trade union. Direct financial contributions based on the check off of union dues is prohibited by Bill 42, passed by the Social Credit government in 1961 for the explicit purpose of containing the exercise of political power by the trade union movement. While the Bill has hindered the growth of a direct organic tie between the party and many trade unions, obstructed the regular flow of labour funds into the party coffers, and lessened the magnitude of financial contribution, it has not prevented labour from resorting to various expedients, such as setting up "educational funds," to facilitate the conversion of trade union into party funds.

The trade unions have served as admirable training schools for political leaders. Six of the fourteen NDP MLA's have held offices in trade unions. The organizational contributions of politically conscious unions have been considerable. Union organizers, labour newspaper editors, and other officials contribute regularly to party campaigns in urban and industrial constituencies. Educational campaigns and party propaganda within the structure of the trade union movement have guaranteed a high turn-out of rank and file NDP party workers and voters. . . .

The political radicalism of the labour movement of British Columbia is opposed by the strong conservatism of the farm community. This is the reverse of the situation in the prairies and Alberta where the farm movements have been militant, class conscious and cohesive, and the labour movements, with the exception of Winnipeg, relatively weak and poorly organized. . . .

There are many reasons for the conservatism of the British Columbia farmers. Of primary importance is the diversified nature of British Columbia agriculture. There exists in British Columbia no monolithic wheat economy such as developed in Saskatchewan where the farming community sought a common solution to common problems affecting a homogeneous area and class structure. British Columbia agriculture is highly varied. Dairy production is concentrated in the Okanagan, the Lower Fraser Valley and Vancouver Island; tree fruits in the Okanagan; small fruits, special horticultural crops, vegetables and potatoes are found predominantly in the Fraser Valley; beef cattle in the Kamloops and the Cariboo areas; cereal crops in the Peace River area and poultry products and fur bearers mainly in the Fraser Valley. With few exceptions, British Columbia can and does produce any type of farm crop grown elsewhere in Canada. The heterogeneity of cultivation with its concomitant diversification of problems and outlooks has arrested the development of a homogeneous rural culture and leadership such as provided the solid base of the Saskatchewan CCF.

The British Columbia farmer is also comparatively affluent. Favourable climatic conditions and cost structures have allowed many agricultural commodities prevalent in British Columbia to compete successfully in foreign markets. Tree fruits, milk and, to a lesser extent, vegetables, have shown a remarkable price stability. There is little absentee ownership in farm areas and a high percentage of farms are free from financial encumbrances. Approximately 85 per cent of the farm operators in 1964 held the title to their land while nearly 75 per cent of the total number of farms were free from mortgages or agreements for sale. Farming activities like dairy ranching and tree fruit growing required a high initial capital investment and attracted capitalistically oriented farmers. Accustomed to accept a slow but steady return on their investment, to wait patiently until the fruit trees grew and matured or the dairy herd was sufficiently augmented, the farmers developed a placid and patient temperament far removed from the idiosyncratic vacillations of the prairies farmers.

The lack of corporate integration of the farming community derived not only from divergent pursuits but also from a great diversity in background, education and outlook. There are some British Columbia farmers well-read in Marxist economic theory and socialist doctrine, but these are not nearly as numerous as in Saskatchewan where more than a few farmers had first hand experience in radical labour politics. The British Columbia farmer is more likely to be found reading Kipling than Marx. The Duncan, Victoria and Saanich areas of Vancouver Island are populated by remittance men. The interior is peopled with gentlemen farmers and ranchers who take their tea and crumpets and observe the weekly ritual of a tennis match while their neighbours, the Mennonites in Chilliwack or the Portuguese in the Okanagan, toil mightily over the soil. British Columbia agrarians are a diverse lot, and, for the most part, content with things as they are.

Rural conservatism is reflected in the rather sparse and brief history of agrarian radicalism. The early Farmers' Alliance and Grange were dismal failures. The United Farmers of British Columbia, formed in 1917, lacked leadership and ideological conviction as well as a mass following. It avoided independent political action until the provincial election of 1924 when it joined forces with the Provincial Party, a weak and opportunistic movement of dissident conservatives led by the maverick millionaire, Maj-Gen. A. D. McRae. The UF of BC expired shortly thereafter and was replaced by the United Farmers of Canada which enjoyed limited success. Compared to the prairie provinces, the agrarian reaction to the depression in British Columbia during the 1930's was remarkably mild.

Predominantly rural constituencies provide the solid electoral base of the Social Credit Party. When Social Credit suddenly began to spread in 1951-52 it was in the rural areas that it received its greatest support. Rural constituencies like Chilliwack, North Peace River and South Peace River, North Okanagan and South Okanagan, still provide the safe solid base of Social Credit representation. The rural sector is heavily over-represented in the legislature. The 4 per cent of the population classed as rural exercise an electoral strength far out of proportion to their actual numbers. Farmers make up 10 per cent of the legislature and all sit for the Social Credit Party. The agrarian-worker cleavage in British Columbia runs deep and the NDP and its predecessor have largely failed to enroll the farmer in the socialist movement. The Cooperative Commonwealth Federation, whose avowed aim it was to federate farm and labour groups into a single radical party, enjoyed only limited success in rural areas. The British Columbia New Democratic Party is not a farm-labour party.

The farmers may provide a solid bread and butter core of Social Credit support, but the Social Credit Party is not an agrarian party and it is certainly not an agrarian protest party. The Social Credit Party today recruits its following from a wide social base. Although extensive quantitative voting surveys have yet to be done, it is clear that the Social Credit Party enjoys a sizeable working class vote. Without this vote the party could not have gained over 40 per cent of the vote in the last provincial election or elected candidates in urban seats like Vancouver-Burrard and Burnaby.

The manual labourer who supports the government is best described as a working man who votes Social Credit rather than a Social Credit working man. There is little ideological in his support; it is essentially pragmatic. The Social Credit administration has staked its career on a policy of rapid and unbridled economic development. With its vast power and communications projects, and wholehearted support of large and prospering firms in the lumber, construction, and mining industries, the government has made good its claim to supply jobs. Social Credit is a prosperity party and to many workers it spells employment.

Workers who vote Social Credit are more likely to be non-union members unexposed to the pro-NDP propaganda disseminated within the structure of the organized labour movement. The Bennett regime has actively wooed the unorganized worker by enacting legislation on matters like medicare and annual vacations with pay, conferring benefits on the unorganized which the trade unionists gained independently through collective bargaining. Social Credit supporters within the trade union movement are likely to be found in the older anti-socialist craft unions, among politically apathetic members or alienated workers who resent the highly bureaucratized union oligarchy, and within sections of dissident dual unions like the Mine Mill and Smelter Workers Union which is presently engaged in a fierce struggle for survival with the United Steelworkers, a strong supporter of the NDP.

The working man who votes Social Credit is not, of course, a deference voter. Frequently, lower class support for free enterprise parties is based on sentiments of deference to what are considered "natural leaders." The tory working man in Britain, whose support for the Conservative Party derives often from deferential sentiments, is a standing problem for the electoral strategists of the Labour Party. In British Columbia, however, hierarchical sentiments are weak, and, in any case, the Social Credit politicians, and the Premier in particular, hardly fit the tory image. As undistinguished populist products of the old middle class, they command little respect or prestige. The danger to the New Democratic Party stems not from the Premier's dignity, which barely exists, but from his maverick and anti-establishment political style. Workingmen identify with, rather than defer to, politicians who flout the niceties and decorum of gentlemanly politics.

But few Social Credit leaders or MLA's are recruited from the working class and the party's ideology, image and policies hardly reflect the pressures of working class interests. Social Credit is essentially anti-labour and certainly anti-trade union. Party leadership is recruited principally from the self-employed old middle classes which also provide solid electoral support. The farmers provide about 15 per cent of the Social Credit MLA's. About 50 per cent of the legislative group are businessmen, deriving their living from wholesale and retail trade, finance or insurance. Almost all are self-employed and many are self-made men with relatively low educational attainment. Notably absent from the legislative caucus are the higher professionals. There are only three lawyers in the legislative caucus, one professor and no doctors. Higher management officials are rarely active Social Creditors. The paucity of representatives from the higher professions explains in part the administration's remarkable disregard for the rules, normative procedures, and decorum usually associated with liberal democratic politics conducted by politicians recruited from high status groups.

The high incidence of support and participation of the old middle class in both urban and rural areas reflects the status anxieties of a class subject to extreme pressures from above and below. British Columbia is a province of Big Business and Big Labour which, before the advent of the Social Credit government in 1952, expressed themselves politically within the Liberal-Conservative coalition and the CCF parties respectively. Social Credit exhibited from the outset some of the populist characteristics found in the Social Credit movement in Alberta and in western populism; on the one hand, resentment of the upper class financial and business interests, on the other, a fear of socialism and the urban labour movement. But these fears are by no means equal. The opposition to organized labour and socialism far exceeds the mistrust of the economic elite. It would be erroneous to stress the populism, as opposed to the conservatism, of the British Columbia Social Credit Party. . . .

. . . There are important differences between the Alberta and British Columbia movements. British Columbia Social Credit shared little of the radicalism and much of the conservatism of the Alberta movement. Both movements, it is true, grew suddenly, like fungi, at points of decay on the body politic. The 1952 breakthrough election campaign in British Columbia was led by the Alberta president of the National Social Credit Association and MP for McLeod, the Rev. Ernest G. Hansell, a leader virtually thrust on the young and inexperienced British Columbia movement by the Alberta Social Credit government. Hansell conducted the campaign with typical evangelical fervour and British Columbians for the first time tasted radical hell-fire religious rhetoric in political debate. There was much talk during the campaign of Christianizing and purifying politics. But the Social Credit breakthrough occurred during a period of prosperity rather than, as in Alberta, depression. British Columbia Social Credit is a prosperity-born movement. Fundamentalist Douglas' economic and political theory, in any of its weird and confused varieties, was never seriously entertained by the new Premier, W. A. C. Bennett, and most of his leading colleagues. The Premier himself was a dissident former conservative who knew little and cared less about Douglasite monetary mysticism. Nor were the dissident old party supporters who cast their votes for the new movement emotionally carried away by a charismatic messiah, such as Aberhart was in 1935. The party in the 1952 campaign was officially leaderless, since Rev. Hansell, an outsider, served only as a temporary campaign leader and quickly left the province after the vote was in.

The British Columbia movement was not in its origins, and is not today, a charismatic movement of the dispossessed. The Social Credit electorate in both urban and rural areas were comparatively affluent and free from severe economic deprivation. They viewed the new premier, as they see him today, as a capable, aggressive and dynamic leader, but not as a man of extraordinary or supernatural powers. The remarkable upset campaign of 1952, which culminated in the election of nineteen Social Credit representatives who formed a minority government, can be traced to a variety of non-economic causes and issues: the dissolution of the discredited ruling Liberal-Conservative coalition, the aid to Catholic Schools question, the bungled Hospital Insurance scheme, and, what is perhaps most important, the new alternative ballot electoral system which, almost through sheer accident, favoured the Social Credit Party.

British Columbia Social Credit was not born and elected to remake the world. There are a few government back benchers, and a larger number of party workers, who profoundly mistrust big business and see Social Credit politics as a way of limiting if not eliminating the power of the magnates over the masses. But the power within the party in British Columbia, as in Alberta, lies primarily in the Premier and cabinet. To Bennett and his leading colleagues, Social Credit is an instrument of power rather than a means of reform or a way of life. It is not, however, power divorced from principle. The fundamental principle of Social Credit legislation, and the basic rationale of the movement, is to preserve intact the modified free enterprise system and, the necessary corollary of this, to keep the New Democratic Party from gaining power. When asked to define Social Credit during a campaign speech, the Premier replied simply: "It is the opposite of Socialism." British Columbia Social Credit is, as Professor Angus has written, free enterprise's second team.

The first team was the Liberal-Conservative Coalition, formed in 1941, and cemented by the close personal relationship of Liberal premier John Hart and Conservative leader R. J. Maitland. The coalition was continued by Byron Johnson and Herbert Anscomb, the successors of Hart and Maitland, although with much less success. It was formed ostensibly to handle the pressing war problems but endured long after the war crisis disappeared. The Coalition's basic objective was to keep the CCF from power. Had there been three-party constituency contests in the provincial election of 1945, and, possibly, of 1949, the CCF would have gained power through a split in the free enterprise vote. The Liberal-Conservative coalition effectively represented the economic elite, just as the CCF acted as labour's political arm. The most ardent business support came from powerful firms in the power and lumber industries which were acutely sensitive to the CCF's nationalization proposals. In a province in which a radical socialist party has been on the verge of power for decades, the insecurities of the economic magnates are great, and their intervention in politics direct and uninhibited.

The sudden accession of Social Credit to power in 1952 changed the direction but not the character of big business support. The economic elite's traditional allies had been routed and the corporations floundered momentarily between the old CCF dragon and the new crusaders. But it soon became apparent that the Bennett administration was the new effective free enterprise force. Elite financial support was accordingly shifted from the prostrate old party politicians to the new men of power. The support of the economic elite for the Social Credit Party, as the recent Williamson trial revealed, has continued uninterrupted from the 1953 provincial election to the present day.

This is not to say that Social Credit is a captive of the economic elite or that the Bennett cabinet is, in the crude sense, an executive committee of the ruling class. As new men of power recruited from undistinguished middle strata, the Social Credit politicians are mistrustful of the economic giants. None of the Social Credit legislators are recruited from the economic elite and older political families, and none have gained a measure of prestige and power in the economic or social system. They are resentful of those who have. The sentiment of resentment, characteristic of the old middle class, is a distinguishing mark of the Social Credit politician. Resentment is an ambivalent feeling compounded of admiration and hatred of the object resented. The Social Crediter accepts the premises of the free enterprise system and necessarily admires and identifies with the flower of business civilization, the business magnate. But the very conditions which guarantee the power and position of the elite—concentration and monopoly—have conspired to restrict the freedom of opportunity of the forgotten man, the small entrepreneur.

Middle class resentment of the elite is not, however, extreme in British Columbia because prosperity has buttressed the stability and position of all classes, and especially the old middle class, both rural and urban. The insurance agents, farmers, and car dealers, sitting for Social Credit in the legislature may not have earned a fortune at the free enterprise game, but they have certainly avoided the declassification and deprivations resulting from depressed conditions. Their mistrust of the financial elite is correspondingly mild. And, if the Social Credit legislator has not arrived economically and socially, he has certainly risen politically. Resentment of the elite, born of status deprivation, has been partially overcome through accession to positions of political power.

Status, however, is a scarce and slippery commodity and there exists in British Columbia today a high concentration of status outside of, rather than within, the political system. After thirteen years in office, the longest administration in provincial history, Social Credit is still not thoroughly respectable and claims few open adherents among the prestigious classes. Social Credit legislators are hard put to overcome their undistinguished backgrounds, low education and modest skills. Their low prestige derives as well from a long-standing element of the British Columbia political culture which places a low value on the political career. In a weakly integrated community in which cleavages run deep and where the brokerage function of the liberal politician has not been effective, politics has been discredited. The British Columbia politician is more likely to be broken than a broker.

There is, of course, the added factor of the New Democratic Party. The existence of a Socialist Party as the principal viable
alternative increases the independence of the Bennett administration from
the economic elite. In a non-polarized political system, such as exists
federally in Canada, in which there is wide class support for both major
parties, the large firms characteristically split their financial contributions
60-40 between the government and major opposition. But Social Credit
gains the lion's share of corporation funds in British Columbia because
there is no viable free enterprise opposition. By switching the bulk of its
support to either or both of the minor parties, business runs the fatal risk
of helping split the anti-socialist opposition and bringing in a minority
New Democratic Party government. Furthermore, the Premier cannot
emulate E. C. Manning and turn a deaf ear to opposition demands.
Alberta's is virtually a one party system. The NDP in British Columbia,
with almost 30 per cent of the popular vote, always stands as a ready
alternative administration and therefore does exercise some influence over
government policy.

Finally, friction between the elite and the government is
magnified by the amateur composition of the Social Credit regime. There
is a notable lack of administrative skills within the Cabinet and legislative
caucus. Only two members of the legislative group elected in 1952 had
previous legislative experience. While party legislators have gained considerable experience during the thirteen years in office, the cabinet is still
sorely lacking in the administrative competence found primarily in members of the legal profession and higher management. The skills of the
Social Credit politician are more evident on the hustings than in legislative
debate or departmental administration.

It is, of course, ironic that a party which elevates the
technocratic ideal should be so devoid of technical talents, rational methods, and administrative skills. The Premier and his cabinet talk of efficient
results, and liken the new administration to a sound and profitable business enterprise. They have never gone as far as the Alberta movement
which advocated, in its early phase, rule by experts, but they do see Social
Credit as the infusion of rational, efficient, and, one might add, Christian
principles into the sphere of public government. Social Credit holds out
the Saint-Simonian hope that the government of men will be replaced by
the administration of things. In an environment of high tensions, it promises the end of politics and enjoys the ardent support of groups, especially
the old middle class, disillusioned with the chicanery, corruption, and
compromises of class-based politics.

But the Saint-Simonian promise has not been fulfilled. The
Sommers case, the system of allocation of liquor licences and timber
rights, the patchwork social welfare programme, the crude mode of ex-
propriation of BC Hydro, all negate the government's claims to either
rationality or Christian morality. The money lenders, their pockets bulg-
ing, lie fat in the temple. Rationality implies predictability, but few can
chart the legislative course or decision-making pattern of a regime acutely

sensitive to the waves and eddies of the public mood. Social Credit is not a-political but hyper-political. The government of men, within the structure of the modified free enterprise system, is its only concern. The genius of British Columbia Social Credit lies in its ability to manipulate, rather than eliminate, group conflict and resentment.

British Columbia politics is a politics of high moral tension. Norms of legitimacy are weakly anchored and cross-group consensus is weak. Social cleavages run deep. The Doukhobor question and the earlier oriental problem have a history of violence and rancour. Anti-metropolitanism pervades the interior while xenophobic sentiments flourish in a society divided into distinct and separate geographical and cultural entities. But the class cleavage, cutting across all of the other divisions, is deepest of all. In no other province have the socialists hovered on the brink of power for so long, feeding the indignation and fears of the possessing classes. In a community where cross-class consensus is at a minimum, the temperature of political debate is white hot. It is standard fare during election campaigns to remind the electorate that a vote for the New Democratic Party is a vote for the abolition of the Church, family, morality and, not least, property. The Social Credit Party is the legitimate expression of the indignation of the possessing classes and the effective guarantee of their hegemony.

British Columbia's anomalous party system cannot be correctly designated a protest party system. The New Democratic Party, it is true, still holds out the Utopian promise of the Cooperative Commonwealth in a province whose bountiful wealth and magnificent beauty nurture the vision of the end of scarcity and inequality. But the present is Utopia enough for the government party. British Columbia Social Credit advertises neither the populist idyllic past, nor the socialist golden future. Its vision extends no further than the next highway or bridge.

Election Results 1878-1965

*

I am indebted to Professor Howard A. Scarrow who provided most of the data that follow.[1] The 1962 percentages of votes are calculated from the preliminary results issued by the Chief Electoral Officer on August 8, 1962 and published in the *Kingston Whig-Standard,* August 9, 1962.

The 1962 information relating to seats is from the Canadian Press summary published in the *Kingston Whig-Standard,* June 21, 1962, adjusted for the two Liberal victories after the tabulation of the service vote and the Liberal victory in the deferred Stormont election.

The 1963 percentages of votes and apportionment of seats are computed from the Canadian Press summary published in the *Kingston Whig-Standard, May 10, 1963.*

The 1965 percentages of votes are computed from returns issued by the Chief Electoral Officer, published in the *Daily Star,* December 29, 1965. The apportionment of seats is taken from the Canadian Press summary published in the *Kingston Whig-Standard,* November 9, 1965.

---

[1]Complete details can be found in his book *Canada Votes: A Handbook of Federal and Provincial Election Data* (New Orleans: Hauser Press. 1962).

PRINCE EDWARD ISLAND

Election Year	Party Forming Government	Total Seats	Conservative Seats	Conservative Votes (%)	Liberal Seats	Liberal Votes (%)	Other Seats	Other Votes (%)
1878	Con.	6	5	57	1	43		
1882	"	6	1	48	5	52		
1887	"	6	0	46	6	54		
1891	"	6	2	48	4	52		
1896	Lib.	5	3	49	2	51		
1900	"	5	2	48	3	52		
1904	"	4	3	51	1	49		
1908	"	4	1	50	3	50		
1911	Con.	4	2	51	2	49		
1917	" [1]	4	2	50	2	50		
1921	Lib.	4	0	37	4	46		17[2]
1925	"	4	2	48	2	52		
1926	"	4	1	47	3	53		
1930	Con.	4	3	50	1	50		
1935	Lib.	4	0	39	4	58		3[3]
1940	"	4	0	45	4	55		
1945	"	4	1	47	3	49		4[4]
1949	"	4	1	48	3	49		3[5]
1953	"	4	1	48	3	51		1
1957	Con.	4	4	52	0	47		1
1958	"	4	4	62	0	38		
1962	"	4	4	51	0	44		5[6]
1963	Lib.	4	2	51	2	47		2[7]
1965	"	4	4	54	0	44		2[8]

1. Wartime Coalition.
2. Including 12 per cent Progressive.
3. "   3 "   "   Reconstruction Party.
4. "   4 "   "   C.C.F.
5. "   2 "   "   C.C.F.
6. "   5 "   "   N.D.P.
7. "   2 "   "   N.D.P.
8. "   2 "   "   N.D.P.

NEWFOUNDLAND

Election Year	Party Forming Government	Total Seats	Conservative Seats	Conservative Votes (%)	Liberal Seats	Liberal Votes (%)	Other Seats	Other Votes (%)
1949	Lib.	7	2	28	5	72		
1953	"	7	0	28	7	67		5[1]
1957	Con.	7	2	38	5	62		
1958	"	7	2	45	5	54		1
1962	"	7	1	36	6	59		5[2]
1963	Lib.	7	0	30	7	65		5[3]
1965	"	7	0	32	7	64		4[4]

1. Including 4 per cent C.C.F.
2.   "   5 "   " N.D.P.
3.   "   4 "   " N.D.P.
4.   "   1 "   " N.D.P., and 2 per cent Social Credit.

NOVA SCOTIA

Election Year	Party Forming Government	Total Seats	Conservative Seats	Conservative Votes (%)	Liberal Seats	Liberal Votes (%)	C.C.F.—N.D.P. Seats	C.C.F.—N.D.P. Votes (%)	Other Seats	Other Votes (%)
1878	Con.	21	14	52	6	44			1	4
1882	"	21	14	55	7	45				
1887	"	21	14	50	7	47				3
1891	"	21	16	54	5	45				1
1896	Lib.	20	10	50	10	49				1
1900	"	20	5	48	15	52				
1904	"	18	0	44	18	55				1
1908	"	18	6	49	12	51				
1911	Con.	18	9	49	9	51				
1917	" [1]	16	12[2]	48	4	46				6
1921	Lib.	16	0	32	16	53				15
1925	"	14	11	56	3	42				2
1926	"	14	12	54	2	43				3
1930	Con.	14	10	53	4	47				
1935	Lib.	12	0	32	12	52				16
1940	"	12	1	40	10	51	1	6		3
1945	"	12	2	37	9	46	1	17		
1949	"	13	2	37	10	53	1	10		
1953	"	12	1	40	10	53	1	7		
1957	Con.	12	10	50	2	45	0	5		
1958	"	12	12	57	0	38	0	5		
1962	"	12	9	47	2	42	1	10		1
1963	Lib.	12	7	47	5	47	0	6		
1965	"	12	10	49	2	42	0	9		

1. Wartime Coalition.
2. Including three Liberal Unionists.

NEW BRUNSWICK

Election Year	Party Forming Government	Total Seats	Conservative Seats	Conservative Votes (%)	Liberal Seats	Liberal Votes (%)	Other Seats	Other Votes (%)
1878	Con.	16	5	45	11	55		
1882	"	16	9	55	7	45		
1887	"	16	10	51	6	49		
1891	"	16	13	59	3	38		3
1896	Lib.	14	9	49	5	44		7
1900	"	14	5	48	9	52		
1904	"	13	6	49	7	51		
1908	"	13	2	46	11	54		
1911	Con.	13	5	49	8	51		
1917	"	11	7[1]	59	4	41		
1921	Lib.	11	5	39	5	50	1[2]	11
1925	"	11	10	60	1	40		
1926	"	11	7	54	4	46		
1930	Con.	11	10	59	1	41		
1935	Lib.	10	1	32	9	57		11
1940	"	10	5	43	5	55		2
1945	"	10	3	38	7	50		12
1949	"	10	2	39	8	54		7
1953	"	10	3	42	7	53		5
1957	Con.	10	5	49	5	48		3
1958	"	10	7	54	3	43		3
1962	"	10	4	46	6	45		9[3]
1963	Lib.	10	4	40	6	47		13[4]
1965	"	10	4	43	6	47		9[5]

1. Including four Liberal Unionists.
2. Progressive.
3. Including 5 per cent N.D.P. and 5 per cent Social Credit.
4. Including 4 per cent N.D.P. and 9 per cent Social Credit.
5. Including 9 per cent N.D.P.

QUEBEC

Election Year	Party Forming Government	Total Seats	Conservative Seats	Conservative Votes (%)	Liberal Seats	Liberal Votes (%)	Other Seats	Other Votes (%)
1878	Con.	65	45	56	20	40		4
1882	"	65	52	59	13	41		
1887	"	65	36	51	29	49		
1891	"	65	29	52	34	45		3
1896	Lib.	65	16	46	49	54		
1900	"	65	8	44	57	56		
1904	"	65	11	43	54	56		1
1908	"	65	11	41	54	57		2
1911	Con.	65	27	49	38	51		
1917	" [1]	65	3[2]	25	62	73		2
1921	Lib.	65	0	18	65	70		12
1925	"	65	4	34	59	59	2	7
1926	"	65	4	34	60	62	1	4
1930	Con.	65	24	45	40	53	1	2
1935	Lib.	65	5	28	55	54	5	18[3]
1940	"	65	1[5]	20	61	63	3[4]	17
1945	"	65	2[7]	8	53	51	10[6]	41
1949	"	73	2	25	68	60	3	15
1953	"	75	4	29	66	61	5[8]	10
1957	Con.	75	9	31	62	58	4[9]	11
1958	"	75	50	50	25	46		4
1962	"	75	14	30	35	40	26[11]	30[10]
1963	Lib.	75	8	20	47	46	20[11]	34[12]
1965	"	75	8	21	56	46	11[13]	33[14]

1. Wartime Coalition.
2. Including one Liberal Unionist.
3. Including 9 per cent cast for Reconstruction Party.
4. Independent Liberals.
5. Independent Conservative.
6. Six Independents, one Independent Liberal, two Bloc Populaire Canadien, one Labour Progressive.
7. Including one Independent Conservative.
8. Three Independents and two Independent Liberals.
9. Two Independents and two Independent Liberals.
10. Including 26 per cent Social Credit and 4 per cent N.D.P.
11. Social Credit.
12. Including 27 per cent Social Credit and 7 per cent N.D.P.
13. Including nine Créditistes, one Independent Progressive Conservative and one Independent.
14. Including 18 per cent Créditiste and 12 per cent N.D.P.

ONTARIO

Election Year	Party Forming Government	Total Seats	Conservative Seats	Conservative Votes (%)	Liberal Seats	Liberal Votes (%)	Progressive Seats	Progressive Votes (%)	C.C.F.—N.D.P. Seats	C.C.F.—N.D.P. Votes (%)	Other Seats	Other Votes (%)
1878	Con.	88	62	52	26	47						1
1882	"	92	54	51	38	49						
1887	"	92	54	51	38	49						
1891	"	92	48	49	44	49						2
1896	Lib.	92	43	45	43	40					6[1]	15
1900	"	92	56	50	36	50						
1904	"	86	48	50	38	50						
1908	"	86	48	51	37[2]	47					1[3]	2
1911	Con.	86	73[4]	56	13	43						1
1917	"	82	74[5]	62	8	34						4
1921	Lib.	82	37	39	21	30	24	28				3
1925	"	82	68	57	11	31	2	9			1[6]	3
1926	"	82	53	54	26[7]	39	2	4			1[8]	3
1930	Con.	82	59	54	22	44	1	1			1[9]	1
1935	Lib.	82	25	35	56	43					1[9]	22[10]
1940	"	82	25	43	57[11]	51						6
1945	"	82	48	42	34	41				14		3
1949	"	83	25	37	56	46			1	15	1[12]	2
1953	"	85	33	40	51	47			1	11		2
1957	Con.	85	61	49	21	37			3	12		2
1958	"	85	67	56	15	33			3	11		
1962	"	85	35	39	44	42			6	17		2
1963	Lib.	85	27	35	52	46			6	16		3[13]
1965	"	85	25	34	51	44			9	22		

1. Three McCarthyite, two Patrons of Industry, one Independent.
2. Including one Independent Liberal.
3. Independent.
4. Including one Independent Conservative.
5. Including twelve Liberal Unionists.
6. Independent Liberal.
7. Including two Liberal Progressives and one Independent Liberal.
8. Independent Liberal.
9. United Farmers of Ontario-Labour.
10. Including 12 per cent for Reconstruction Party.
11. Including two Liberal Progressives.
12. Independent.
13. Including two per cent Social Credit.

MANITOBA

Election Year	Party Forming Government	Total Seats	Conservative Seats	Conservative Votes (%)	Liberal Seats	Liberal Votes (%)	Progressive Seats	Progressive Votes (%)	Labour—C.C.F.—N.D.P. Seats	Labour—C.C.F.—N.D.P. Votes (%)	Other Seats	Other Votes (%)
1878	Con.	4	3	50	1	50						
1882	"	5	2	47	3	53						
1887	"	5	4	51	1	49						
1891	"	5	4	53	1	47						
1896	Lib.	7	4	47	2	35					1[1]	18
1900	"	7	3	48	4	52						3
1904	"	10	3	42	7	55						3
1908	"	10	8	52	2	45						3
1911	Con.	10	8	52	2	45						3
1917	" [2]	15	14[3]	80	1	20						
1921	Lib.	15	0	24	1	11	12	44	1	6	1[4]	15
1925	"	17	7	42	1	20	7	27	2	11		
1926	"	17	0	42	11[5]	38	4	11	2	9		
1930	Con.	17	11	48	4[6]	37		4	2	11		
								C.C.F.				
1935	Lib.	17	1	27	14[7]	41			2	19		13[8]
1940	"	17	1	26	15[9]	48			1	19		7
1945	"	17	2	25	10	35			5	32		8
1949	"	16	1	22	12	48			3	26		4
1953	"	14	3	27	8	40			3	24		9[10]
1957	Con.	14	8	36	1	26			5	24		14[11]
1958	"	14	14	57	0	22			0	20		1
								N.D.P.				
1962	"	14	11	41	1	31			2	20		8[12]
1963	Lib.	14	10	42	2	34			2	17		7[13]
1965	"	14	10	41	1	31			3	24		4[14]

1. McCarthyite.
2. Wartime Coalition.
3. Including six Liberal Unionists.
4. Independent Liberal.
5. Including seven Liberal Progressives.
6.   "   three   "   "
7.   "   two   "   "
8.   "   6 per cent Reconstruction Party.
9.   "   one Liberal Progressive.
10.   "   6 per cent Social Credit.
11.   "   13 "   "   "   "
12.   "   7 "   "   "   "
13.   "   7 "   "   "   "
14.   "   4 "   "   "   "

SASKATCHEWAN

Election Year	Party Forming Government	Total Seats	Conservative Seats	Conservative Votes (%)	Liberal Seats	Liberal Votes (%)	C.C.F.—N.D.P. Seats	C.C.F.—N.D.P. Votes (%)	Progressive Seats	Progressive Votes (%)	Other Seats	Other Votes (%)
1908	Lib	10	1	37	9	57						6
1911	Con.	10	1	39	9	59						2
1917	"	16	16[1]	74	0	26						1
1921	Lib.	16	0	17	1	21			15	61		1
1925	"	21	0	25	15	42			6	32		1
1926	"	21	0	27	18[2]	57			3	16		1
1930	Con.	21	8	38	11	47			2	12		3
1935	Lib.	21	1	19	16	41	2	21			2[3]	19[4]
1940	"	21	2	14	12	43	5	29			2[5]	14
1948	"	21	1	19	2	33	18	44				4[6]
1949	"	20	1	14	14	44	5	41				1
1953	"	17	1	12	5	38	11	44				6[7]
1957	Con.	17	3	23	4	30	10	36				11[8]
1958	"	17	16	51	0	20	1	28				1
1962	"	17	16	50	1	23	0	22				5
1963	Lib.	17	17	54	0	24	0	18				4[9]
1965	"	17	17	48	0	24	0	26				2[10]

1. Including seven Liberal Unionists.
2. Including two Liberal Progressives.
3. Social Credit.
4. Including 16 per cent Social Credit.
5. One Unity, one Unity Reform.
6. Including 3 per cent Social Credit.
7.   "   5 "   "   "   "
8.   " 10 "   "   "   "
9.   "   4 "   "   "   "
10.   "   2 "   "   "   "

ALBERTA

Election Year	Party Forming Government	Total Seats	Conservative Seats	Conservative Votes (%)	Liberal Seats	Liberal Votes (%)	Progressive Seats	Progressive Votes (%)	Social Credit Seats	Social Credit Votes (%)	Other Seats	Other Votes (%)
1878	Con.											
1882	"											
1887	"											
1891	"											
1896	Lib.											
1900	"											
1904	"											
1908	"	7	3	44	4	50						6
1911	Con.	7	1	43	6	53						4
1917	" [11]	12	11[1]	61	1	36						3
1921	Lib.	12	0	20	0	16	11	57			1[2]	7
1925	"	16	3	32	4	26	9	32				10
1926	"	16	1	32	3	24	11	39			1[2]	5
1930	Con.	16	4	34	3	30	9	30				6
1935	Lib.	17	1	17	1	21			15	48		14[3]
1940	"	17	0	13	7	38			10	35		14[4]
1945	"	17	2	19	2	22			13	37		22[5]
1949	"	17	2	17	5	35			10	37		11[6]
1953	"	17	2	15	4	35			11	41		9[7]
1957	Con.	17	3	28	1	28			13	38		6[8]
1958	"	17	17	60	0	14			0	22		4[9]
1962	"	17	15	43	0	19			2	29		9[10]
1963	Lib.	17	14	45	1	22			2	26		7[12]
1965	"	17	15	47	0	22			2	23		8[13]

1. Including four Liberal Unionists.
2. Labour.
3. Including 13 per cent C.C.F.
4. " 13 " " "
5. " 18 " " "
6. " 9 " " "
7. " 7 " " "
8. " 6 " " "
9. " 4 " " "
10. " 9 " " N.D.P.
11. Wartime Coalition.
12. Including 7 per cent N.D.P
13. " 8 " " "

BRITISH COLUMBIA

Election Year	Party Forming Government	Total Seats	Conservative Seats	Conservative Votes (%)	Liberal Seats	Liberal Votes (%)	C.C.F.—N.D.P. Seats	C.C.F.—N.D.P. Votes (%)	Social Credit Seats	Social Credit Votes (%)	Other Seats	Other Votes (%)
1878	Con.	6	6	89	0							11
1882	"	6	6	83	0	11						6
1887	"	6	6	87	0	13						
1891	"	6	6	72	0	28						
1896	Lib.	6	2	51	4	49						
1900	"	6	2	41	4	49						10[1]
1904	"	7	0	39	7	49						12[2]
1908	"	7	5	47	2	36						17[3]
1911	Con.	7	7	59	0	37						4[4]
1917	"	13	13	68	0	26						6[5]
1921	Lib.	13	7	48	3	30					3[6]	22[7]
1925	"	14	10	49	3	35					1[8]	16[9]
1926	"	14	12	54	1	37					1[10]	9[11]
1930	Con.	14	7	49	5	41					2[12]	10[13]
1935	Lib.	16	5	25	6	32	3	34			2[14]	9[15]
1940	"	16	4	31	10	37	1	28			1[16]	4[17]
1945	"	16	5	30	5	28	4	29		2	2[18]	11[19]
1949	"	18	3	28	11	37	3	31		1	1[20]	3
1953	"	22	3	14	8	31	7	27	4	26		2
1957	Con.	22	7	33	2	21	7	22	6	24		
1958	"	22	18	49	0	16	4	25	0	10		
1962	"	22	6	27	4	27	10	31	2	14		1
1963	Lib.	22	4	23	7	33	9	30	2	13		1
1965	"	22	3	19	7	30	9	33	3	17		1

1. Labour.
2. Including 4 per cent Socialist, 8 per cent Independent.
3. Including 7 per cent Socialist and 10 per cent Independent.
4. Including 3 per cent Socialist.
5. Including 5 per cent Labour.
6. Two Progressives and one Independent.
7. Including 9 per cent Progressive; 5 per cent Labour; 5 per cent Socialist; 2 per cent Independent.
8. Independent.
9. Including 6 per cent Labour and 6 per cent Progressive.
10. Independent.
11. Including 7 per cent Labour.
12. One Independent; one Independent Labour.
13. Including 6 per cent Independent Labour.
14. One Reconstruction; one Independent.
15. Including 7 per cent Reconstruction.
16. Independent.
17. Including 3 per cent Independent.
18. One Independent CCF; one Independent.
19. Including 5 per cent Labour Progressive.
20. Independent.

THE TERRITORIES

Election Year	Party Forming Government	Total Seats	Conservative Seats	Conservative Votes (%)	Liberal Seats	Liberal Votes (%)	Other Votes (%)
1887	Con.	4	4	69		31	
1891	"	4	4	81		19	
1896	Lib.	4	1	44	3	46	10[1]
1900	"	4		45	4	55	
1904	"	11	4	43	7	57	
1908	"	1	0	11	1	40	49[2]
1911	Con.	1	1	61	0	39	
1917	"	1	1	54	0	46	
1921	Lib.	1	1	51	0	48	1[3]
1925	"	1	1	59	0	41	
1926	"	1	1	56	0	44	
1930	Con.	1	1	60	0	40	
1935	Lib.	1	1	56	0	44	
1940	"	1	1	54	0	46	
1945	"	1	1	40	0	0	60[4]
1949	"	1	0	0	1	49	51[5]
1953	"	2	0	27	2	54	19[6]
1957	Con.	2	0	41	2	59	
1958	"	2	1	49	1	50	1[7]
1962	"	2	1	47	1	46	7[8]
1963	Lib.	2	2	54	0	42	4[10]
1965	"	2	1	45	1	52	3

1968
1972

1. Independent.
2. Independent.
3. Independent.
4. Including 28 per cent C.C.F. and 32 per cent Labour Progressive.
5. Including 17 per cent C.C.F. and 34 per cent Independent.
6. Including 14 per cent Social Credit.
7. Including 1 per cent Independent Progressive Conservative.
8. Including 7 per cent Social Credit.
9. Wartime Coalition.
10. Including 4 per cent Social Credit.

TOTAL

Election Year	Party Forming Government	Total Seats	Conservative Seats	Conservative Votes (%)	Liberal Seats	Liberal Votes (%)	Progressive Seats	Progressive Votes (%)	C.C.F.–N.D.P. Seats	C.C.F.–N.D.P. Votes (%)	Social Credit Seats	Social Credit Votes (%)	Reconstruction / Créditiste Seats	Reconstruction / Créditiste Votes (%)	Other Seats	Other Votes (%)
1878	Con.	206	140	53	65	45									1	2
1882	"	211	138	53	73	47									2	2
1887	"	215	128	51	87	49									7	9
1891	Lib.	215	122	52	91	46									1	1
1896	"	213	88	46	118	45										2
1900	"	213	81	47	132	52										1
1904	"	214	75	47	139	52										3
1908	"	221	85	47	135	51									4	6
1911	Con.	221	134	51	87	48									6	5
1917	" [1]	235	153[2]	57	82[3]	40									6	4
1921	Lib.	235	50	30	116	41	65	23							5	3
1925	"	245	116	46	99	40	24	9							7	3
1926	"	245	91	45	128	46	20	5							6	7
1930	Con.	245	137	49	91	45	12	3							12	12
1935	Lib.	245	40	30	173	45			7	9	17	4	1	9	5	4
1940	"	245	40	31	181	51			8	8	10	3			5	4
1945	"	245	67	27	125	41			28	16	13	4			4	2
1949	"	262	41	30	193	49			13	13	10	4				1
1953	"	265	51	31	171	49			23	11	15	5				
1957	Con.	265	112	39	105	41			25	11	19	7				
1958	"	265	208	54	49	34			8	9		2				
1962	"	265	116	37	100	37			19	14	30	12				
1963	Lib.	265	95	33	129	42			17	13	24	12	9	5		
1965	"	265	97	32	131	40			21	18	5	4			2	1

1. Wartime Coalition.
2. Government.
3. Opposition.

Readings

*

Section One: Historical Background

Ayearst, Morely, "The Parti Rouge and the Clergy," *Canadian Historical Review*, XV (1934), 390.

Borden, Sir Robert, *Robert Laird Borden: His Memoirs*. Toronto: Macmillan Co. of Canada, Ltd., 1938.

Bovey, Wilfred, "French Canada and the Problem of Quebec," *The Nineteenth Century*, CXXIII (January, 1938).

Brady, Alexander, *Canada*. New York: Charles Scribner's Sons, 1932, Chap. 3.

Brown, George, "The Grit Party and the Great Reform Convention of 1859," *Canadian Historical Review*, XVI (1935), 245.

Careless, J. M. S., *Brown of the Globe*, I: *The Voice of Upper Canada, 1818-1859*. Toronto: Macmillan Co. of Canada, Ltd., 1959.

Cornell, P. G., "The Alignment of Political Groups in the United Province of Canada 1854-1864." *Canadian Historical Review*, XXX (1949), 22.

Creighton, Donald, *John A. Macdonald: The Old Chieftain*. Toronto: Macmillan Co. of Canada, Ltd., 1955.

Dafoe, J. W., *Laurier: A Study in Canadian Politics*. Toronto: Thomas Allen, Ltd., 1922.

Dobie, Edith, "Party History in British Columbia, 1903-1933," *Pacific Northwest Quarterly* (April, 1936).

MacFarlane, R. O., "Manitoba Politics and Parties After Confederation," *Canadian Historical Association Report*, 1940.

Meighen, Arthur, *Unrevised and Unrepented*. Toronto: Clarke, Irwin & Company, Ltd., 1949.

Reid, Escott M., "Canadian Political Parties: A Study of the Economic and Racial Bases of Conservation and Liberalism in 1930," *Contributions to Canadian Economics*, VI (1930).

Skelton, O. D., *Life and Letters of Sir Wilfrid Laurier*. London: The Century Company, 1921.

Thomson, D. C., *Alexander MacKenzie: Clear Grit*. Toronto: Macmillan Co. of Canada, Ltd., 1960.

Underhill, Frank H., *Canadian Political Parties*, Canadian Historical Association, Historical Booklets, No. 8 (1957).

———"The Development of National Parties in Canada," *Canadian Historical Review*, XVI (1935), 367. Reprinted in F. H. Underhill, *In Search of Canadian Liberalism*. Toronto: Macmillan Co. of Canada, Ltd., 1960, p. 21.

Section Two: The Canadian Party System

Alford, Robert R., *Social Class and Voting in Four Anglo-Saxon Democracies,* Berkeley: Survey Research Center, 1961.

Beck, J. M., *The Government of Nova Scotia*. Toronto: University of Toronto Press, 1957.

———"The Election of 1957 and the Canadian Electoral System," *The Dalhousie Review*, XXXVII, 4, Winter (1958).

Beck, J. M., "The Nomination of Candidates in Nova Scotia," *The Dalhousie Review*, XXXVI, No. 4, Winter (1957).

Corbett, David C., Some Implications of the Canadian Election," *The Australian Quarterly*, XXIX, No. 3 (September, 1957).

Dawson, R. MacGregor, *The Government of Canada*. Toronto: University of Toronto Press, 1954, Chaps. 21-23.

Dean, Edgar Packard, "How Canada Has Voted: 1867-1945," *The Canadian Historical Review*, XXX, 3 (1949).

Epstein, Leon D., "A Comparative Study of Canadian Parties," *The American Political Science Review*, LVIII, 1 (1964).

Fox, P. W., *Politics: Canada*. Toronto, 2nd ed.: McGraw-Hill Co. of Canada, Ltd., 1966.

Heasman, D. J., "Political Alignments in Canada," *Parliamentary Affairs*, XVI, 4 (1963), 419.

Kamin, L. G., "Ethnic and Party Affiliations of Candidates as Determinants of Voting," *Canadian Journal of Psychology*, XII (1958).

Kornberg, Alan, "Perception and Constituency Influence on Legislative Behaviour," *Western Political Quarterly*, XIX, 2 (1966), 285.

Kornberg, Alan and Thomas, Norman, "The Political Socialization of National Legislative Elites in the United States and Canada," *Journal of Politics*, XXVII, 4 (1965), 761.

Lederle, J. W., "Party Forms in the Canadian Senate," *Queen's Quarterly*, LVII (1950), 21.

Lower, Arthur R. M., "Political Partyism in Canada," *Canadian Historical Association Report*, 1955.

Meisel, John, *The 1957 Canadian General Election*. Toronto: University of Toronto Press, 1962.

———, *Papers on the 1962 Election*. Toronto: University of Toronto Press, 1965.

———, "The Stalled Omnibus: Canadian Parties in the 1960's," *Social Research*, XXX, No. 3, Autumn (1963).

Reid, Escott M., "The Canadian Election of 1935 and After," *American Political Science Review*, XXX (1936), 111.

———"The Effects of the Depression on Canadian Politics," *American Political Science Review*, XXVII (1933), 455.

Scarrow, Howard A., "By-Elections and Public Opinion in Canada," *The Public Opinion Quarterly*, XXV, Spring (1961).

———, "Distinguishing Between Political Parties—The Case of Canada," *Midwest Journal of Political Science*, IX, No. 1 (February, 1965).

———, "Nomination and Local Party Organization in Canada: A Case Study," *The Western Political Quarterly*, XVII No. 1 (March, 1964), 55.

———, "Patterns of Voter Turnout in Canada," *Midwest Journal of Political Science*, V, No. 4 (November, 1961).

Smiley, Donald V., "Canada's Poujadists: A New Look at Social Credit," *Canadian Forum*, XLII (1962), 121.

———, "One Partyism and Canadian Democracy," *Canadian Forum*, XXXVIII (1958), 79.

———"The Two Party System and One Party Dominance in the Liberal Democratic State," *Canadian Journal of Economics and Political Science*, XXIV (1958), 312.

Thorburn, H. G., *Politics in New Brunswick*. Toronto: University of Toronto Press, 1961.

Underhill, Frank H., "Canadian Liberal Democracy in 1955," in G. Ferguson & F. H. Underhill, *Press and Party in Canada.* Toronto: The Ryerson Press, 1955.

———"The Canadian Party System in Transition," *The Canadian Journal of Economics and Political Science,* IX (August, 1953), 300.

———"The Party System in Canada," *Papers and Proceedings of the Canadian Political Science Association,* IV (1932).

Wrong, Dennis H., "Canadian Politics in the Sixties," *Political Science Quarterly,* LXXVIII, 1 (March, 1963).

———, "Parties and Voting in Canada—A Backward and Forward Glance in the Light of the Last Election," *Political Science Quarterly,* LXXIII, 3 (September, 1958).

———, "The Pattern of Party Voting in Canada," *Public Opinion Quarterly,* XXI (1957), 252.

Section Three: The Two Old Parties

Aitken, Margaret, *Hey Ma, I Did It!* Toronto: Clarke, Irwin & Company, Ltd., 1953.

Allen, Ralph, *Ordeal by Fire, Canada: 1910-1945.* Toronto: Doubleday & Company, 1961, Chap. 36.

Banks, M. A., "The Change in Liberal Party Leadership in 1887," *Canadian Historical Review,* XXXVIII (1957), 109.

Bennett, R. B., *Canadian Problems.* Toronto: Oxford University Press, 1933.

Breslin, Cathie, "I Sold My Vote — Twenty Times," *Maclean's Magazine,* LXXIII (August 13, 1960).

Ferns, H. S. and Bernard Ostry, *The Age of Mackenzie King: The Rise of the Leader.* London: William Heinemann, Ltd., 1955.

Fisher, D. M., "An Interesting Campaign," *Canadian Forum,* XXXVII (September, 1957), 121.

Fraser, Blair, "How the Grits' Power Play Backfired," *Maclean's Magazine,* LXIX (July 7, 1956).

Graham, W. R., *Arthur Meighen,* I: *The Door of Opportunity.* Toronto: Clarke, Irwin & Company, Ltd., 1960.

———"Arthur Meighen and the Conservative Party in Quebec: The Election of 1925," *Canadian Historical Review,* XXXVI (1955), 17.

———"Meighen and the Montreal Tycoons: Railway Policy and the 1921 Election," *Canadian Historical Association Report,* 1957.

Heppe, P. H., *The Liberal Party of Canada,* Ph.D. Dissertation, University of Michigan, 1957.

Hutchison, Bruce, *The Incredible Canadian.* Toronto: Longmans, Green, & Co., 1952.

Jewett, Pauline, "C. D. Howe," *Canadian Forum,* XXXVII (September, 1957), 126.

Laurier, Wilfrid, *Lecture on Political Liberalism.* Lecture in the Music Hall, Quebec, June 26, 1877.

Lederle, J. W., "The Liberal Convention of 1893," *Canadian Journal of Economics and Political Science,* XVI (1950), 42.

———"The Liberal Convention of 1919 and the Selection of Mackenzie King," *Dalhousie Review,* XXVII (1948), 85.

———*The National Organization of the Liberal and Conservative Parties in Canada,* Ph.D. Dissertation, University of Michigan, 1942.

MacKay, R. A., "After Beauharnois, What?," *Maclean's Magazine*, XLIV (October 15, 1931).

McNaught, Kenneth, "The Failure of Television in Politics," *Canadian Forum*, XXXVIII (August, 1958), 104.

Meighen, Arthur, "Beauharnois and Implicated Senators," *Unrevised and Unrepented*. Toronto: Clarke, Irwin & Company, Ltd., 1949.

Meisel, John, "The Formulation of Liberal and Conservative Programmes in the 1957 Canadian Election," *Canadian Journal of Economics and Political Science*, XXVI (1960), 565.

Neatby, H. B., and J. T. Saywell, "Chapleau and the Conservative Party in Quebec," *Canadian Historical Review*, XXXVII (1956), 1.

Pickersgill, J. W., *The Liberal Party*. Toronto: McClelland and Stewart, Ltd., 1962.

——*The Mackenzie King Record*, I: *1939-1944*. Toronto: University of Toronto Press, 1960.

Power, C. G., "What's Wrong with The Liberals," *Maclean's Magazine*, LX (February 1, 1947).

Quinn, H. F., "The Role of the Liberal Party in Recent Canadian Politics," *Political Science Quarterly*, LXVIII (September, 1953), 396.

——"Third National Convention of the Liberal Party," *Canadian Journal of Economics and Political Science*, XVII (1951), 228.

Roberts, Leslie, *C.D.: The Life and Times of Clarence Decatur Howe*. Toronto: Clarke, Irwin & Company, Ltd., 1957.

Scott, James, "A Political Primer," *The Globe and Mail*, October 11, 12, 13, 16, 17, 18, 19, 20, and 21, 1961.

——"Political Slush Funds Corrupt All Parties," *Maclean's Magazine*, LXXIV (September 9, 1961).

Williams, J. R., *The Conservative Party of Canada*. Durham: Duke University Press, 1956.

——"The Selection of Arthur Meighen as Conservative Party Leader in 1941," *Canadian Journal of Economics and Political Science*, XVII (1951), 234.

Wrong, D. H., "Parties and Voting in Canada: A Backward and Forward Glance in the Light of the Last Election," *Political Science Quarterly*, LXXIII (September, 1958), 397.

——"Patterns of Party Voting in Canada," *Public Opinion Quarterly*, XXI (1957), 252.

Section Four: The Minor Parties

Engelmann, F. C., "Membership Participation in Policy-Making in the C.C.F.," *Canadian Journal of Economics and Political Science*, XXII (1956), 161.

Irving, J. A. "The Evolution of the Social Credit Movement," *Canadian Journal of Economics and Political Science*, XIV (1948), 321.

Knowles, Stanley, *The New Party*. Toronto: McClelland & Stewart, Ltd., 1961.

McHenry, Dean E., *The Third Force in Canada: The Cooperative Commonwealth Federation, 1932-1948*. Berkeley: University of California Press, 1950.

MacInnis, Grace, *J. S. Woodsworth: A Man to Remember*. Toronto: Macmillan Co. of Canada, Ltd., 1953.

McNaught, Kenneth, "C.C.F. Town and Country," *Queen's Quarterly*, LXI (1954), 213.

McNaught, Kenneth, "J. S. Woodsworth and a Political Party for Labour, 1896-1921," *Canadian Historical Review*, XXX (1949), 123.

――――*A Prophet in Politics: A Biography of J. S. Woodsworth*. Toronto: University of Toronto Press, 1959.

Mallory, J. R., "Social Credit: Party or Movement?" *Canadian Forum*, XXXV (1955).

Schultz, H. J., "The Social Credit: Back-Benchers' Revolt, 1937," *Canadian Historical Review*, XLI (1960).

Smiley, D. V., "Canada's Poujadists: A New Look at Social Credit," *Canadian Forum*, XLII (1962), 121.

Thompson, R. N., *Canadians, It's Time You Knew*, 2nd ed. Ottawa: Aavangen Press, 1961.

Tyre, Robert, *Douglas in Saskatchewan: The Story of a Socialist Experiment*. Vancouver: Mitchell Press, 1962.

Whalen, Hugh, "Social Credit Measures in Alberta," *Canadian Journal of Economics and Political Science*, XVIII (1952), 500.

Section Five: Regional Politics

Bergeron, Gérard, "Political Parties in Quebec," *University of Toronto Quarterly*, XXVII (1958), 352.

Cité Libre, Numéro Spécial sur les Elections, XIII, 51 (1962).

Cité Libre, Numéro Spécial, Le Québec Politique, XVI, 80 (1965).

Cité Libre, Numéro Spécial, Séparatisme, XIII, 46 (1926).

Cliche, Paul, "Double Allégeance et unitarisme," *Cité Libre*, XV (1964).

――――, "Le parti Libéral Fédéral au Québec," *Cité Libre*, XV (1964).

Dion, Léon, "The Origin and Character of the Nationalism of Growth," *The Canadian Forum*, XLII (1964), 229.

Falardeau, Jean-C., "Le Canada français politique vu de l'intérieur," *Recherches Sociographiques*, II, 3-4 (1961), 343.

Filley, W. O., "Social Structure and Canadian Political Parties: The Quebec Case," *Western Political Quarterly*, IX (1956).

Gagnon, Serge, "Pour une conscience historique de le révolution québecoise," *Cité Libre*, XVI, 83 (1966), 4.

Hamelin, Jean and Marcel Hamelin, *Les moeurs électorales dans le Québec de 1791 à nos jours*. Montréal: Les Editions du Jour, 1962.

Hamilton, Alvin, "The Saskatchewan Election, An Analysis," *Canadian Forum*, XXXVI (1956), 103.

Irving, J. A., *The Social Credit Movement in Alberta*. Toronto: University of Toronto Press, 1959.

Keate, Stuart, "Maurice, The Magnificent," *Maclean's Magazine*, LXI (September 1, 1948).

Kelley, G. A., "French Canada's New Left," *Orbis*, IX, 2 (1965).

Laporte, Pierre, "Les élections ne se font pas avec des prières, *Le Devoir*, October 1-6 and October 10-November 15, 1956.

――――*The True Face of Duplessis*. Montreal: Harvest House, 1960.

Lemieux, Vincent, "La structure des partis politiques," *Cité Libre* XV, 81 (1965), 17.

――――, "Les dimensions sociologiques du vote créditiste au Quebec," *Recherches Sociographiques*, VI, 2 (1965), 181.

――――, "Les élections provinciales dans le comté de Lévis, de 1912 a 1960," *Recherches Sociographiques*, II, 3-4 (1961), 367.

――――, "Le législateur et le médiateur: analysis d'une campagne électoral," *Recherches Sociographiques*, III, 3 (1962).

Lipset, S. M., *Agrarian Socialism*. Berkeley: University of California Press, 1950.
———"The Rural Community and Political Leadership in Saskatchewan," *Canadian Journal of Economics and Political Science*, XIII (1947), 410.
Macpherson, C. B., *Democracy in Alberta*. Toronto: University of Toronto Press, 1953.
Mallory, J. R., *Social Credit and the Federal Power in Canada*. Toronto: University of Toronto Press, 1954.
Martin, Harold, "Quebec's Little Strong Man," *Saturday Evening Post*, CCXXI (January 15, 1949).
Morton, W. L., "The Bias of Prairie Politics," *Transactions of the Royal Society of Canada*, XLIX, Series III (June, 1955), 57.
———*The Progressive Party in Canada*. Toronto: University of Toronto Press, 1950.
———"The Western Progressive Movement and Cabinet Domination," *Canadian Journal of Economics and Political Science*, XII (1946), 136.
Oliver, Michael, "Duplessis and Quebec's Intellectual," *Canadian Forum*, XXXVIII (1958), 55.
———"Quebec and Canadian Democracy," *Canadian Journal of Economics and Political Science*, XXIII (1957), 504.
Ormsby, M. A., *British Columbia: A History*. Toronto: Macmillan Co. of Canada, Ltd., 1958.
Pellerin, Jean, "Le Neo-charlatanisme," *Cité Libre*, XIV, 53 (1963) 10.
Pelletier, Gérard, " 'Parti Pris' ou la grande illusion," *Cité Libre*, XV, 66 (1964), 3.
———, "Profil d'un demagogue: M. Réal Caouette," *Cité Libre*, XIV, 53 (1963), 1.
Poznanska, Alice, "Ce fut un 'vote blanc'," *Cité Libre*, XIII, 49 (1962), 5.
Quinn, H. F., "The Changing Pattern of Quebec Politics," *Canadian Forum*, XXXII (1952), 129.
———"The Role of the Union Nationale in Quebec Politics, 1935-48," *Canadian Journal of Economics and Political Science*, XV (1949), 523.
———"The Union Nationale Party," *Canadian Forum*, XXXV (1955), 29.
———"The Union Nationale Returns to Power," *Canadian Forum*, XXXVI (1956), 101.
Rolph, W. K., *Henry Wise Wood of Alberta*. Toronto: University of Toronto Press, 1951.
Sharp, P. F., *The Agrarian Revolt in Western Canada*. Minneapolis: University of Minnesota Press, 1948.
Taylor, Charles, "Nationalism and the Political Intelligentsia: A Case Study," *Queen's Quarterly*, LXXII, 1 (1965), 150.
Thomas, L. G., *The Liberal Party in Alberta*, Toronto: University of Toronto Press, 1959.
Trudeau, Pierre Elliott, "Contre-révolution séparatiste," *Cité Libre*, XV, 67 (1964), 2.
———, "Note sur la conjoncture politique," *Cité Libre*, XIII, 49 (1962), 1.
———"Reflections sur la politique au Canada français," *Cité Libre*, II (December, 1952), 53.
———"Some Obstacles to Democracy in Quebec," in *Canadian Dualism*, M. Wade, ed. Toronto: University of Toronto Press, 1960.